1973

MASTERWORKS OF
PHILOSOPHY
VOLUME 1

MASTERWORKS OF
PHILOSOPHY

VOLUME 1

EDITED BY S. E. FROST, JR.

DIGESTS OF

PLATO: DIALOGUES

ARISTOTLE: NICOMACHEAN ETHICS

FRANCIS BACON: NOVUM ORGANUM

RENE DESCARTES: PRINCIPLES OF PHILOSOPHY

McGraw-Hill Book Company

New York • St. Louis • San Francisco • London • Düsseldorf

Kuala Lumpur • Mexico • Montreal • Panama • Rio de Janeiro

Sydney • Toronto • Johannesburg • New Delhi • Singapore

Masterworks of Philosophy, Volume I

Copyright 1946 by Copeland & Lamm, Inc. All rights reserved.
Printed in the United States of America. No part of this publication
may be reproduced, stored in a retrieval system, or transmitted,
in any form or by any means, electronic, mechanical, photocopying,
recording, or otherwise, without the prior written permission of
the publisher.

First McGraw-Hill Paperback Edition, 1972
07-040801-7

1 2 3 4 5 6 7 8 9   MU MU   7 9 8 7 6 5 4 3 2

CONTENTS

DIALOGUES

by

PLATO

CONTENTS

Dialogues

PLATO

427–347 B.C.

GREEK LIFE was becoming dangerously confused in the later years of the Peloponnesian War—the struggle between Athens and Sparta that had been dragging on for more than a quarter of a century. The old standards were crumbling, and moral and civic virtues were being discarded for an easy, unthinking existence. Many, especially the young men, were accepting the new ways without discrimination, and the greatness that was Athens was being sneered at. Others, largely the older men, were yearning for the "good old days," but found themselves able to do little more than yearn.

Into this situation came two individuals whose names and ideas are so closely interwoven that it is impossible to speak of one without considering the other. Socrates and Plato sought a way out of the confusion. They realized that the old order was going and that nothing could be done to save it. They also saw the dangers of the new. Consequently they endeavored to think their way through the perplexity of the times to a firm basis for right living and for a high moral idealism.

Little is known of the life of Plato. It is certain that he was born of wealthy and noble parents. His father was a descendant of Codrus, the last king of Athens. His mother traced her ancestry to the great lawgiver, Solon.

Thus Plato was heir to the finest tradition of Athenian aristocracy, and this aristocratic tradition colored much of his thinking.

During Plato's early manhood he was a devoted pupil of Socrates, and his first writings are believed to reflect the teachings of this "wisest man of the ages." The contrast between teacher and pupil was unique. Socrates was ungainly in appearance, a man of no wealth or family prestige, a "vagabond saint" who wrote nothing but who spent his time walking about the streets of Athens and talking to anyone who cared to listen. Plato was stately in face and figure, a dashing young nobleman whose wealth made it possible for him to enjoy tranquillity and to perfect himself in all the social and cultural graces of his time. He wrote extensively, developing his philosophy in the form of *Dialogues*—that is, dramatic conversations in which his characters clashed with one another.

The chief character in Plato's dialogues is Socrates, whose method of developing a philosophic idea has become known as "Socratic." Whenever he met with a group of Athenians, Socrates feigned ignorance and encouraged them to express themselves on some matter of general interest. Then he began to question them in such a way as to reveal their ignorance and to impart to them "a glimmering of the truth" as he saw it.

It was under this system of "modest inquiry" after the truth that Plato got his early training in philosophy. When he himself became a teacher, he opened a school in a public garden known as the *Akademia.* This academy became world-famous and continued to function long after his death. It was here that Plato wrote many of his immortal dialogues.

In all Plato wrote twenty-four dialogues, out of which we have selected nineteen for this book. Two of the remaining dialogues, the *Republic* and the *Laws,* deal largely with matters of government. The *Republic* is included in another volume of this series. The other three dialogues, the *Cratylus,* the *Sophist,* and the *Statesman,* have been omitted since they make no significant additional contribution to the understanding of Plato's philosophy.

The philosophy of Plato is coextensive with the world. Referring to the universality of Plato's work, Emerson exclaims: "Burn the libraries; for their value is in this book." Indeed, there is hardly a subject of human interest that Plato did not touch upon in his pilgrimage of thought. The brotherhood of man, eugenics, socialism, communism, feminism, birth control, free love, free speech, the double and the single standards of morality, the public ownership of wealth, of women, of children—these are only a few of the problems that he discusses in his dialogues. But underlying all these discussions there is a single purpose, Plato's steadfast desire to see *rightness*—today we call it *righteousness*—established on earth. The world, he maintains, is founded upon the Idea of Rightness, of Harmony of Justice.

The Idea of Justice—this is the centermost core of the Platonic philosophy, the Doctrine of Ideas. This Doctrine of Ideas has stimulated not only the thinking of the Christian Church, but a great many other branches of modern thought.

Here, in brief, is the Platonic philosophy of Ideas: Every object in the world, believes Plato, is an imperfect copy of a perfect idea. Every human being is a material and temporary image of the eternal idea of Man. The temporary image dies; the eternal idea lives on. The world of our earthly experience is but a fleeting picture of the Ideal World in the mind of God. This Idea of God, the Divine Secret of Life, is like a shining light in heaven. But our ordinary minds here below are distorted bits of mirrors in which the Idea becomes broken up into blurred and grotesque and unrecognizable reflections. "Now [in the perishable material of our human body]," writes the Christian Platonist, St. Paul, "we see in a mirror, darkly; but then [when the material of our body is dissolved] we shall see face to face." It is the business of the philosopher, says Plato, so to shape and to polish the mirror of his mind as to get a clear image of the Idea of God, the Divine Secret, the Harmonious Pattern that guides the stars in the heavens and the affairs of men. And having received this clear indication of God's purpose, it is the further business of the philosopher to reveal it to his fellows so that they may adjust their lives to the harmony of beauty, under the light of reason, in the interest of justice between nation and nation and between man and man.

DIALOGUES

LACHES, OR COURAGE

Socrates. The question is, Which of us is skilful or successful in the treatment of the soul, and which of us has had good teachers?

Laches. Well but, Socrates; did you never observe that some persons, who have had no teachers, are more skilful than those who have, in some things?

Socrates. Yes, Laches, I have observed that; but you would not be very willing to trust them if they only professed to be masters of their art, unless they could show some proof of their skill or excellence in one or more works.

Laches. That is true.

Socrates. And therefore, Laches and Nicias, as Lysimachus and Melesias, in their anxiety to improve the minds of their sons, have asked our advice about them, we too should inform them who our teachers were, if we say that we have any, and prove them to be men of merit and experienced trainers of the minds of youth and really our teachers. Or if any of us says that he has no teacher, but that he has works to show of his own; then he should point out to them, what Athenians or strangers, bond or free, he is generally acknowledged to have improved. But if he can show neither teachers nor works, then they should ask him to look out for others; and not to run the risk of spoiling the children of friends, which is the most formidable accusation that can be brought against any one by his near and dear relations. As for myself, Lysimachus and Melesias, I am the first to confess that I have never had a teacher; although I have always from my earliest youth desired to have one. But I am too poor to give money to the Sophists, who are the only professors of moral improvement; and to this day I have never been able to discover the art myself, though I should not be surprised if Nicias or Laches may have learned or discovered it; for they are far wealthier than I am, and may therefore have learned of others. And they are older too; so that they have had more time to make the discovery. And I really believe that they are able to educate a man; for unless they had been confident in their own knowledge, they would never have spoken thus decidedly of the pursuits which are advantageous or hurtful to a young man. I repose confidence in both of them; but I do not understand why they differ from one another. And therefore, Lysimachus, as Laches suggests that you should detain me, and not let me go until I have answered, I in turn earnestly beseech and advise you to detain Laches and Nicias, and question them. I would have you say to them: Socrates says that he has no knowledge of the matter, and that he is unable to decide which of you speaks truly; neither discoverer nor student is he of anything of the kind. But you, Laches and Nicias, should either of you tell us who is the most skilful educator whom you have ever known; and whether you invented the art yourselves, or learned of another; and if you learned, who were your respective teachers, and who were their brothers in the art; and then, if you are too much occupied in politics to teach us yourselves, let us go to them, and present them with gifts, or make interest with them, or both, in the hope that they may be induced to take charge of all our families, in order that they may not grow up inferior, and disgrace their ancestors. But if you are yourselves original discoverers in that field, give us some proof of your skill. Who are they who, having been inferior persons, have become under your care good and noble? For if this is your first attempt at education, there is a danger that you may be trying the experiment, not on the "vile corpus" of a Carian slave, but on your own sons, or the sons of your friend; and as the proverb says, "break the large vessel in learning to make pots."

CHARMIDES, OR TEMPERANCE

Socrates Is the Narrator

I THINK, I said, that I had better begin by asking you, What is Temperance?

At first Charmides hesitated, and was very unwilling to answer: then he said that he thought temperance was doing things orderly and quietly, such things for example as walking in the streets, and talking, or anything else of that nature. In a word, he said, I should answer that, in my opinion, temperance is quietness.

Are you right, Charmides? I said. No doubt the opinion is held that the quiet are the temperate; but let us see whether they are right who say this; and first tell me whether you would not acknowledge temperance to be of the class of the honorable and good?

Yes.

But which is the best when you are at the writing-master's, to write the same letters quickly or quietly?

Quickly.

And to read quickly or slowly?

Quickly again.

And when the soul inquires, and in deliberations, not the quietest, as I imagine, and he who with difficulty deliberates and discovers, is thought worthy of praise, but he who does this most easily and quickly?

That is true, he said.

And in all that concerns either body or soul, swiftness and activity are clearly better than slowness and quietness?

That, he said, is the inference.

Then temperance is not quietness, nor is the temperate life quiet, upon this view; for the life which is temperate is supposed to be the good. And of two things, one is true,—either never, or very seldom, do the quiet actions in life appear to be better than the quick and energetic ones; or, granting ever so much that of the nobler sort of actions, there are as many quiet, as quick and vehement ones: still, even if we admit this, temperance will not be acting quietly any more than acting quickly and vehemently, either in walking, talking, or anything else; nor will the quiet life be more temperate than the unquiet, seeing that temperance is reckoned by us in the class of good and honorable, and the quick have been shown to be as good as the quiet.

I think, he said, Socrates, that you are right in saying that.

Critias had long been showing uneasiness, for he felt that he had a reputation to maintain with Charmides and the rest of the company. He had, however, hitherto managed to restrain himself; but now he could no longer forbear, and his eagerness satisfied me of the truth of my suspicion, that Charmides had heard this answer about temperance from Critias. And Charmides, who did not want to answer himself, but to make Critias answer, tried to stir him up. He went on pointing out that he had been refuted, and at this Critias got angry, and, as I thought, was rather inclined to quarrel with him; just as a poet might quarrel with an actor who spoiled his poems in repeating them; so he looked hard at him and said—

Do you imagine, Charmides, that the author of the definition of temperance did not understand the meaning of his own words, because you don't understand them?

Why, at his age, I said, most excellent Critias, he can hardly be expected to understand; but you, who are older, and have studied, may well be assumed to know the meaning of them; and therefore, if you agree with him, and accept his definition of temperance, I would much rather argue with you than with him about the truth or falsehood of the definition.

Well, he answered; I mean to say, that he who does evil, and not good, is not temperate; and that he is temperate who does good, and not evil: for temperance I define in plain words to be the doing of good actions.

And you may be very likely right in that, I said; but I am curious to know whether you imagine that temperate men are ignorant of their own temperance?

I do not imagine that, he said.

And yet were you not saying, not so very long ago, that craftsmen might be temperate in doing another's work, as well as their own?

Yes, I was, he replied; but why do you refer to that?

I have no particular reason, but I wish you would tell me whether a physician who cures a patient may do good to himself and good to another also?

I think that he may.

And he who does this does his duty. And does not he who does his duty act temperately or wisely?

Yes, he acts wisely.

But must the physician necessarily know when his treatment is likely to prove beneficial, and when not? or must the craftsman necessarily know when he is likely to be benefited, and when not to be benefited, by the work which he is doing?

I suppose not.

Then, I said, he may sometimes do good or harm, and not know what he is himself doing, and yet, in doing good, as you say, he has done temperately or wisely. Was not that your statement?

Yes.

Then, as would seem, in doing good, he may act wisely or temperately, and be wise or temperate, but not know his own wisdom or temperance?

But that, Socrates, he said, is impossible; and therefore if that is, as you imply, the necessary consequence of any of my previous admissions, I would rather withdraw them, and not be ashamed to confess that I was mistaken, than admit that a man can be temperate or wise, who does not know himself.

Shall I tell you, Socrates, why I say all this? My object is to leave the previous discussion (in which I know not whether you or I are more right, but, at any rate, no clear result was attained), and to raise a new one in which I will attempt to prove, if you deny, that temperance is self-knowledge.

Yes, I said, Critias; but you come to me as though I professed to know about the questions which I ask, and as though I could, if only I would, agree with you. Whereas the fact is that I am, as you are, an inquirer into the truth of your proposition; and when I have inquired, I will say whether I agree with you or not. Please then to allow me time to reflect.

Reflect, he said.

I am reflecting, I replied, and discover that temperance, or wisdom, if implying a knowledge of anything, must be a science, and a science of something.

Yes, he said; the science of itself.

Now I want you, Critias, to answer a similar question about temperance, or wisdom, to which you ought to know the answer, if, as you say, wisdom or temperance is the science of itself. Admitting this, I ask, what good work, worthy of the name, does wisdom effect? Answer me that.

That is not the true way of pursuing the inquiry, Socrates, he said; for wisdom is not like the other sciences, any more than they are like one another: but you proceed as if they were alike. For tell me, he said, what result is there of computation or geometry, in the same sense as a house is the result of building, or a garment of weaving, or any other work of any other art? Can you show me any such result of them? You can not.

Tell me, then, I said, what you mean to affirm about wisdom.

I mean, he said, that wisdom is the only science which is the science of itself and of the other sciences as well.

But the science of science, I said, will also be the science of the absence of science.

Very true, he said.

Then the wise or temperate man, and he only, will know himself, and be able to examine what he knows or does not know, and see what others know, and think that they know and do really know; and what they do not know, and fancy that they know, when they do not. No other person will be able to do this. And this is the state and virtue of wisdom, or temperance, and self-knowledge, which is just knowing what a man knows, and what he does not know. That is your view?

Yes, he said.

Now then, I said, making an offering of the third or last argument to Zeus the Savior, let us once more begin, and ask, in the first place, whether this knowledge that you know and do not know what you know and do not know is possible; and in the second place, whether, even if quite possible, such knowledge is of any use.

That is what we must consider, he said.

And here, Critias, I said, I hope that you will find a way out of a difficulty into which I have got myself. Shall I tell you the difficulty?

By all means, he replied.

Does not what you have been saying, if true, amount to this: that there must be a science which is wholly a science of itself, and also of other sciences, and that the same is also the science of the absence of science?

True.

But surely we are assuming a science of this kind, which, having no subject-matter, is a science of itself and of the other sciences; for that is what is affirmed. Now this is strange, if true: however, we must not as yet absolutely deny the possibility of such a science; let us rather consider the matter.

You are quite right.

Well then, this science of which we are speaking is a science of something, and is of a nature to be a science of something?

Yes.

Just as that which is greater is of a nature to be greater than something?

Yes.

Which is less, if the other is to be conceived as greater?

To be sure.

And if we could find something which is at once greater than self, and greater than other great things, but not greater than those things in comparison of which the others are greater, then that thing would have the property of being greater and also less than itself?

That, Socrates, he said, is the inevitable inference.

Or if there be a double which is double of other doubles and of itself, they will be halves; for the half is relative to the double?

That is true.

And that which is greater than itself will also be less, and that which is heavier will also be lighter, and that which is older will also be younger: and the same of other things; that which has a nature relative to self will retain also the nature of its object. I mean to say, for example, that hearing is, as we say, of sound or voice. Is that true?

Yes.

And therefore, O son of Callaeschrus, as you maintain that temperance or wisdom is a science of science, and also of the absence of science, I will request you to show in the first place, as I was saying before, the possibility, and in the second place, the advantage, of such a science; and then perhaps you may satisfy me that you are right in your view of temperance.

Critias heard me say this, and saw that I was in a difficulty; and as one person when another yawns in his presence catches the infection of yawning from him, so did he seem to be driven into a difficulty by my difficulty. But as he had a reputation to maintain, he was ashamed to admit before the company that he could not answer my challenge or decide the question at issue; and he made an unintelligible attempt to hide his perplexity. In order that the argument might proceed, I said to him, Well then, Critias, if you like, let us assume that there may be this science of science; whether the assumption is right or wrong may be hereafter investigated. But fully admitting this, will you tell me how such a science enables us to distinguish what we know or do not know, which, as we were saying, is self-knowledge or wisdom. That is what we were saying?

Yes, Socrates, he said; and that I think is certainly true: for he who has that science or knowledge which knows itself will become like that knowledge which he has, in the same way that he who has swiftness will be swift, and he who has beauty will be beautiful, and he who has knowledge will know. In the same way he who has that knowledge which is the knowledge of itself, will know himself.

I do not doubt, I said, that a man will know himself, when he possesses that which has self-knowledge: but what necessity is there that, having this, he should know what he knows and what he does not know?

Because, Socrates, they are the same.

Very likely, I said; but I remain as stupid as ever; for still I fail to comprehend how this knowing what you know and do not know is the same as the knowledge of self.

What do you mean? he said.

This is what I mean, I replied: I will admit that there is a science of science, but can this do more than determine that of two things one is and the other is not science or knowledge?

No, just that.

But how will this knowledge or science teach him to know what he knows? Say that he knows health;—not wisdom or temperance, but the art of medicine has taught him that;—and he has learned harmony from the art of music, and building from the art of building,—neither, from wisdom or temperance: and the same of other things.

That is evident.

But how will wisdom, regarded only as a knowledge of knowledge or science of science, ever teach him that he knows health, or that he knows building?

That is impossible.

Then he who is ignorant of this will only know that he knows, but not what he knows?

True.

Then wisdom or being wise appears to be not the knowledge of the things which we do or do not know, but only the knowledge that we know and do not know?

That is the inference.

Then he who has this knowledge will not be able to examine whether a pretender knows or does not know that which he says that he knows: he will only know that he has a knowledge of some kind; but wisdom will not show him of what the knowledge is?

Plainly not.

But then what profit, Critias, I said, is there any longer in wisdom or temperance which yet remains, if this is wisdom? If, indeed, as we were supposing at first, the wise man had been able to distinguish what he knew and did not know, and that he knew the one and did not know the other, and to recognize a similar faculty of discernment in others, there would certainly have been a great advantage in being wise; for then we should never have made a mistake, but have passed through life the un-erring guides of ourselves and of those who were under us; and we should not have attempted to do what we did not know, but we should have found out those who knew, and confided in them; nor should we have allowed those who were under us to do anything which they were not likely to do well; and they would be likely to do well just that of which they had knowledge; and the house or state which was ordered or ad-ministered under the guidance of wisdom would have been well ordered, and everything else of which wisdom was the lord; for truth guiding, and error having been expelled, in all their doings, men would have done well, and would have been happy. Was not this, Critias, what we spoke of as the great advantage of wisdom—to know what is known and what is un-known to us?

Very true, he said.

And now you perceive, I said, that no such science is to be found any-where.

I perceive, he said.

May we assume then, I said, that wisdom, viewed in this new light merely as a knowledge of knowledge and ignorance, has this advantage:— that he who possesses such knowledge will more easily learn anything that he learns; and that everything will be clearer to him, because, in addi-tion to the knowledge of individuals, he sees the science, and this also will better enable him to test the knowledge which others have of what he knows himself; whereas the inquirer who is without this knowledge may be supposed to have a feebler and weaker insight? Are not these, my friend, the real advantages which are to be gained from wisdom? And are not we looking and seeking after something more than is to be found in her?

That is very likely, he said.

That is very likely, I said; and very likely, too, we have been inquiring to no purpose. I am led to infer this, because I observe that if this is wis-dom, some strange consequences would follow. Let us, if you please, assume the possibility of this science of sciences, and further admit and allow, as was originally suggested, that wisdom is the knowledge of what we know and do not know. Assuming all this, still, upon further consider-ation, I am doubtful, Critias, whether wisdom, if such as this, would do us any good. For I think we were wrong in supposing, as we were saying just now, that such wisdom ordering the government of house or state would be a great benefit.

How is that? he said.

Why, I said, we were far too ready to admit the great benefits which mankind would obtain from their severally doing the things which they knew, and committing to others who knew the things of which they are ignorant.

Were we not right, he said, in making that admission?

I think not, I said.

That is certainly strange, Socrates.

By the dog of Egypt, I said, I am of your opinion about that: and that was in my mind when I said that strange consequences would follow, and that I was afraid we were on the wrong track; for however ready we may be to admit that this is wisdom, I certainly can not make out what good this sort of thing does to us.

What do you mean? he said; I wish that you could make me understand what you mean.

I dare say that what I am saying is nonsense, I replied; and yet if a man has any feeling of what is due to himself, he can not let the thought which comes into his mind pass away unheeded and unexamined.

I like that, he said.

Hear, then, I said, my own dream; whether coming through the horn or the ivory gate, I can not tell. The dream is this: Let us suppose that wisdom is such as we are now defining, and that she has absolute sway over us; then each action will be done according to the arts or sciences, and no one professing to be a pilot when he is not, or any physician or general, or any one else pretending to know matters of which he is ignorant, will deceive or elude us; our health will be improved; our safety at sea, and also in battle, will be assured; our coats and shoes, and all other instruments and implements will be well made, because the workmen will be good and true. Aye, and if you please, you may suppose that prophecy, which is the knowledge of the future, will be under the control of wisdom, and that she will deter deceivers and set up the true prophet in their place as the revealer of the future. Now I quite agree that mankind, thus provided, would live and act according to knowledge, for wisdom would watch and prevent ignorance from intruding on us. But we have not as yet discovered why, because we act according to knowledge, we act well and are happy, my dear Critias.

Yet I think, he replied, that you will hardly find any other end of right action, if you reject knowledge.

And of what is this knowledge? I said. Just answer me that small question. Do you mean a knowledge of shoemaking?

God forbid.

Or of working in brass?

Certainly not.

Or in wool, or wood, or anything of that sort?

No, I do not.

Then, I said, we are giving up the doctrine that he who lives according to knowledge is happy, for these live according to knowledge, and yet they are not allowed by you to be happy; but I think that you mean to confine happiness to particular individuals who live according to knowledge, such for example as the prophet, who, as I was saying, knows the future.

Yes, I mean him, but there are others as well.

Yes, I said, some one who knows the past and present as well as the future, and is ignorant of nothing. Let us suppose that there is such a person, and if there is, you will allow that he is the most knowing of all living men.

Certainly he is.

Yet I should like to know one thing more: which of the different kinds of knowledge makes him happy? or do all equally make him happy?

Not all equally, he replied.

But which most tends to make him happy? the knowledge of what past, present, or future thing? May I infer this to be the knowledge of the game of draughts?

Nonsense about the game of draughts.

Or of computation?

No.

Or of health?

That is nearer the truth, he said.

And that knowledge which is nearest of all, I said, is the knowledge of what?

The knowledge with which he discerns good and evil.

Monster! I said; you have been carrying me round in a circle, and all this time hiding from me the fact that the life according to knowledge is not that which makes men act rightly and be happy, not even if all the sciences be included, but that this has to do with one science only, that of good and evil. For, let me ask you, Critias, whether, if you take away this science from all the rest, medicine will not equally give health, and shoemaking equally produce shoes, and the art of the weaver clothes?—whether the art of the pilot will not equally save our lives at sea, and the art of the general in war?

Quite so.

And yet, my dear Critias, none of these things will be well or beneficially done, if the science of the good be wanting.

That is true.

But that science is not wisdom or temperance, but a science of human advantage; not a science of other sciences, or of ignorance, but of good and evil: and if this be of use, then wisdom or temperance will not be of use.

And why, he replied, will not wisdom be of use? For if we really assume that wisdom is a science of sciences, and has a sway over other sciences, surely she will have this particular science of the good under her control, and in this way will benefit us.

And will wisdom give health? I said; is not this rather the effect of medicine? Or does wisdom do the work of any of the other arts, and do not they do, each of them, their own work? Have we not long ago asseverated that knowledge is only the knowledge of knowledge and of ignorance, and of nothing else?

That is clear.

Another art is concerned with health.

Another?

The art of health is different.

Yes, different.

Nor does wisdom give advantage, my good friend; for that again we have just now been attributing to another art.

Very true.

How then can wisdom be advantageous, giving no advantage?

That, Socrates, is certainly inconceivable.

You see then, Critias, that I was not far wrong in fearing that I could have no sound notion about wisdom; I was quite right in depreciating myself; for that which is admitted to be the best of all things would never have seemed to us useless, if I had been good for anything at an inquiry. But now I have been utterly defeated, and have failed to discover what that is to which the imposer of names gave this name of temperance or wisdom. And yet many more admissions were made by us than could be really granted; for we admitted that there was a science of science, although the argument said No, and protested against this; and we admitted further, that this science knew the works of the other sciences (although this too was denied by the argument), because we wanted to show that the wise man had knowledge of what he knew and did not know; also we nobly disregarded, and never even considered, the impossibility of a man knowing in a sort of way that which he does not know at all; for our assumption was, that he knows that which he does not know; than which nothing, as I think, can be more irrational. And yet, after finding us so easy and good-natured, the inquiry is still unable to discover the truth; but mocks us to a degree, and has gone out of its way to prove the inutility of that which we admitted only by a sort of supposition and fiction to be the true definition of temperance or wisdom: which result, as far as I am concerned, is not so much to be lamented, I said. But for your sake,

Charmides, I am very sorry—that you, having such beauty and such wisdom and temperance of soul, should have no profit or good in life from your wisdom and temperance. And still more am I grieved about the charm which I learned with so much pain, and to so little profit, from the Thracian, for the sake of a thing which is nothing worth. I think indeed that there is a mistake, and that I must be a bad inquirer, for I am persuaded that wisdom or temperance is really a great good; and happy are you if you possess that good. And therefore examine yourself, and see whether you have this gift and can do without the charm; for if you can, I would rather advise you to regard me simply as a fool who is never able to reason out anything; and to rest assured that the more wise and temperate you are, the happier you will be.

LYSIS, OR FRIENDSHIP

Socrates Is the Narrator

Here is Lysis, who does not understand something that I was saying, and wants me to ask Menexenus, who, as he thinks, will be able to answer.

And why don't you ask him? he said.

Very well, I said, I will ask him; and do you, Menexenus, answer. But first I must tell you that I am one who from my childhood upward have set my heart upon a certain thing. All people have their fancies; some desire horses, and others dogs; and some are fond of gold, and others of honor. Now, I have no violent desire of any of these things; but I have a passion for friends; and I would rather have a good friend than the best cock or quail in the world: I would even go further, and say than a horse or dog. Yea, by the dog of Egypt, I should greatly prefer a real friend to all the gold of Darius, or even to Darius himself: I am such a lover of friends as that. And when I see you and Lysis, at your early age, so easily possessed of this treasure, and so soon, he of you, and you of him, I am amazed and delighted, seeing that I myself, although I am now advanced in years, am so far from having made a similar acquisition, that I do not even know in what way a friend is acquired. But this is the question which I want to ask you, as you have experience: tell me then, when one loves another, is the lover or the beloved the friend; or may either be the friend?

Either, he said, may be the friend.

Do you mean, I said, that if only one of them loves the other, they are mutual friends?

Yes, he said; that is my meaning.

But what if the lover is not loved in return? That is a possible case.

Yes.

Or is, perhaps, even hated? for that is a fancy which lovers sometimes have. Nothing can exceed their love; and yet they imagine either that they are not loved in return, or that they are hated. Is not that true?

Yes, he said, quite true.

In that case, the one loves, and the other is loved?

Yes.

Then which is the friend of which? Is the lover the friend of the beloved, whether he be loved in return, or hated; or is the beloved the friend; or is there no friendship at all on either side, unless they both love one another?

There would seem to be none at all.

Then that is at variance with our former notion.

That appears to be true.

Then no one is a friend to his friend who does not love in return?

I think not.

Then they are not lovers of horses, whom the horses do not love in return; nor lovers of quails, nor of dogs, nor of wine, nor of gymnastic exercises, who have no return of love; no, nor of wisdom, unless wisdom loves them in return. Or perhaps they do love them, but they are not beloved by them; and the poet was wrong who sings:—

"Happy the man to whom his children are dear, and steeds having single hoofs, and dogs of chase, and the stranger of another land."

I do not think that he was wrong.

Then you think that he is right?

Yes.

Then, Menexenus, the conclusion is, that what is beloved may be dear, whether loving or hating: for example, very young children, too young to love, or even hating their father or mother when they are punished by them, are never dearer to them than at the time when they are hating them.

I think that is true, he said.

Then on this view, not the lover, but the beloved, is the friend or dear one; and the hated one, and not the hater, is the enemy?

That is plain.

Then many men are loved by their enemies, and hated by their friends, and are the friends of their enemies, and the enemies of their friends— that follows if the beloved is dear, and not the lover: but this, my dear friend, is an absurdity, or, I should rather say, an impossibility.

That, Socrates, I believe to be true.

But then, if not the enemy, the lover will be the friend, of that which is loved?

True.

And the hater will be the enemy of that which is hated?

Certainly.

Yet there is no avoiding the admission in this, as in the preceding instance, that a man may love one who is not his friend, or who may be his enemy. There are cases in which a lover loves, and is not loved, or is perhaps hated; and a man may be the enemy of one who is not his enemy, and is even his friend: for example, when he loves that which does not hate him, or even hates that which loves him.

That appears to be true.

But if the lover is not a friend, nor the beloved a friend, nor both together, what are we to say? Whom are we to call friends to one another? Do any remain?

Indeed, Socrates, I can not find any.

Then are we to say that the greatest friendship is of opposites?

Exactly.

Yes, Menexenus; but will not that be a monstrous answer? and will not the all-wise eristics be down upon us in triumph, and ask, fairly enough, whether love is not the very opposite of hate? and what answer shall we make to them? must we not admit that they speak truly?

That we must.

They will ask whether the enemy is the friend of the friend, or the friend the friend of the enemy?

Neither, he replied.

Well, but is a just man the friend of the unjust, or the temperate of the intemperate, or the good of the bad?

I do not see how that is possible.

And yet, I said, if friendship goes by contraries, the contraries must be friends.

They must.

Then neither like and like nor unlike and unlike are friends.

I suppose not.

And yet there is a further consideration: may not all these notions of friendship be erroneous? but still may there not be cases in which that which is neither good nor bad is the friend of the good?

How do you mean? he said.

Why really, I said, the truth is that I don't know; but my head is dizzy with thinking of the argument, and therefore I hazard the conjecture, that the beautiful is the friend, as the old proverb says. Beauty is certainly a soft, smooth, slippery thing, and therefore of a nature which easily slips in and permeates our souls. And I further add that the good is the beautiful. You will agree to that?

Yes.

This I say from a sort of notion that what is neither good nor evil is the friend of the beautiful and the good, and I will tell you why I am inclined to think this: I assume that there are three principles—the good, the bad, and that which is neither good nor bad. What do you say to that?

I agree.

And neither is the good the friend of the good, nor the evil of the evil, nor the good of the evil;—that the preceding argument will not allow; and therefore the only alternative is—if there be such a thing as friendship or love at all—that what is neither good nor evil must be the friend, either of the good, or of that which is neither good nor evil, for nothing can be the friend of the bad.

True.

Nor can like be the friend of like, as we were just now saying.

True.

Then that which is neither good nor evil can have no friend which is neither good nor evil.

That is evident.

Then the good alone is the friend of that only which is neither good nor evil.

That may be assumed to be certain.

And does not this seem to put us in the right way? Just remark, that the body which is in health requires neither medical nor any other aid, but is well enough; and the healthy man has no love of the physician, because he is in health.

He has none.

But the sick loves him, because he is sick?

Certainly.

And sickness is an evil, and the art of medicine a good and useful thing?

Yes.

But the human body, viewed as a body, is neither good nor evil?

True.

And the body is compelled by reason of disease to court and make friends of the art of medicine?

Yes.

Then that which is neither good nor evil becomes the friend of good, by reason of the presence of evil?

That is the inference.

And clearly this must have happened before that which was neither good nor evil had become altogether corrupted with the element of evil, for then it would not still desire and love the good; for, as we were saying, the evil can not be the friend of the good.

That is impossible.

And therefore we say that those who are already wise, whether gods or men, are no longer lovers of wisdom; nor can they be lovers of wisdom, who are ignorant to the extent of being evil, for no evil or ignorant person is a lover of wisdom. There remain those who have the misfortune to be ignorant, but are not yet hardened in their ignorance, or void of understanding, and do not as yet fancy that they know what they do not know: and therefore those who are the lovers of wisdom are as yet neither good nor bad. But the bad do not love wisdom any more than the good; for, as we have already seen, neither unlike is the friend of unlike, nor like of like. You remember that?

Yes, they both said.

And so, Lysis and Menexenus, we have discovered the nature of friendship: there can be no doubt of that. Friendship is the love which the neither good nor evil has of the good, when the evil is present, either in the soul, or in the body, or anywhere.

They both agreed and entirely assented, and for a moment I rejoiced and was satisfied like a huntsman whose prey is within his grasp. But then a suspicion came across me, and I fancied unaccountably that the conclusion was untrue, and I felt pained, and said, Alas! Lysis and Menexenus, I am afraid that we have been grasping at a shadow.

Why do you say that? said Menexenus.

I am afraid, I said, that the argument about friendship is false: arguments, like men, are often pretenders.

How is that? he asked.

Well, I said; look at the matter in this way: a friend is the friend of some one.

Certainly he is.

And has he a motive and object in being a friend, or has he no motive and object?

He has a motive and object.

And is the object which makes him a friend dear to him, or neither dear nor hateful to him?

I don't quite follow you, he said.

I do not wonder at that, I said. But perhaps, if I put the matter in another way, you will be able to follow me, and my own meaning will be clearer to myself. The sick man, as I was just now saying, is the friend of the physician—is he not?

Yes.

And he is the friend of the physician because of disease, and for the sake of health?

Yes.

And disease is an evil?

Certainly.

And what of health? I said. Is that good or evil, or neither?

Good, he replied.

And we were saying, I believe, that the body being neither good nor evil, because of disease, that is to say because of evil, is the friend of medicine, and medicine is a good: and medicine has entered into this friendship for the sake of health, and health is a good.

True.

And is health a friend, or not a friend?

A friend.

And disease is an enemy?

Yes.

Then that which is neither good nor evil is the friend of the good because of the evil and hateful, and for the sake of the good and the friend?

That is clear.

Then the friend is a friend for the sake of the friend, and because of the enemy?

That is to be inferred.

Then at this point, my boys, let us take heed, and be on our guard against deceptions. I will no more say that the friend is the friend of the friend, and the like of the like, which has been declared by us to be an impossibility; but, in order that this new statement may not delude us, let us attentively examine another point, which is this: medicine, as we were saying, is a friend, or dear to us for the sake of health?

Yes.

And health is also dear?

Certainly.

And if dear, then dear for the sake of something?

Yes.

And surely this object must also be dear, as is implied in our previous admissions?

Yes.

And that something dear involves something else dear?

Yes.

But then, proceeding in this way, we shall at last come to an end, and arrive at some first principle of friendship or dearness which is not capable of being referred to any other, for the sake of which, as we maintain, all other things are dear.

Certainly.

My fear is that all those other things, which, as we say, are dear for the sake of that other, are illusions and deceptions only, of which that other is the reality or true principle of friendship. Let me put the matter thus: Suppose the case of a great treasure (this may be a son, who is more precious to his father than all his other treasures); would not the father, who values his son above all things, value other things also for the sake of his son? I mean, for instance, if he knew that his son had drunk hemlock, and the father thought that wine would save him, he would value the wine?

Certainly.

And also the vessel which contains the wine?

Certainly.

But he does not therefore value the three measures of wine, or the earthen vessel which contains them, equally with his son? Is not this rather the true state of the case? All this anxiety of his has regard not to the means which are provided for the sake of an object, but to the object for the sake of which they are provided. And although we may often say that gold and silver are highly valued by us, that is not the truth; for the truth is that there is a further object, whatever that may be, which we value most of all, and for the sake of which gold and all our other possessions are acquired by us. Am I not right?

Yes, certainly.

And may not the same be said of the friend? That which is only dear to us for the sake of something else is improperly said to be dear, but the truly dear is that in which all these so-called dear friendships terminate.

That, he said, appears to be true.

And the truly dear or ultimate principle of friendship is not for the sake of any other or further dear.

True.

Then the notion is at an end that friendship has not any further object. But are we therefore to infer that the good is the friend?

That is my view.

Then is the good loved for the sake of the evil? Let me put the case in this way: Suppose that of the three principles, good, evil, and that which is neither good nor evil, there remained only the good and the neutral, and that evil went far away, and in no way affected soul or body, nor ever at all that class of things which, as we say, are neither good nor evil in themselves;—would the good be of any use, or other than useless to us? For if there were nothing to hurt us any longer, we should have no need of anything that would do us good. Then would be clearly seen that we did but love and desire the good because of the evil, and as the remedy of the evil, which was the disease; but if there had been no disease, there would have been no need of a remedy. Is not this the nature of the good—to be loved because of the evil, by us who are between the two? but there is no use in the good for its own sake.

I suppose that is true.

Then the final principle of friendship, in which all other friendships which are relative only were supposed by us to terminate, is of another and a different nature from them. For they are called dear because of another dear or friend. But with the true friend or dear, the case is quite the reverse; for that is proved to be dear because of the hated, and if the hated were away, the loved would no longer stay.

That is true, he replied: at least, that is implied in the argument.

But, oh! will you tell me, I said, whether if evil were to perish, we should hunger any more, or thirst any more, or have any similar affection? Or may we suppose that hunger will remain while men and animals remain, but not so as to be hurtful? And the same of thirst and the other affections,—that they will remain, but will not be evil because evil has perished? Or shall I say rather, that to ask what either would be or would not be has no meaning, for who can tell? This only we know, that in our present condition hunger may injure us, and may also benefit us. Is not that true?

Yes.

And in like manner thirst or any similar desire may sometimes be a good and sometimes an evil to us, and sometimes neither one nor the other?

To be sure.

But is there any reason why, because evil perishes, that which is not evil should also perish?

None.

Then, even if evil perishes, the desires which are neither good nor evil will remain?

That is evident.

And must not a man love that which he desires and affects?

He must.

Then, even if evil perishes, there may still remain some elements of love or friendship?

Yes.

But not, if evil is the cause of friendship: for in that case nothing will be the friend of any other thing after the destruction of evil; for the effect can not remain when the cause is destroyed.

True.

And have we not been saying that the friend loves something for a reason? and the reason was because of the evil which leads the neither good nor evil to love the good?

Very true.

But now our view is changed, and there must be some other cause of friendship?

I suppose that there must.

May not the truth be that, as we were saying, desire is the cause of friendship; for that which desires is dear to that which is desired at the time of desire? and may not the other theory have been just a long story about nothing?

That is possibly true.

But surely, I said, he who desires, desires that of which he is in want?

Yes.

And that of which he is in want is dear to him?

True.

And he is in want of that of which he is deprived?

Certainly.

Then love, and desire, and friendship would appear to be of the natural or congenial. That, Lysis and Menexenus, is the inference.

They assented.

Then if you are friends, you must have natures which are congenial to one another?

Certainly, they both said.

And I say, my boys, that no one who loves or desires another would ever have loved or desired or affected him, if he had not been in some way congenial to him, either in his soul, or in his character, or in his manners, or in his form.

Yes, yes, said Menexenus. But Lysis was silent.

Then, I said, the conclusion is, that what is of a congenial nature must be loved.

That follows, he said.

Then the true lover, and not the counterfeit, must be loved by his love.

Lysis and Menexenus gave a faint assent to this; and Hippothales changed into all manner of colors with delight.

Here, intending to revise the argument, I said: Can we point out any difference between the congenial and the like? For if that is possible, then I think, Lysis and Menexenus, there may be some sense in our argument about friendship. But if the congenial is only the like, how will you get rid of the other argument, of the uselessness of like to like in as far as they are like; for to say that what is useless is dear, would be absurd? Suppose, then, that we agree to distinguish between the congenial and the like—in the intoxication of argument, that may perhaps be allowed.

Very true.

And shall we further say that the good is congenial, and the evil uncongenial to every one? Or again that the evil is congenial to the evil, and the good to the good; or that which is neither good nor evil to that which is neither good nor evil.

They agreed to the latter alternative.

Then, my boys, we have again fallen into the old discarded error; for the unjust will be the friend of the unjust, and the bad of the bad, as well as the good of the good.

That appears to be true.

But again if we say that the congenial is the same as the good, in that case the good will only be the friend of the good.

True.

But that too was a position of ours which, as you will remember, has been already refuted by ourselves.

We remember.

Then what is to be done? Or rather is there anything to be done? I can only, like the wise men who argue in courts, sum up the arguments. If neither the beloved, nor the lover, nor the like, nor the unlike, nor the good, nor the congenial, nor any other of whom we spoke—for there were such a number of them that I can't remember them—if, I say, none of these are friends, I know not what remains to be said.

PROTAGORAS

Socrates Is the Narrator

WHEN we were all seated, Protagoras said: Now that the company are assembled, Socrates, tell me about the young man of whom you were just now speaking.

I replied: I will begin again at the same point, Protagoras, and tell you once more the purport of my visit: this is my friend Hippocrates, who is desirous of making your acquaintance; he wants to know what will happen to him if he associates with you. That is all I have to say.

Protagoras answered: Young man, if you associate with me, on the very first day you will return home a better man than you came, and better on the second day than on the first, and better every day than you were on the day before.

When I heard this, I said: Protagoras, I do not at all wonder at hearing you say this: even at your age, and with all your wisdom, if any one were to teach you what you did not know before, you would become better no doubt: but please to answer in a different way; I will explain how by an example. Let me suppose that Hippocrates, instead of desiring your acquaintance, wished to become acquainted with the young man Zeuxippus of Heraclea, who has newly come to Athens, and he were to go to him as he has gone to you, and were to hear him say, as he has heard you say, that every day he would grow and become better if he associated with him: and then suppose that he were to ask him, "In what would he be better, and in what would he grow?" Zeuxippus would answer, "In painting." And suppose that he went to Orthagoras the Theban, and heard him say the same, and asked him, "In what would he become better day by day?" he would reply, "In flute-playing." Now I want you to make the same sort of answer to this young man and to me, who am asking questions on his account. When you say that on the first day on which he associates with you he will return home a better man, and on every day will grow in like manner—in what, Protagoras, will he be better? and about what?

When Protagoras heard me say this, he replied: You ask questions fairly, and I like to answer a question which is fairly put. If Hippocrates comes to me he will not experience the sort of drudgery with which other Sophists are in the habit of insulting their pupils; who, when they have just escaped from the arts, are taken and driven back into them by these teachers, and made to learn calculation, and astronomy, and geometry, and music (he gave a look at Hippias as he said this); but if he comes to me, he will learn that which he comes to learn. And this is prudence in affairs private as well as public; he will learn to order his own house in the best manner, and he will be best able to speak and act in the affairs of the state.

Do I understand you, I said; and is your meaning that you teach the art of politics, and that you promise to make men good citizens?

That, Socrates, is exactly the profession which I make.

Then, I said, you do indeed possess a noble art, if there is no mistake about this; for I will freely confess to you, Protagoras, that I have a doubt whether this art is capable of being taught, and yet I know not how to disbelieve your assertion. And I ought to tell you why I am of opinion that this art can not be taught or communicated by man to man. I say that the Athenians are an understanding people, as indeed they are esteemed by the other Hellenes. Now I observe that when we are met together in the assembly, and the matter in hand relates to building, the builders are summoned as advisers; when the question is one of ship-building, then the ship-builders; and the like of other arts which they think capable of being taught and learned. And if some person offers to give them advice who is not supposed by them to have any skill in the art, even though he be good-looking, and rich, and noble, they don't listen to him, but laugh at him, and hoot him, until either he is clamored down and retires of himself; or if he persist, he is dragged away or put out by the constables at the command of the prytanes. This is their way of behaving about the arts which have professors. When, however, the question is an affair of state, then everybody is free to have a say— carpenter, tinker, cobbler, sailor, passenger; rich and poor, high and low—any one who likes gets up, and no one reproaches him, as in the former case, with not having learned, and having no teacher, and yet giving advice; evidently because they are under the impression that this sort of knowledge can not be taught. And not only is this true of the state, but of individuals; the best and wisest of our citizens are unable to impart their political wisdom to others: as for example, Pericles, the father of these young men, who gave them excellent instruction in all that could be learned from masters, in his own department of politics taught them nothing; nor did he give them teachers, but they were allowed to wander at their own free will in a sort of hope that they would light upon virtue of their own accord. Or take another example: there was Cleinias the younger brother of our friend Alcibiades, of whom this very same Pericles was the guardian; and he being in fact under the apprehension that Cleinias would be corrupted by Alcibiades, took him away, and placed him in the house of Ariphron to be educated; but before six months had elapsed, Ariphron sent him back, not knowing what to do with him. And I could mention numberless other instances of persons who were good themselves, and never yet made any one else good, whether friend or stranger. Now I, Protagoras, when I reflect on all this, am inclined to think that virtue can not be taught. But then again, when I listen to your words, I am disposed to waver; and I believe that there must be something in what you say, because I know that you have great experience, and learning, and invention. And I wish that you would, if possible, show me a little more clearly that virtue can be taught. Will you be so good?

That I will, Socrates, and gladly. But what would you like? Shall I, as an elder, speak to you as younger men in an apologue or myth, or shall I argue the question?

Now I want you to tell me truly whether virtue is one whole, of which justice and temperance and holiness are parts; or whether all these are only the names of one and the same thing: that is the doubt which still lingers in my mind.

There is no difficulty, Socrates, in answering that the qualities of which you are speaking are the parts of virtue which is one.

And are they parts, I said, in the same sense in which mouth, nose, and eyes, and ears, are the parts of a face; or are they like the parts of gold, which differ from the whole and from one another only in being larger or smaller?

I should say that they differed, Socrates, in the first way; as the parts of a face are related to the whole face.

And do men have some one part and some another part of virtue? Or if a man has one part, must he also have all the others?

By no means, he said; for many a man is brave and not just, or just and not wise.

Why then, I said, courage and wisdom are also parts of virtue?
Most undoubtedly, he said; and wisdom is the noblest of the parts.
And they are all different from one another? I said.
Yes.

And each of them has a distinct function like the parts of the face;—
the eye, for example, is not like the ear, and has not the same functions;
and the other parts are none of them like one another, either in their
functions, or in any other way? Now I want to know whether the parts
of virtue do not also differ in themselves and in their functions; as that
is clearly what the simile would imply.

Yes, Socrates, you are right in that.

Then, I said, no other part of virtue is like knowledge, or like
justice, or like courage, or like temperance, or like holiness?

No, he answered.

Well then, I said, suppose that you and I inquire into their natures.
And first, you would agree with me that justice is of the nature of a
thing, would you not? That is my opinion, would not that be yours also?

Yes, he said; that is mine also.

And suppose that some one were to ask us, saying, O Protagoras,
and you Socrates, what about this thing which you just now called
justice, is it just or unjust? And I were to answer, just: and you—would
you vote for me or against me?

With you, he said.

Thereupon I should answer to him who asked me, that justice is of
the nature of the just: would not you?

Yes, he said.

And suppose that he went on to say: Well now, is there such a thing
as holiness?—we should answer, Yes, if I am not mistaken?

Yes, he said.

And that you acknowledge to be a thing—should we admit that?
He assented.

And is this a sort of thing which is of the nature of the holy, or of
the nature of the unholy? I should be angry at his putting such a question,
and should say, Peace, man; nothing can be holy if holiness is not holy.
What do you say to that? Would you not answer in the same way?

Certainly, he said.

And then after this suppose that he came and asked us, What were
you saying just now? Perhaps I may not have heard you rightly, but
you seemed to me to be saying that the parts of virtue were not the
same as one another. I should reply, You certainly heard that said, but
you did not, as you think, hear me say that; for Protagoras gave the
answer, and I did but ask the question. And suppose that he turned to
you and said, Is this true, Protagoras? and do you maintain that one

part of virtue is unlike another, and is this your position? how would you answer him?

Well, he said, I admit that justice bears a resemblance to holiness, for there is always some point of view in which everything is like every other thing; white is in a certain way like black, and hard is like soft, and the most extreme opposites have some qualities in common; even the parts of the face which, as we were saying before, are distinct and have different functions, are still in a certain point of view similar, and one of them is like another of them. And you may prove that they are like one another on the same principle that all things are like one another; and yet things which are alike in some particular ought not to be called alike, nor things which are unlike in some particular, however slight, unlike.

And do you think, I said, in a tone of surprise, that justice and holiness have but a small degree of likeness?

Certainly not, he said; but I do not agree with what I understand to be your view.

Well, I said, as you appear to have a difficulty about this, let us take another of the examples which you mentioned instead. Do you admit the existence of folly?

I do.

And is not wisdom the very opposite of folly?

That is true, he said.

And when men act rightly and advantageously they seem to you to be temperate or moderate?

Yes, he said.

And moderation makes them moderate?

Certainly.

And they who do not act rightly act foolishly, and in thus acting are not moderate?

I agree to that, he said.

Then to act foolishly is the opposite of acting moderately?

He assented.

And foolish actions are done by folly, and moderate or temperate actions by moderation?

He agreed.

And that is done strongly which is done by strength, and weakly which is done by weakness?

He assented.

And that which is done with swiftness is done swiftly, and that which is done with slowness, slowly?

He acknowledged that.

And if anything is done in the same way, that is done by the same; and if anything is done in an opposite way, by the opposite?

He agreed.

Once more, I said, is there anything beautiful?

Yes.

To which the only opposite is the ugly?

There is no other.

And is there anything good?

There is.

To which the only opposite is the evil?

There is no other.

And there is the acute in sound?

True.

To which the only opposite is the grave?

There is no other, he said, but that.

Then every opposite has one opposite only and no more?

He assented.

Then now, I said, let us recapitulate our admissions. First of all we admitted that everything has one opposite and not more than one?

To that he assented.

And we admitted also that what was done in opposite ways was done by opposites?

Yes.

And that which was done foolishly, as we also admitted, was done in the opposite way to that which was done moderately?

Yes.

And that which was done moderately was done by moderation or temperance, and that which was done foolishly by folly?

He agreed.

And that which is done in opposite ways is done by opposites?

Yes.

And one thing is done by moderation or temperance, and quite another thing by folly?

Yes.

And those are opposite ways?

Certainly.

And therefore done by opposites. Then folly is the opposite of moderation or temperance?

That is evident.

And do you remember that folly has already been acknowledged by us to be the opposite of wisdom?

He assented.

And we said that everything has only one opposite?

Yes.

Then, Protagoras, which of the two assertions shall we renounce? One says that everything has but one opposite; the other that wisdom is distinct from temperance or moderation, and that both of them are parts of virtue; and that they are not only distinct, but unlike, both in themselves and in their functions, like the parts of a face. Which of these two assertions shall we renounce? For both of them together are certainly not in harmony; they do not accord or agree: for how can they be said to agree if everything is assumed to have only one opposite and not more than one, and yet folly, which is one, has clearly the two opposites —wisdom and temperance? Is not that true, Protagoras? I said. What else would you say?

He assented, but with great reluctance.

Then temperance and wisdom are the same, as before justice and holiness appeared to us to be nearly the same. And now, Protagoras, I said, do not let us be faint-hearted, but let us complete what remains. Do you think that an unjust man can be temperate in his injustice?

I should be ashamed, Socrates, he said, to acknowledge this, which nevertheless many may be found to assert.

And shall I argue with them or with you? I replied.

I would rather, he said, that you should argue with the many first, if you will.

Whichever you please, if you will only answer me and say whether you are of their opinion or not. My object is to test the validity of the argument; and yet the result may be that I and you who ask and answer may also be put on our trial.

Protagoras at first made a show of refusing, as he said that the argument was not encouraging; at length, however, he consented to answer.

Now then, I said, begin at the beginning and answer me. You think that some men are moderate or temperate, and yet unjust?

Yes, he said; let that be admitted.

And moderation is good sense?

Yes.

And good sense is good counsel in doing justice?

Granted.

If they succeed, I said, or if they don't succeed?

If they succeed.

And you would admit the existence of good?

Yes.

And is the good that which is expedient for man?

Yes, indeed, he said; and there are some things which may be inexpedient, and yet I call them good.

I thought that Protagoras was getting ruffled and excited; he seemed to be setting himself in an attitude of war. Seeing this, I minded my business and gently said:—

When you say, Protagoras, that things inexpedient are good, do you mean inexpedient for man only, or inexpedient altogether? and do you call the latter good?

Certainly not the last, he replied; for I know of many things, meats, drinks, medicines, and ten thousand other things, which are partly expedient for man, and partly inexpedient; and some which are expedient for horses, and not for men; and some for oxen only, and some for dogs; and some for no animals, but only for trees; and some for the roots of trees and not for their branches, as for example, manure, which is a good thing when laid about the roots, but utterly destructive if thrown upon the shoots and young branches; or I may instance olive oil, which is mischievous to all plants, and generally most injurious to the hair of every animal with the exception of man, but beneficial to human hair and to the human body generally; and even in this application (so various and changeable is the nature of the benefit) that which is the greatest good to the outward parts of a man, is a very great evil to his inward parts: and for this reason physicians always forbid their patients the use of oil in their food, except in very small quantities, just sufficient to take away the disagreeable sensation of smell in meats and sauces.

ION

Ion. I am conscious in my own self that I do speak better and have more to say about Homer than any other man, and this is the general opinion. But I do not speak equally well about other poets—tell me the reason of this?

Socrates. I perceive, Ion; and I will proceed to explain to you what I imagine to be the reason of this. This gift which you have of speaking excellently about Homer is not an art, but an inspiration; there is a divinity moving you, like that in the stone which Euripides calls a magnet, but which is commonly known as the stone of Heraclea. For that stone not only attracts iron rings, but also imparts to them a similar power of attracting other rings; and sometimes you may see a number of pieces of iron and rings suspended from one another so as to form quite a long chain: and all of them derive their power of suspension from the original stone. Now this is like the Muse, who first gives to men inspiration herself; and from these inspired persons a chain of other persons is suspended, who take the inspiration from them. For all good poets, epic as well as lyric, compose their beautiful poems not as works of art, but because they are inspired and possessed. And as the Corybantian revellers when they dance are not in their right mind, so the lyric poets are not in their right mind when they are composing their beautiful strains: but when falling under the power of music and metre they are inspired and possessed; like Bacchic maidens who draw milk and honey from the rivers, when they are under the influence of Dionysus, but not when they are in their right mind. And the soul of the lyric poet does the same, as they themselves tell us; for they tell us that they gather their strains from honied fountains out of the gardens and dells of the Muses; thither, like the bees, they wing their way. And this is true. For the poet is a light and winged and holy thing, and there is no invention in him until he has been inspired and is out of his senses, and the mind is no longer in him: when he has not attained to this state, he is powerless and is unable to utter his oracles. Many are the noble words in which poets speak of actions like your own words about Homer; but they do not speak of them by any rules of art: only when they make that to which the Muse impels them are their inventions inspired; and then one of them will make dithyrambs, another hymns of praise, another choral strains, another epic or iambic verses— and he who is good at one is not good at any other kind of verse: for not by art does the poet sing, but by power divine. Had he learned by rules of art, he would have known how to speak not of one theme only, but of all; and therefore God takes away the minds of poets, and uses them as his ministers, as he also uses diviners and holy prophets, in order that we who hear them may know that they speak not of themselves who utter these priceless words in a state of unconsciousness, but that God is the speaker, and that through them he is conversing with us. And Tynnichus the Chalcidian affords a striking instance of what I am saying: he wrote nothing that any one would care to remember but the famous paean which is in every one's mouth, and is one of the finest poems ever written, and is certainly an invention of the Muses, as he himself says. For in this way the God would seem to indicate to us and not allow us to doubt that these beautiful poems are not human, or the work of man, but divine and the word of God; and that the poets are only the interpreters of the gods by whom they are severally possessed. Was not this the lesson which the God intended to teach when by the mouth of the worst of poets he sang the best of songs? Am I not right, Ion?

Ion. Yes, indeed, Socrates, I feel that you are; for your words touch my soul, and I am persuaded somehow that good poets are the inspired interpreters of the gods.

MENO

Meno. Can you tell me, Socrates, whether virtue is acquired by teaching or by practice; or if neither by teaching nor by practice, then whether it comes to man by nature, or in what other way?

Socrates. I am certain that if you were to ask any Athenian whether virtue was natural or acquired, he would laugh in your face, and say: Stranger, you have far too good an opinion of me; if I were inspired I might answer your question. But now I literally do not know what virtue is, and much less whether it is acquired by teaching or not. And I myself, Meno, living as I do in this region of poverty, am as poor as the rest of the citizens; and I confess with shame that I know literally nothing about virtue. How, if I knew nothing at all of Meno, could I tell if he was fair, or the opposite of fair; rich and noble, or the reverse of rich and noble? Do you think that I could?

Meno. There will be no difficulty, Socrates, in answering that. Take first the virtue of a man: his virtue is to know how to administer the state, in the administration of which he will benefit his friends and damage his enemies, and will take care not to suffer damage himself. A woman's virtue may also be easily described: her virtue is to order her house, and keep what is indoors, and obey her husband. Every age, every condition of life, young or old, male or female, bond or free, has a different virtue: there are virtues numberless, and no lack of definitions of them; for virtue is relative to the actions and ages of each of us in all that we do. And the same may be said of vice, Socrates.

Socrates. How fortunate I am, Meno! When I ask you for one virtue, you present me with a swarm of them, which are in your keeping. Suppose that I carry on the figure of the swarm, and ask of you, What is the nature of the bee? and you answer that there are many kinds of bees, and I reply: But do bees differ as bees, because there are many and different kinds of them; or are they not rather to be distinguished by some other quality, as for example beauty, size, or shape? How would you answer that?

Meno. I should answer that bees do not differ from one another, as bees.

Socrates. And suppose that I went on to say: That is what I want to know, Meno; tell me what is that quality in which they do not differ, but are all alike;—you would be able to answer that?

Meno. I should.

Socrates. And so of the virtues, however many and different they may be, they have all a common nature which makes them virtues; and on this he who would answer the question, What is virtue? would do well to have his eye fixed.

Meno. Certainly.

Socrates. Then both men and women, if they are to be good men and women, must have the same virtues of temperance and justice?

Meno. Yes, Socrates; I agree to that, for justice is virtue.

Socrates. Would you say "virtue," Meno, or "a virtue?"

Meno. What do you mean?

Socrates. I mean as I might say about anything; that a round, for example, is "a figure" and not simply "figure," and I should say this because there are other figures.

Meno. Quite right; and that is just what I am saying about virtue—that there are other virtues as well as justice.

Socrates. What are they? tell me the names of them, as I would tell you the names of the other figures if you asked me.

Meno. Courage and temperance and wisdom and magnificence are virtues; and there are many others.

Socrates. No wonder; but I will try to arrive a little nearer if I can, for you know that all things have a common notion. Suppose now that some one asked you the question which I asked before: Meno, he would say, what is figure? And if you answered "roundness," he would reply to you, in my way of speaking, by asking whether you would say that roundness is "figure" or "a figure"; and you would answer, "a figure."

Meno. Certainly.

Socrates. And for this reason—that there are other figures?

Meno. Yes.

Socrates. And suppose that he were to pursue the matter in my way, he would say: Ever and anon we are landed in particulars, but this is not what I want; tell me then, since you call them by a common name, and say that they are all figures, even when opposed to one another, what is that common nature which you designate as figure—which comprehends straight as well as round, and is no more one than the other—would you not say that?

Meno. Yes.

Socrates. And in saying that, you do not mean to say that the round is round any more than straight, or the straight any more straight than round?

Meno. Certainly not.

Socrates. You only assert that the round figure is not more a figure than the straight, or the straight than the round?

Meno. That is true.

Socrates. What then is this which is called figure? Try and answer. Suppose that when a person asked you this question either about figure or color, you were to reply, Man, I do not understand whàt you want, or know what you are saying; he would look rather astonished and say: Do you not understand that I am looking for the "simile in multis?" And then he might put the question in another form: Meno, he might say, what is that "simile in multis" which you call figure, and which includes not only round and straight figures, but all? Could you not answer that question, Meno? I wish that you would try; the attempt will be good practice with a view to the answer about virtue.

Meno. I would rather that you should answer, Socrates.

Socrates. Well, I will try and explain to you what figure is. What do you say to this answer?—Figure is the only thing that always follows color. I hope that you are satisfied with that, as I am sure I should be content if you would let me have a similar definition of virtue.

Meno. But that, Socrates, is a simple answer.

Socrates. Why simple?

Meno. Because you say that figure is that which always follows color; but if a person says that he does not know what color is, any more than what figure is—what sort of answer would you have given him?

Socrates. And now, as Pindar says, "read my meaning":—color is an effluence of form, commensurate with sight, and sensible.

Meno. That, Socrates, appears to me to be an admirable answer.

Socrates. And now, in your turn, you are to fulfil your promise, and tell me what virtue is in the universal; and do not make a singular into a plural, as the facetious say of those who break a thing, but deliver virtue to me whole and sound and not broken into a number of pieces. I have given you the pattern.

Meno. Well then, Socrates, virtue, as I take it, is the love and attainment of the honorable; that is what the poet says, and I say too—

"Virtue is the desire and power of attaining the honorable."

Socrates. Then, according to your definition, virtue would appear to be the power of attaining good?

Meno. I entirely approve, Socrates, of the manner in which you view this matter.

Socrates. Then now let us see whether this is true from another point of view; for I dare say that you are right. What you say is, that virtue is the power of attaining good?

Meno. Yes.

Socrates. Then justice or temperance or holiness, or some other part of virtue, as would appear, must accompany the acquisition, and without them the mere acquisition of good will not be virtue.

Meno. Why, how can there be virtue without these?

Socrates. Then the acquisition of such goods is no more virtue than the non-acquisition of them, but whatever is accompanied by justice or honesty is virtue, and whatever is devoid of justice is vice?

Meno. There can be no doubt about that, in my judgment.

Socrates. And were we not saying just now that justice, temperance, and the like, were each of them a part of virtue?

Meno. Yes.

Socrates. And so, Meno, this is the way in which you mock me.

Meno. Why do you say that, Socrates?

Socrates. Why, because I asked you to deliver virtue into my hands whole and unbroken, and I gave you a pattern according to which you were to frame your answer; and you have already forgotten this, and tell me that virtue is the power of attaining good justly, or with justice—thus acknowledging justice to be a part of virtue.

Meno. Yes.

Socrates. Then begin again, and answer me, What, according to you and your friend, is the definition of virtue?

Meno. O Socrates; I used to be told, before I knew you, that you are always puzzling yourself and others; and now you are casting your spells over me, and I am simply getting bewitched and enchanted, and am at my wits' end. And I think that you are very wise in not voyaging and going away from home, for if you did in other places as you do in Athens, you would be cast into prison as a magician.

Socrates. You are a rogue, Meno, and had all but caught me.

Meno. What do you mean, Socrates?

Socrates. I perplex others, not because I am clear, but because I am utterly perplexed myself. And now I know not what virtue is, and you seem to be in the same case, although you did once know before you touched me. However, I have no objection to join with you in the inquiry.

Meno. And how will you inquire, Socrates, into that which you know not? What will you put forth as the subject of inquiry? And if you find what you want, how will you ever know that this is what you did not know?

Socrates. I have heard from certain wise men and women who spoke of things divine that—

Meno. What was that? and who were they?

Socrates. Some of them were priests and priestesses, who have studied how they might be able to give a reason of their profession: there have been poets also, such as the poet Pindar and other inspired men. And what they say is—mark, now, and see whether their words are true—they say that the soul of man is immortal, and at one time has an end, which is termed dying, and at another time is born again, but is never destroyed. The soul, then, as being immortal, and having been born again many times, and having seen all things that there are, whether in this world or in the world below, has knowledge of them all; and it is no wonder that she should be able to call to remembrance all that she ever knew about virtue, and about everything; for as all nature is akin, and the soul has learned all things, there is no difficulty in her eliciting, or as men say learning, all out of a single recollection, if a man is strenuous and does not faint; for all inquiry and all learning is but recollection.

Meno. I feel, somehow, that I like what you are saying.

Socrates. And I, Meno, like what I am saying. Some things I have said of which I am not altogether confident. But that we shall be better and braver and less helpless if we think that we ought to inquire, than we should have been if we indulged in the idle fancy that there was no knowing and no use in searching after what we know not;—that is a theme upon which I am ready to fight, in word and deed, to the utmost of my power.

Meno. That again, Socrates, appears to me to be well said.

Socrates. Then, as we are agreed that a man should inquire about that which he does not know, shall you and I make an effort to inquire together into the nature of virtue?

Meno. By all means, Socrates. And yet I would rather return to my original question, Whether virtue comes by instruction, or by nature, or is gained in some other way?

Socrates. Had I the command of you as well as of myself, Meno, I would not have inquired whether virtue is given by instruction or not, until we had first ascertained "what virtue is." But as you never think of controlling yourself, but only of controlling him who is your slave, and this is your notion of freedom, I must yield to you, for I can not help. And therefore I have now to inquire into the qualities of that of which I do not at present know the nature. At any rate, will you condescend a little, and allow the question, "Whether virtue is given by instruction, or in any other way," to be argued upon hypothesis? Let the first hypothesis be that virtue is or is not knowledge,—in that case will it be taught or not? or, as we were just now saying, "remembered"? For there is no use in disputing about the name. But is virtue taught or not? or rather, does not every one see that knowledge alone is taught?

Meno. I agree.

Socrates. Then if virtue is knowledge, virtue will be taught?

Meno. Certainly.

Socrates. And the next question is, whether virtue is knowledge or of another species?

Meno. Well; and why are you so slow of heart to believe that knowledge is virtue?

Socrates. I will try and tell you why, Meno. I do not retract the assertion that if virtue is knowledge it may be taught; but I fear that I have some reason in doubting whether virtue is knowledge: for consider now and say whether virtue, or anything that is taught, must not have teachers and disciples?

Meno. Surely.

Socrates. And again, may not that art of which there are neither teachers nor disciples be assumed to be incapable of being taught?

Meno. True; but do you think that there are no teachers of virtue?

Socrates. I have certainly often inquired whether there were any, and taken great pains to find them, and have never succeeded; and many have assisted me in the search, and they were the persons whom I thought the most likely to know.

Meno. But I can not believe, Socrates, that there are no good men in the state. And if there are, how did they come into existence?

Socrates. I am afraid, Meno, that you and I are not good for much, and that Gorgias has been as poor an educator of you as Prodicus has been of me. Certainly we shall have to look to ourselves, and try to find some one who will help to improve us. This I say, because I observe that in the previous discussion none of us remarked that right and good action is possible to man under other guidance than that of knowledge;—and indeed if this be denied, there is no seeing how there can be any good men at all.

Meno. How do you mean, Socrates?

Socrates. I will explain. If a man knew the way to Larisa, or anywhere else, and went to the place and led others thither, would he not be a right and good guide?

Meno. Certainly.

Socrates. And a person who had a right opinion about the way, but had never been and did not know, might be a good guide also, might he not?

Meno. Certainly.

Socrates. And while he has true opinion about that which the other knows, he will be just as good a guide if he thinks the truth, as if he knows the truth?

Meno. Exactly.

Socrates. Then true opinion is as good a guide to correct action as wisdom; and that was the point which we omitted in our speculation about the nature of virtue, when we said that wisdom only is the guide of right action; whereas there is also right opinion.

Meno. True.

Socrates. Then right opinion is not less useful than knowledge?

Meno. I admit the cogency of that, and therefore, Socrates, allowing this, I wonder that knowledge should be preferred to right opinion—or why they should ever differ.

Socrates. You would not wonder if you had ever observed the images of Daedalus; but perhaps you have not got them in your country?

Meno. Why do you refer to them?

Socrates. Because they require to be fastened in order to keep them, and if they are not fastened they will run away.

Meno. Well, what of that?

Socrates. I mean to say that it is not much use possessing one of them if they are at liberty, for they will walk off like runaway slaves; but when fastened, they are of great value, for they are really beautiful works of art. Now this is an illustration of the nature of true opinions: while they abide with us they are beautiful and fruitful, but they run away out of the human soul, and do not remain long, and therefore they are not of much value until they are fastened by the tie of the cause; and this fastening of them, friend Meno, is recollection, as has been already agreed by us. But when they are bound, in the first place, they have the nature of knowledge; and, in the second place, they are abiding. And this is why knowledge is more honorable and excellent than true opinion, because fastened by a chain.

Meno. Yes indeed, Socrates, that I should conjecture to be the truth.

Socrates. Seeing then that men become good and useful to states, not only because they have knowledge, but because they have right opinion, and neither knowledge nor right opinion is given to man by nature or acquired by him—if they are not given by nature, neither are the good by nature good?

Meno. Certainly not.

Socrates. And nature being excluded, the next question was whether virtue is acquired by teaching?

Meno. Yes.

Socrates. But if virtue is not taught, neither is virtue knowledge.

Meno. Clearly not.

Socrates. Then of two good and useful things, one, which is knowledge, has been set aside, and can not be supposed to be our guide in political life.

Meno. I think not.

Socrates. But if not by knowledge, the only alternative which remains is that statesmen must have guided states by right opinion, which is in politics what divination is in religion; for diviners and also prophets say many things truly, but they know not what they say.

Meno. Very true.

Socrates. To sum up our inquiry—the result seems to be, if we are at all right in our view, that virtue is neither natural nor acquired, but an instinct given by God to the virtuous. Nor is the instinct accompanied by reason, unless there may be supposed to be among statesmen any one who is also the educator of statesmen.

Meno. That is excellent, Socrates.

Socrates. Then, Meno, the conclusion is that virtue comes to the virtuous by the gift of God.

EUTHYPHRO

Socrates. What is piety, and what is impiety?

Euthyphro. Piety is doing as I am doing; that is to say, prosecuting any one who is guilty of murder, sacrilege, or of any other similar crime—whether he be your father or mother, or some other person, that makes no difference—and not prosecuting them is impiety. And please to consider, Socrates, what a notable proof I will give you of the truth of what I am saying, which I have already given to others:—of the truth, I mean, of the principle that the impious, whoever he may be, ought not to go unpunished. For do not men regard Zeus as the best and most righteous of the gods?—and even they admit that he bound his father (Cronos) because he wickedly devoured his sons, and that he too had punished his own father (Uranus) for a similar reason, in a nameless manner.

Socrates. May not this be the reason, Euthyphro, why I am charged with impiety—that I can not approve of these stories about the gods? and therefore I suppose that people think me wrong. But, as you who are well informed about them approve of them, I can not do better than assent to your superior wisdom. For what else can I say, confessing as I do, that I know nothing of them. I wish you would tell me whether you really believe that they are true?

Euthyphro. Yes, Socrates; and things more wonderful still, of which the world is in ignorance.

Socrates. I dare say; and you shall tell me them at some other time when I have leisure. But just at present I would rather hear from you a more precise answer, which you have not as yet given, my friend, to the question, What is "piety"? In reply, you only say that piety is, Doing as you do, charging your father with murder?

Euthyphro. And that is true, Socrates.

Socrates. Tell me what this is, and then I shall have a standard to which I may look, and by which I may measure the nature of actions, whether yours or any one's else, and say that this action is pious, and that impious?

Euthyphro. Piety, then, is that which is dear to the gods, and impiety is that which is not dear to them.

Socrates. That, my good friend, we shall know better in a little while.

The point which I should first wish to understand is whether the pious or holy is beloved by the gods because it is holy, or holy because it is beloved of the gods. And what do you say of piety, Euthyphro: is not piety, according to your definition, loved by all the gods?

Euthyphro. Yes.

Socrates. Because it is pious or holy, or for some other reason?

Euthyphro. No, that is the reason.

Socrates. It is loved because it is holy, not holy because it is loved?

Euthyphro. Yes.

Socrates. And that which is in a state to be loved of the gods, and is dear to them, is in a state to be loved of them because it is loved of them?

Euthyphro. Certainly.

Socrates. Then that which is loved of God, Euthyphro, is not holy, nor is that which is holy loved of God, as you affirm; but they are two different things.

Euthyphro. How do you mean, Socrates?

Socrates. I mean to say that the holy has been acknowledged by us to be loved of God because it is holy, not to be holy because it is loved.

Euthyphro. Yes.

Socrates. But that which is dear to the gods is dear to them because it is loved by them, not loved by them because it is dear to them.

Euthyphro. True.

Socrates. But, friend Euthyphro, if that which is holy is the same as that which is dear to God, and that which is holy is loved as being holy, then that which is dear to God would have been loved as being dear to God; but if that which is dear to God is dear to him because loved by him, then that which is holy would have been holy because loved by him. But now you see that the reverse is the case, and that they are quite different from one another. And what is impiety?

Euthyphro. I really do not know, Socrates, how to say what I mean. For somehow or other our arguments, on whatever ground we rest them, seem to turn round and walk away.

Socrates. Tell me, then,—Is not that which is pious necessarily just?

Euthyphro. Yes.

Socrates. And is, then, all which is just pious? or, is that which is pious all just, but that which is just only in part and not all pious?

Euthyphro. Yes; that, I think, is correct.

Socrates. Then, now, if piety is a part of justice, I suppose that we inquire what part? If you had pursued the inquiry in the previous cases; for instance, if you had asked me what is an even number, and what part of number the even is, I should have had no difficulty in replying, a number which represents a figure having two equal sides. Do you agree?

Euthyphro. Yes.

Socrates. In like manner, I want you to tell me what part of justice is piety or holiness; that I may be able to tell Meletus not to do me injustice, or indict me for impiety; as I am now adequately instructed by you in the nature of piety or holiness, and their opposites.

Euthyphro. I have told you already, Socrates, that to learn all these things accurately will be very tiresome. Let me simply say that piety is learning how to please the gods in word and deed, by prayers and sacrifices. That is piety, which is the salvation of families and states, just as the impious, which is unpleasing to the gods, is their ruin and destruction.

Socrates. I think that you could have answered in much fewer words the chief question which I asked, Euthyphro, if you had chosen. But I see plainly that you are not disposed to instruct me: else why, when we had reached the point, did you turn aside? Had you only answered me I should have learned of you by this time the nature of piety. Now, as the asker of a question is necessarily dependent on the answerer, whither he leads I must follow; and can only ask again, what is the pious, and what is piety? Do you mean that they are a sort of science of praying and sacrificing?

Euthyphro. Yes, I do.

Socrates. And sacrificing is giving to the gods, and prayer is asking of the gods?

Euthyphro. Yes, Socrates.

Socrates. Then piety, Euthyphro, is an art which gods and men have of doing business with one another?

Euthyphro. That is an expression which you may use, if you like.

Socrates. But I have no particular liking for anything but the truth. I wish, however, that you would tell me what benefit accrues to the gods from our gifts. That they are the givers of every good to us is clear; but how we can give any good thing to them in return is far from being equally clear. If they give everything and we give nothing, that must be an affair of business in which we have very greatly the advantage of them.

Euthyphro. And do you imagine, Socrates, that any benefit accrues to the gods from what they receive of us?

Socrates. But if not, Euthyphro, what sort of gifts do we confer upon the gods?

Euthyphro. What should we confer upon them, but tributes of honor; and, as I was just now saying, what is pleasing to them?

Socrates. Piety, then, is pleasing to the gods, but not beneficial or dear to them?

Euthyphro. I should say that nothing could be dearer.

Socrates. Then once more the assertion is repeated that piety is dear to the gods?

Euthyphro. No doubt.

Socrates. Then we must begin again and ask, What is piety? That is an inquiry which I shall never be weary of pursuing as far as in me lies; and I entreat you not to scorn me, but to apply your mind to the utmost, and tell me the truth.

Euthyphro. Another time, Socrates; for I am in a hurry, and must go now.

APOLOGY

Socrates Is the Speaker

LET US REFLECT and we shall see that there is great reason to hope that death is a good, for one of two things:—either death is a state of nothingness and utter unconsciousness, or, as men say, there is a change and migration of the soul from this world to another. Now if you suppose that there is no consciousness, but a sleep like the sleep of him who is undisturbed even by the sight of dreams, death will be an unspeakable gain. For if a person were to select the night in which his sleep was undisturbed even by dreams, and were to compare with this the other days and nights of his life, and then were to tell us how many days and nights he had passed in the course of his life better and more pleasantly than this one, I think that any man, I will not say a private man, but even the great king will not find many such days or nights, when compared with the others. Now if death is like this, I say that to die is gain; for eternity is then only a single night. But if death is the journey to another place, and there, as men say, all the dead are, what good, O my friends and judges, can be greater than this? If indeed when the pilgrim arrives in the world below, he is delivered from the professors of justice in this world, and finds the true judges who are said to give judgment there, Minos and Rhadamanthus and Aeacus and Triptolemus, and other sons of God who were righteous in their own life, that pilgrimage will be worth making. What would not a man give if he might converse with Orpheus and Musaeus and Hesiod and Homer? Nay, if this be true, let me die again and again. I, too, shall have a wonderful interest in a place where I can converse with Palamedes, and Ajax the son of Telamon, and other heroes of old, who have suffered death through an unjust judgment; and there will be no small pleasure, as I think, in comparing my own sufferings with theirs. Above all, I shall be able to continue my search into true and false knowledge; as in this world, so also in that; I shall find out who is wise, and who pretends to be wise, and is not. What would not a man give, O judges, to be able to examine the leader of the great Trojan expedition; or Odysseus or Sisyphus, or numberless others, men and women too! What infinite delight would there be in conversing with them and asking them questions! For in that world they do not put a man to death for this; certainly not. For besides being happier in that world than in this, they will be immortal, if what is said is true.

Wherefore, O judges, be of good cheer about death, and know this of a truth—that no evil can happen to a good man, either in life or after death. He and his are not neglected by the gods; nor has my own approaching end happened by mere chance. But I see clearly that to die and be released was better for me; and therefore the oracle gave no sign. For which reason, also, I am not angry with my accusers or my condemners; they have done me no harm, although neither of them meant to do me any good; and for this I may gently blame them.

CRITO

Socrates. Dear Crito, your zeal is invaluable, if a right one; but if wrong, the greater the zeal the greater the evil; and therefore we ought to consider whether these things shall be done or not. For I am and always have been one of those natures who must be guided by reason, whatever the reason may be which upon reflection appears to me to be the best; and now that this fortune has come upon me, I can not put away the reasons which I have before given: the principles which I have hitherto honored and revered I still honor, and unless we can find other and better principles on the instant, I am certain not to agree with you; no, not even if the power of the multitude could inflict many more imprisonments, confiscations, deaths, frightening us like children with hobgoblin terrors. But what will be the fairest way of considering the question? Shall I return to your old argument about the opinions of men? some of which are to be regarded, and others are not to be regarded. Now were we right in maintaining this before I was condemned? And has the argument which was once good now proved to be talk for the sake of talking;—in fact an amusement only, and altogether vanity? That is what I want to consider with your help, Crito:—whether, under my present circumstances, the argument appears to be in any way different or not; and is to be allowed by me or disallowed. That argument, which, as I believe, is maintained by many who assume to be authorities, was to the effect, as I was saying, that the opinions of some men are to be regarded, and of other men not to be regarded. Now you, Crito, are a disinterested person who are not going to die to-morrow—at least, there is no human probability of this, and you are therefore not liable to be deceived by the circumstances in which you are placed. Tell me then, whether I am right in saying that some opinions, and the opinions of some men only, are to be valued, and other opinions, and the opinions of other men, are not to be valued. I ask you whether I was right in maintaining this?

Crito. Certainly.

Socrates. The good are to be regarded, and not the bad?

Crito. Yes.

Socrates. And the opinions of the wise are good, and the opinions of the unwise are evil?

Crito. Certainly.

Socrates. Very good; and is not this true, Crito, of other things which we need not separately enumerate? In the matter of just and unjust, fair and foul, good and evil, which are the subjects of our present consultation, ought we to follow the opinion of the many and to fear them; or the opinion of the one man who has understanding, and whom we ought to fear and reverence more than all the rest of the world: and whom deserting we shall destroy and injure that principle in us which may be assumed to be improved by justice and deteriorated by injustice;—is there not such a principle?

Crito. Certainly there is, Socrates.

Socrates. Then, my friend, we must not regard what the many say of us: but what he, the one man who has understanding of just and unjust, will say, and what the truth will say. And therefore you begin in error when you suggest that we should regard the opinion of the many about just and unjust, good and evil, honorable and dishonorable.

Crito. Yes, that holds.

Socrates. From these premises I proceed to argue the question whether I ought or ought not to try and escape without the consent of the Athenians: and if I am clearly right in escaping, then I will make the attempt; but if not, I will abstain. The other considerations which you mention, of money and loss of character and the duty of educating children, are, as I fear, only the doctrines of the multitude, who would be as ready to call people to life, if they were able, as they are to put them to death—and with as little reason. But now, since the argument has thus far prevailed, the only question which remains to be considered is, whether we shall do rightly either in escaping or in suffering others to aid in our escape and paying them in money and thanks, or whether we shall not do rightly; and if the latter, then death or any other calamity which may ensue on my remaining here must not be allowed to enter into the calculation.

Crito. I think that you are right, Socrates; how then shall we proceed?

Socrates. Are we to say that we are never intentionally to do wrong, or that in one way we ought and in another way we ought not to do wrong, or is doing wrong always evil and dishonorable, as I was just now saying, and as has been already acknowledged by us? Are all our former admissions which were made within a few days to be thrown away? And have we, at our age, been earnestly discoursing with one another all our

life long only to discover that we are no better than children? Or are we
to rest assured, in spite of the opinion of the many, and in spite of consequences whether better or worse, of the truth of what was then said, that
injustice is always an evil and dishonor to him who acts unjustly? Shall we
affirm that?

Crito. Yes.

Socrates. Then I will proceed to the next step, which may be put in
the form of a question:—Ought a man to do what he admits to be right,
or ought he to betray the right?

Crito. He ought to do what he thinks right.

Socrates. Then consider the matter in this way:—Imagine that I am
about to play truant, and the laws and the government come and interro-
gate me: "Tell us, Socrates," they say; "what are you about? are you going
by an act of yours to overturn us—the laws and the whole state, as far as
in you lies? Do you imagine that a state can subsist and not be overthrown, in which the decisions of law have no power, but are set aside
and overthrown by individuals?" What will be our answer, Crito, to these
and the like words? Any one, and especially a clever rhetorician, will have
a good deal to urge about the evil of setting aside the law which requires
a sentence to be carried out; and we might reply, "Yes; but the state has
injured us and given an unjust sentence." Suppose I say that?

Crito. Very good, Socrates.

Socrates. "And was that our agreement with you?" the law would say;
"or were you to abide by the sentence of the state?" And if I were to express astonishment at their saying this, the law would probably add: "Answer, Socrates, instead of opening your eyes: you are in the habit of asking
and answering questions. Tell us what complaint you have to make against
us which justifies you in attempting to destroy us and the state? In the
first place did we not bring you into existence? Your father married your
mother by our aid and begat you. Say whether you have any objection to
urge against those of us who regulate marriage?" None, I should reply.
"Or against those of us who regulate the system of nurture and education
of children in which you were trained? Were not the laws, who have the
charge of this, right in commanding your father to train you in music and
gymnastic?" Right, I should reply. "Well then, since you were brought
into the world and nurtured and educated by us, can you deny in the first
place that you are our child and slave, as your fathers were before you?
And if this is true you are not on equal terms with us; nor can you think
that you have a right to do to us what we are doing to you. Would you
have any right to strike or revile or do any other evil to a father or to your
master, if you had one, when you have been struck or reviled by him, or
received some other evil at his hands?—you would not say this? And because we think right to destroy you, do you think that you have any right

to destroy us in return, and your country as far as in you lies? And will you, O professor of true virtue, say that you are justified in this? Has a philosopher like you failed to discover that our country is more to be valued and higher and holier far than mother or father or any ancestor, and more to be regarded in the eyes of the gods and of men of understanding? also to be soothed, and gently and reverently entreated when angry, even more than a father, and if not persuaded, obeyed? And when we are punished by her, whether with imprisonment or stripes, the punishment is to be endured in silence; and if she lead us to wounds or death in battle, thither we follow as is right; neither may any one yield or retreat or leave his rank, but whether in battle or in a court of law, or in any other place, he must do what his city and his country order him; or he must change their view of what is just: and if he may do no violence to his father or mother, much less may he do violence to his country." What answer shall we make to this, Crito? Do the laws speak truly, or do they not?

Crito. I think that they do.

Socrates. Then the laws will say: "Consider, Socrates, if this is true, that in your present attempt you are going to do us wrong. For, after having brought you into the world, and nurtured and educated you, and given you and every other citizen a share in every good that we had to give, we further proclaim and give the right to every Athenian, that if he does not like us when he has come of age and has seen the ways of the city, and made our acquaintance, he may go where he pleases and take his goods with him; and none of us laws will forbid him or interfere with him. Any of you who does not like us and the city, and who wants to go to a colony or to any other city, may go where he likes, and take his goods with him. But he who has experience of the manner in which we order justice and administer the state, and still remains, has entered into an implied contract that he will do as we command him. And he who disobeys us is, as we maintain, thrice wrong; first, because in disobeying us he is disobeying his parents; secondly, because we are the authors of his education; thirdly, because he has made an agreement with us that he will duly obey our commands; and he neither obeys them nor convinces us that our commands are wrong; and we do not rudely impose them, but give him the alternative of obeying or convincing us;—that is what we offer, and he does neither. These are the sort of accusations to which, as we were saying, you, Socrates, will be exposed if you accomplish your intentions; you, above all other Athenians." Suppose I ask, why is this? they will justly retort upon me that I above all other men have acknowledged the agreement. "There is clear proof," they will say, "Socrates, that we and the city were not displeasing to you. Of all Athenians you have been the most constant resident in the city, which, as you never leave, you may be supposed to love. For you never went out of the city either to see the games, except once when you went to the Isthmus, or to any other place unless when you were on military service; nor did you travel as other men do. Nor had you any curiosity to know other states or their laws: your affections did not go beyond us and our state; we were your special favorites, and you acquiesced in our government of you; and this is the state in which you begat your children, which is a proof of your satisfaction. Moreover, you might, if you had liked, have fixed the penalty at banishment in the course of the trial—the state which refuses to let you go now would have let you go then. But you pretended that you preferred death to exile, and that you were not grieved at death. And now you have forgotten these fine sentiments, and pay no respect to us the laws, of whom you are the destroyer; and are doing what only a miserable slave would do, running away and turning your back upon the compacts and agreements which you made as a citizen. And first of all answer this very question: Are we right in saying that you agreed to be governed according to us in deed, and not in word only? Is that true or not?" How shall we answer that, Crito? Must we not agree?

Crito. There is no help, Socrates.

Socrates. Then will they not say: "You, Socrates, are breaking the covenants and agreements which you made with us at your leisure, not in any haste or under any compulsion or deception, but having had seventy years to think of them, during which time you were at liberty to leave the city, if we were not to your mind, or if our covenants appeared to you to be unfair. You had your choice, and might have gone either to Lacedaemon or Crete, which you often praise for their good government, or to some other Hellenic or foreign state. Whereas you, above all other Athenians, seemed to be so fond of the state, or, in other words, of us her laws that you never stirred out of her; the halt, the blind, the maimed were not more stationary in her than you were. And now you run away and forsake your agreements. Not so, Socrates, if you will take our advice; do not make yourself ridiculous by escaping out of the city.

"For just consider, if you transgress and err in this sort of way, what good will you do either to yourself or to your friends? That your friends will be driven into exile and deprived of citizenship, or will lose their property, is tolerably certain; and you yourself, if you fly to one of the neighboring cities, as, for example, Thebes or Megara, both of which are well-governed cities, will come to them as an enemy, Socrates, and their government will be against you, and all patriotic citizens will cast an evil eye upon you as a subverter of the laws, and you will confirm in the minds of the judges the justice of their own condemnation of you. For he who is a corruptor of the laws is more than likely to be corruptor of the young and foolish portion of mankind. Will you then flee from well-ordered cities and virtuous men? and is existence worth having on these terms? Or will you go to them without shame, and talk to them, Socrates? And what will you say to them? What you say here about virtue and justice and institutions and laws being the best things among men. Would that be decent of you? Surely not. But if you go away from well-governed states to Crito's friends in Thessaly, where there is a great disorder and license, they will be charmed to have the tale of your escape from prison, set off with ludicrous particulars of the manner in which you were wrapped in a goatskin or some other disguise, and metamorphosed as the fashion of runaways is—that is very likely; but will there be no one to remind you that in your old age you violated the most sacred laws from a miserable desire of a little more life? Perhaps not, if you keep them in a good temper; but if they are out of temper you will hear many degrading things; you will live, but how?—as the flatterer of all men, and the servant of all men; and doing what?—eating and drinking in Thessaly, having gone abroad in order that you may get a dinner. And where will be your fine sentiments about justice and virtue then? Say that you wish to live for the sake of your children, that you may bring them up and educate them— will you take them into Thessaly and deprive them of Athenian citizenship? Is that the benefit which you would confer upon them? Or are you under the impression that they will be better cared for and educated here if you are still alive, although absent from them; for that your friends will take care of them? Do you fancy that if you are an inhabitant of Thessaly they will take care of them, and if you are an inhabitant of the other world they will not take care of them? Nay; but if they who call themselves friends are truly friends, they surely will.

"Listen, then, Socrates, to us who have brought you up. Think not of life and children first, and of justice afterwards, but of justice first, that you may be justified before the princes of the world below. For neither will you nor any that belong to you be happier or holier or juster in this life, or happier in another, if you do as Crito bids. Now you depart in innocence, a sufferer and not a doer of evil; a victim, not of the laws, but of men. But if you go forth, returning evil for evil, and injury for injury, breaking the covenants and agreements which you have made with us, and wronging those whom you ought least to wrong, that is to say, yourself, your friends, your country, and us, we shall be angry with you while you live, and our brethren, the laws in the world below, will receive you as an enemy; for they will know that you have done your best to destroy us. Listen, then, to us and not to Crito."

This is the voice which I seem to hear murmuring in my ears, like the sound of the flute in the ears of the mystic; that voice, I say, is humming in my ears, and prevents me from hearing any other. And I know that anything more which you may say will be vain. Yet speak, if you have anything to say.

Crito. I have nothing to say, Socrates.

Socrates. Then let me follow the intimations of the will of God.

PHAEDO

Phaedo Is the Narrator

WHY do you say, inquired Cebes, that a man ought not to take his own life, but that the philosopher will be ready to follow the dying?

Socrates replied: And have you, Cebes and Simmias, who are acquainted with Philolaus, never heard him speak of this?

I never understood him, Socrates.

My words, too, are only an echo; but I am very willing to say what I have heard: and indeed, as I am going to another place, I ought to be thinking and talking of the nature of the pilgrimage which I am about to make. What can I do better in the interval between this and the setting of the sun?

Would you not say that he is entirely concerned with the soul and not with the body? He would like, as far as he can, to be quit of the body and turn to the soul.

That is true.

In matters of this sort philosophers, above all other men, may be observed in every sort of way to dissever the soul from the body.

That is quite true.

What again shall we say of the actual acquirement of knowledge?— is the body, if invited to share in the inquiry, a hinderer or a helper? I mean to say, have sight and hearing any truth in them? Are they not, as the poets are always telling us, inaccurate witnesses? and yet, if even they are inaccurate and indistinct, what is to be said of the other senses?—for you will allow that they are the best of them?

Certainly, he replied.

Then when does the soul attain truth?—for in attempting to consider anything in company with the body she is obviously deceived.

Yes, that is true.

Then must not existence be revealed to her in thought, if at all?

Yes.

And thought is best when the mind is gathered into herself and none of these things trouble her—neither sounds nor sights nor pain nor any pleasure,—when she has as little as possible to do with the body, and has no bodily sense or feeling, but is aspiring after being?

That is true.

And in this the philosopher dishonors the body; his soul runs away from the body and desires to be alone and by herself?

That is true.

Well, but there is another thing, Simmias: Is there or is there not an absolute justice?

Assuredly there is.

And an absolute beauty and absolute good?

Of course.

But did you ever behold any of them with your eyes?

Certainly not.

Or did you ever reach them with any other bodily sense? Has the reality of them ever been perceived by you through the bodily organs? or rather, is not the nearest approach to the knowledge of their several natures made by him who so orders his intellectual vision as to have the most exact conception of the essence of that which he considers?

Certainly.

But if this is true, O my friend, then there is great hope that, going whither I go, I shall there be satisfied with that which has been the chief concern of you and me in our past lives. And now that the hour of departure is appointed to me, this is the hope with which I depart, and not I only, but every man who believes that he has his mind purified.

Cebes answered: I agree, Socrates, in the greater part of what you say. But in what relates to the soul, men are apt to be incredulous; they fear that when she leaves the body her place may be nowhere, and that on the very day of death she may be destroyed and perish—immediately on her release from the body, issuing forth like smoke or air and vanishing away into nothingness. For if she could only hold together and be herself after she was released from the evils of the body, there would be good reason to hope, Socrates, that what you say is true. But much persuasion and many arguments are required in order to prove that when the man is dead the soul yet exists, and has any force or intelligence.

True, Cebes, said Socrates; and shall I suggest that we talk a little of the probabilities of these things?

I am sure, said Cebes, that I should greatly like to know your opinion about them.

I reckon, said Socrates, that no one who heard me now, not even if he were one of my old enemies, the comic poets, could accuse me of idle talking about matters in which I have no concern. Let us then, if you please, proceed with the inquiry.

Whether the souls of men after death are or are not in the world below, is a question which may be argued in this manner:—The ancient doctrine of which I have been speaking affirms that they go from hence into the other world, and return hither, and are born from the dead. Now if this be true, and the living come from the dead, then our souls must be in the other world, for if not, how could they be born again? And this would be conclusive, if there were any real evidence that the living are only born from the dead; but if there is no evidence of this, then other arguments will have to be adduced.

That is very true, replied Cebes.

Then let us consider this question, not in relation to man only, but in relation to animals generally, and to plants, and to everything of which there is generation, and the proof will be easier. Are not all things which have opposites generated out of their opposites? I mean such things as good and evil, just and unjust—and there are innumerable other opposites which are generated out of opposites. And I want to show that this holds universally of all opposites; I mean to say, for example, that anything which becomes greater must become greater after being less.

Quite agreed.

Then, suppose that you analyze life and death to me in the same manner. Is not death opposed to life?

Yes.

And they are generated one from the other?

Yes.

What is generated from life?

Death.

And what from death?

I can only say in answer—life.

Then the living, whether things or persons, Cebes, are generated from the dead?

That is clear, he replied.

Then the inference is that our souls are in the world below?

That is true.

And one of the true processes or generations is visible—for surely the act of dying is visible?

Surely, he said.

And may not the other be inferred as the complement of nature, who is not to be supposed to go on one leg only? And if not, a corresponding process of generation in death must also be assigned to her?

Certainly, he replied.

And what is that process?

Revival.

And revival, if there be such a thing, is the birth of the dead into the world of the living?

Quite true.

Then here is a new way in which we arrive at the inference that the

living come from the dead, just as the dead come from the living; and
if this is true, then the souls of the dead must be in some place out of
which they come again. And this, as I think, has been satisfactorily proved.

Yes, Socrates, he said; all this seems to flow necessarily out of our
previous admissions.

But then, O my friends, if the soul is really immortal, what care
should be taken of her, not only in respect of the portion of time which
is called life, but of eternity! And the danger of neglecting her from this
point of view does indeed appear to be awful. If death had only been the
end of all, the wicked would have had a good bargain in dying, for they
would have been happily quit not only of their body, but of their own
evil together with their souls. But now, as the soul plainly appears to be
immortal, there is no release or salvation from evil except the attainment
of the highest virtue and wisdom. For the soul when on her progress to
the world below takes nothing with her but nurture and education; which
are indeed said greatly to benefit or greatly to injure the departed, at the
very beginning of his pilgrimage in the other world.

For after death, as they say, the genius of each individual, to whom
he belonged in life, leads him to a certain place in which the dead are
gathered together for judgment, whence they go into the world below,
following the guide, who is appointed to conduct them from this world
to the other: and when they have there received their due and remained
their time, another guide brings them back again after many revolutions
of ages. Now this journey to the other world is not, as Aeschylus says in
the Telephus, a single and straight path—no guide would be wanted for
that, and no one could miss a single path; but there are many partings of
the road, and windings, as I must infer from the rites and sacrifices which
are offered to the gods below in places where three ways meet on earth.
The wise and orderly soul is conscious of her situation, and follows in the
path; but the soul which desires the body, and which, as I was relating
before, has long been fluttering about the lifeless frame and the world of
sight, is after many struggles and many sufferings hardly and with violence
carried away by her attendant genius, and when she arrives at the place
where the other souls are gathered, if she be impure and have done impure deeds, or been concerned in foul murders or other crimes which are
the brothers of these, and the works of brothers in crime—from that soul
every one flees and turns away; no one will be her companion, no one her
guide, but alone she wanders in extremity of evil until certain times are
fulfilled, and when they are fulfilled, she is borne irresistibly to her own
fitting habitation; as every pure and just soul which has passed through
life in the company and under the guidance of the gods has also her own
proper home.

Now the earth has divers wonderful regions, and is indeed in nature and extent very unlike the notions of geographers, as I believe on the authority of one who shall be nameless.

What do you mean, Socrates? said Simmias. I have myself heard many descriptions of the earth, but I do not know in what you are putting your faith, and I should like to know.

Well, Simmias, replied Socrates, the recital of a tale does not, I think, require the art of Glaucus; and I know not that the art of Glaucus could prove the truth of my tale, which I myself should never be able to prove, and even if I could, I fear, Simmias, that my life would come to an end before the argument was completed. I may describe to you, however, the form and regions of the earth according to my conception of them.

That, said Simmias, will be enough.

Well then, he said, my conviction is, that the earth is a round body in the centre of the heavens, and therefore has no need of air or any similar force as a support, but is kept there and hindered from falling or inclining any way by equability of the surrounding heaven and by her own equipoise. For that which, being in equipoise, is in the centre of that which is equably diffused, will not incline any way in any degree, but will always remain in the same state and not deviate. And this is my first notion.

Which is surely a correct one, said Simmias.

Also I believe that the earth is very vast, and that we who dwell in the region extending from the river Phasis to the Pillars of Heracles along the borders of the sea, are just like ants or frogs about a marsh, and inhabit a small portion only, and that many others dwell in many like places. For I should say that in all parts of the earth there are hollows of various forms and sizes, into which the water and the mist and the air collect; and that the true earth is pure and in the pure heaven, in which also are the stars —that is the heaven which is commonly spoken of as the ether, of which this is but the sediment collecting in the hollows of the earth. But we who live in these hollows are deceived into the notion that we are dwelling above on the surface of the earth; which is just as if a creature who was at the bottom of the sea were to fancy that he was on the surface of the water, and that the sea was the heaven through which he saw the sun and the other stars,—he having never come to the surface by reason of his feebleness and sluggishness, and having never lifted up his head and seen, nor ever heard from one who had seen, this other region which is so much purer and fairer than his own. Now this is exactly our case: for we are dwelling in a hollow of the earth, and fancy that we are on the surface; and the air we call the heaven, and in this we imagine that the stars move. But this is also owing to our feebleness and sluggishness, which prevent our reaching the surface of the air: for if any man could arrive at the exterior limit, or take the wings of a bird and fly upward, like a fish who puts his head out and sees this world, he would see a world beyond; and, if the nature of man could sustain the sight, he would acknowledge that this was the place of the true heaven and the true light and the true stars. For this earth, and the stones, and the entire region which surrounds us, are spoiled and corroded, like the things in the sea which are corroded by the brine; for in the sea too there is hardly any noble or perfect growth, but clefts only, and sand, and an endless slough of mud; and even the shore is not to be compared to the fairer sights of this world. And greater far is the superiority of the other. Now of that upper earth which is under the heaven, I can tell you a charming tale, Simmias, which is well worth hearing.

And we, Socrates, replied Simmias, shall be charmed to listen.

The tale, my friend, he said, is as follows:—In the first place, the earth, when looked at from above, is like one of those balls which have leather coverings in twelve pieces, and is of divers colors, of which the colors which painters use on earth are only a sample. But there the whole earth is made up of them, and they are brighter far and clearer than ours; there is a purple of wonderful lustre, also the radiance of gold, and the white which is in the earth is whiter than any chalk or snow. Of these and other colors the earth is made up, and they are more in number and fairer than the eye of man has ever seen; and the very hollows (of which I was speaking) filled with air and water are seen like light flashing amid the other colors, and have a color of their own, which gives a sort of unity to the variety of earth. And in this fair region everything that grows—trees, and flowers, and fruits—are in a like degree fairer than any here; and there are hills, and stones in them in a like degree smoother, and more transparent, and fairer in color than our highly valued emeralds and sardonyxes and jaspers, and other gems, which are but minute fragments of them: for there all the stones are like our precious stones, and fairer still. The reason of this is, that they are pure, and not, like our precious stones, infected or corroded by the corrupt briny elements which coagulate among us, and which breed foulness and disease both in earth and stones, as well as in animals and plants. They are the jewels of the upper earth, which also shines with gold and silver and the like, and they are visible to sight and large and abundant and found in every region of the earth, and blessed is he who sees them. And upon the earth are animals and men, some in a middle region, others dwelling about the air as we dwell about the sea; others in islands which the air flows round, near the continent: and in a word, the air is used by them as the water and the sea are by us, and the ether is to them what the air is to us. Moreover, the temperament of their season is such that they have no disease, and live much longer than we do, and have sight and hearing and smell, and all the other senses, in far greater perfection, in the same degree that air is purer than water or the ether than air. Also they have temples and sacred places in which the gods really dwell, and they hear their voices and receive their answers, and are conscious of them and hold converse with them, and they see the sun, moon, and stars as they really are, and their other blessedness is of a piece with this.

Such is the nature of the whole earth, and of the things which are around the earth; and there are divers regions in the hollows on the face of the globe everywhere, some of them deeper and also wider than that which we inhabit, others deeper and with a narrower opening than ours, and some are shallower and wider; all have numerous perforations, and passages broad and narrow in the interior of the earth, connecting them with one another; and there flows into and out of them, as into basins, a vast tide of water, and huge subterranean streams of perennial rivers, and springs hot and cold, and a great fire, and great rivers of fire, and streams of liquid mud, thin or thick (like the rivers of mud in Sicily, and the lava streams which follow them), and the regions about which they happen to flow are filled up with them. And there is a sort of swing in the interior of the earth which moves all this up and down. Now the swing is on this wise:—There is a chasm which is the vastest of them all, and pierces right through the whole earth; this is that which Homer describes in the words:—

"Far off, where is the inmost depth beneath the earth";

and which he in other places, and many other poets, have called Tartarus. And the swing is caused by the streams flowing into and out of this chasm, and they each have the nature of the soil through which they flow. And the reason why the streams are always flowing in and out, is that the watery element has no bed or bottom, and is surging and swinging up and down, and the surrounding wind and air do the same; they follow the water up and down, hither and thither, over the earth—just as in respiring the air is always in process of inhalation and exhalation;—and the wind swinging with the water in and out produces fearful and irresistible blasts: when the waters retire with a rush into the lower parts of the earth, as they are called, they flow through the earth into those regions, and fill them up as with the alternate motion of a pump, and then when they leave those regions and rush back hither, they again fill the hollows here, and when these are filled, flow through subterranean channels and find their way to their several places, forming seas, and lakes, and rivers, and springs. Thence they again enter the earth, some of them making a long circuit into many lands, others going to few places and those not distant; and again fall into Tartarus, some at a point a good deal lower than that at which they rose, and others not much lower, but all in some degree lower than the point of issue. And some burst forth again on the opposite side, and some on the same side, and some wind round the earth with one or many folds like the coils of a serpent, and descend as far as they can, but always return and fall into the lake. The rivers on either side can descend only to the centre and no further, for to the rivers on both sides the opposite side is a precipice.

Now these rivers are many, and mighty, and diverse, and there are four principal ones, of which the greatest and outermost is that called Oceanus, which flows round the earth in a circle; and in the opposite direction flows Acheron, which passes under the earth through desert places, into the Acherusian lake: this is the lake to the shores of which the souls of the many go when they are dead, and after waiting an appointed time, which is to some a longer and to some a shorter time, they are sent back again to be born as animals. The third river rises between the two, and near the place of rising pours into a vast region of fire, and forms a lake larger than the Mediterranean Sea, boiling with water and mud; and proceeding muddy and turbid, and winding about the earth, comes, among other places, to the extremities of the Acherusian lake, but mingles not with the waters of the lake, and after making many coils about the earth plunges into Tartarus at a deeper level. This is that Pyriphlegethon, as the stream is called, which throws up jets of fire in all sorts of places. The fourth river goes out on the opposite side, and falls first of all into a wild and savage region, which is all of a dark blue color, like lapis lazuli; and this is that river which is called the Stygian river, and falls into and forms the Lake Styx, and after falling into the lake and receiving strange powers in the waters, passes under the earth, winding round in the opposite direction to Pyriphlegethon and meeting in the Acherusian lake from the opposite side. And the water of this river too mingles with no other, but flows round in a circle and falls into Tartarus over against Pyriphlegethon; and the name of this river, as the poets say, is Cocytus.

Such is the nature of the other world; and when the dead arrive at the place to which the genius of each severally conveys them, first of all, they have sentence passed upon them, as they have lived well and piously or not. And those who appear to have lived neither well nor ill, go to the river Acheron, and mount such conveyances as they can get, and are carried in them to the lake, and there they dwell and are purified of their evil deeds, and suffer the penalty of the wrongs which they have done to others, and are absolved, and receive the rewards of their good deeds according to their deserts. But those who appear to be incurable by reason of the greatness of their crimes—who have committed many and terrible deeds of sacrilege, murders foul and violent, or the like—such are hurled into Tartarus which is their suitable destiny, and they never come out. Those again who have committed crimes, which, although great, are not unpardonable—who in a moment of anger, for example, have done violence to a father or a mother, and have repented for the remainder of their lives, or, who have taken the life of another under the like extenuating circumstances—these are plunged into Tartarus, the pains of which they are compelled to undergo for a year, but at the end of the year the wave casts them forth—mere homicides by way of Cocytus, parricides and matricides by Pyriphlegethon—and they are borne to the Acherusian lake, and there they lift up their voices and call upon the victims whom they have slain or wronged, to have pity on them, and to receive them, and to let them come out of the river into the lake. And if they prevail, then they come forth and cease from their troubles; but if not, they are carried back again into Tartarus and from thence into the rivers unceasingly, until they obtain mercy from those whom they have wronged: for that is the sentence inflicted upon them by their judges. Those also who are remarkable for having led holy lives are released from this earthly prison, and go to their pure home which is above, and dwell in the purer earth; and those who have duly purified themselves with philosophy, live henceforth altogether without the body, in mansions fairer far than these, which may not be described, and of which the time would fail me to tell.

Wherefore, Simmias, seeing all these things, what ought not we to do in order to obtain virtue and wisdom in this life? Fair is the prize, and the hope great!

THE SYMPOSIUM

Apollodorus Is the Narrator

SOCRATES took his place on the couch; and when the meal was ended, and the libations offered, and after a hymn had been sung to the god, and there had been the usual ceremonies,—as they were about to commence drinking, Pausanias reminded them that they had had a bout yesterday, from which he and most of them were still suffering, and they ought to be allowed to recover, and not go on drinking to-day. He would therefore ask, How the drinking could be made easiest?

I entirely agree, said Aristophanes, that we should, by all means, get off the drinking, having been myself one of those who were yesterday drowned in drink.

I think that you are right, said Eryximachus, the son of Acumenus; but I should like to hear one other person speak. What are the inclinations of our host?

I am not able to drink, said Agathon.

All agreed that drinking was not to be the order of the day. Then, said Eryximachus, as you are all agreed that drinking is to be voluntary, and that there is to be no compulsion, I move, in the next place, that the

flute-girl, who has just made her appearance, be told to go away; she may
play to herself, or, if she has a mind, to the women who are within. But
on this day let us have conversation instead; and, if you will allow me, I
will tell you what sort of conversation. This proposal having been accepted, Eryximachus proceeded as follows:—

I will begin, he said, after the manner of Melanippe in Euripides,

"Not mine the word"

which I am about to speak, but that of Phaedrus. For he is in the habit of
complaining that, whereas other gods have poems and hymns made in
their honor by the poets, who are so many, the great and glorious god
Love has not a single panegyrist or encomiast. Now I want to offer Phaedrus a contribution to his feast; nor do I see how the present company
can, at this moment, do anything better than honor the god Love. And if
you agree to this, there will be no lack of conversation; for I mean to propose that each of us in turn shall make a discourse in honor of Love. Let
us have the best which he can make; and Phaedrus, who is sitting first on
the left hand, and is the father of the thought, shall begin.

Phaedrus began by affirming that Love is a mighty god, and wonderful among gods and men, but especially wonderful in his birth. For that
he is the eldest of the gods is an honor to him; and a proof of this is, that
of his parents there is no memorial; neither poet nor prose-writer has ever
affirmed that he had any. Thus numerous are the witnesses which acknowledge Love to be the eldest of the gods. And not only is he the eldest, he is
also the source of the greatest benefits to us. For I know not any greater
blessing to a young man beginning life than a virtuous lover, or to the
lover than a beloved youth. For the principle which ought to be the guide
of men who would nobly live—that principle, I say, neither kindred, nor
honor, nor wealth, nor any other motive is able to implant as surely as
love. Of what am I speaking? Of the sense of honor and dishonor, without
which neither states nor individuals ever do any good or great work. And
I say that a lover who is detected in doing any dishonorable act, or submitting through cowardice when any dishonor is done to him by another,
will be more pained at being detected by his beloved than at being seen
by his father, or his companions, or any one else. And the beloved has the
same feeling about his love, when he again is seen on any disgraceful
occasion.

Love will make men dare to die for their beloved; and women as well
as men. Of this, Alcestis, the daughter of Pelias, is a monument to all
Hellas; for she was willing to lay down her life on behalf of her husband,
when no one else would, although he had a father and mother; but the
tenderness of her love so far exceeded theirs, that they seemed to be as
strangers to their own son, having no concern with him; and so noble did

this action of hers appear, not only to men but also to the gods, that among the many who have done virtuously she was one of the very few to whom the gods have granted the privilege of returning to earth, in admiration of her virtue; such exceeding honor is paid by them to the devotion and virtue of love. These are my reasons for affirming that Love is the eldest and noblest and mightiest of the gods, and the chiefest author and giver of happiness and virtue, in life and after death.

This, or something like this, was the speech of Phaedrus: and some other speeches followed which Aristodemus did not remember; the next which he repeated was that of Pausanias, who observed that the proposal of Phaedrus was too indiscriminate, and that Love ought not to be praised in this unqualified manner. If there were only one Love, then what he said would be well enough; but since there are more Loves than one, he should have begun by determining which of them was to be the theme of our praises. I will amend this defect, he said; and first of all I will tell you which Love is worthy of praise, and then try to hymn the praise-worthy one in a manner worthy of the god. For we all know that Love is inseparable from Aphrodite, and if there were only one Aphrodite there would be only one Love; but as there are two goddesses there must be two Loves. For am I not right in asserting that there are two goddesses? The elder one, having no mother, who is called the heavenly Aphrodite— she is the daughter of Uranus; the younger, who is the daughter of Zeus and Dione, whom we call common; and the other Love who is her fellow-worker may and must also have the name of common, as the other is called heavenly. But the Love who is the son of the common Aphrodite is essentially common, and has no discrimination, being such as the meaner sort of men feel, and is apt to be of women as well as of youths, and is of the body rather than of the soul—the most foolish beings are the objects of this love which desires only to gain an end, but never thinks of accomplishing the end nobly, and therefore does good and evil quite indiscriminately. The goddess who is his mother is far younger, and she was born of the union of the male and female, and partakes of both sexes. But the son of the heavenly Aphrodite is sprung from a mother in whose birth the female has no part, but she is from the male only; this is that love which is of youths only, and the goddess being older has nothing of wantonness. Those who are inspired by this love turn to the male, and delight in him who is the more valiant and intelligent nature; any one may recognize the pure enthusiasts in the very character of their attachments. For they love not boys, but intelligent beings whose reason is beginning to be developed, much about the time at which their beards begin to grow. And in choosing them as their companions, they mean to be faithful to them, and to pass their whole life with them, and be with them, and not to take them in their inexperience, and deceive them, and play the fool with them, or run away from one to another of them. Consider, too, how great is the encouragement which all the world gives to the lover; neither is he supposed to be doing anything dishonorable; but if he succeeds he is praised, and if he fail he is blamed.

Such is the entire liberty which gods and men allow the lover, and which in our part of the world the custom confirms. And this is one side of the question, which may make a man fairly think that in this city to love and to be loved is held to be a very honorable thing. But when there is a new regime, and parents forbid their sons to talk with their lovers, and place them under a tutor's care, and their companions and equals are personal in their remarks when they see anything of this sort going on, and their elders refuse to silence them and do not reprove their words; any one who reflects on this will, on the contrary, think that we hold these practices to be disgraceful. But the truth, as I imagine, and as I said at first, is, that whether such practices are honorable or whether they are dishonorable is not a simple question; they are honorable to him who follows them honorably, dishonorable to him who follows them dishonorably. There is dishonor in yielding to the evil, or in an evil manner; but there is honor in yielding to the good, or in an honorable manner. The custom of our country would have them both proven well and truly, and would have us yield to the one sort of love and avoid the other; testing them in contests and trials, which will show to which of the two classes the lover and the beloved respectively belong. And this is the reason why, in the first place, a hasty attachment is held to be dishonorable, because time is the true test of this as of most other things; and then again there is a dishonor in being overcome by the love of money, wealth, or of political power, whether a man suffers and is frightened into surrender at the loss of them, or is unable to rise above the advantages of them. For none of these things are of a permanent or lasting nature; not to mention that no generous friendship ever sprung from them. There remains, then, only one way of honorable attachment which custom allows in the beloved, and this is the way of virtue; any service which the lover did was not to be accounted flattery or dishonor, and the beloved has also one way of voluntary service which is not dishonorable, and this is virtuous service.

When Pausanias came to a pause, Aristodemus said that the turn of Aristophanes was next, but that either he had eaten too much, or from some other cause he had the hiccough, and was obliged to change with Eryximachus the physician, who was reclining on the couch below him. Eryximachus, he said, you ought either to stop my hiccough, or to speak in my turn until I am better.

I will do both, said Eryximachus: I will speak in your turn, and do you speak in mine; and while I am speaking let me recommend you to hold your breath, and if this fails, then to gargle with a little water; and if the hiccough still continues, tickle your nose with something and sneeze; and if you sneeze once or twice, even the most violent hiccough is sure to go. In the meantime I will take your turn, and you shall take mine. I will do as you prescribe, said Aristophanes, and now get on.

Eryximachus spoke as follows: Seeing that Pausanias made a fair beginning, and but a lame ending, I will endeavor to supply his deficiency. I think that he has rightly distinguished two kinds of love. But my art instructs me that this double love is to be found in all animals and plants, and I may say in all that is; and is not merely an affection of the soul of man towards the fair, or towards anything; that, I say, is a view of the subject which I seem to have gathered from my own art of medicine, which shows me how great and wonderful and universal is this deity, whose empire is over all that is, divine as well as human. And from medicine I will begin that I may do honor to my art. For there are in the human body two loves, which are confessedly different and unlike, and being unlike, have loves and desires which are unlike; and the desire of the healthy is one, and the desire of the diseased is another; and, as Pausanias says, the good are to be accepted, and the bad are not to be accepted; and so too in the body the good and healthy elements are to be indulged, and the bad elements and the elements of desire are not to be indulged, but discouraged. And this is what the physician has to do, and in this the art of medicine consists: for medicine may be regarded generally as the knowledge of the loves and desires of the body, and how to fill or empty them; and the good physician is he who is able to separate fair love from foul, or to convert one into the other; and if he is a skilful practitioner, he knows how to eradicate and how to implant love, whichever is required, and he can reconcile the most hostile elements in the constitution, and make them friends. Now the most hostile are the most opposite, such as hot and cold, moist and dry, bitter and sweet, and the like. And my ancestor, Asclepius, knowing how to implant friendship and accord in these elements, was the creator of our art, as our friends the poets tell us and I believe them; and not only medicine in every branch, but the arts of gymnastic and husbandry are under his dominion. Any one who pays the least attention will also perceive that in music there is the same reconciliation of opposites; and I suppose that this must have been the meaning of Heracleitus, although his words are not accurate; for he says that one is united by disunion, like the harmony of the bow and the lyre. Now there is an absurdity in saying that harmony is disagreement or is composed of elements which are still in a state of disagreement. But perhaps what he really meant to say was that harmony is composed of differing notes of higher or lower pitch which disagreed once, but are now reconciled by the art of music; for if the higher and lower notes still disagree, there could be no harm, as is indeed evident. For harmony is a symphony, and symphony is an agreement; but an agreement of disagreements while they disagree can not exist; there is no harmony of discord and disagreement. This may be illustrated by rhythm, which is composed of elements short and long, once differing and now in accord; which accordance, as in the former instance, medicine, so in this, music implants, making love and unison to grow up among them: and thus music, too, is concerned with the principles of love in their application to harmony and rhythm. Again, in the abstract principles of harmony and rhythm there is no difficulty in discerning them, for as yet love has no double nature. But when you want to use them in actual life, either in the composition of music or in the correct performance of airs or metres composed already, which latter is called education, then the difficulty begins, and the good artist is needed. Then the old tale has to be repeated of fair and heavenly love— the love of Urania the fair and heavenly muse—and of the duty of accepting the temperate, and the intemperate only that they may become temperate, and of preserving their love; and again, of the vulgar Polyhymnia who must be used with circumspection that the pleasure may not generate licentiousness; just as in my own art great skill is shown in gratifying the taste of the epicure without inflicting upon him the attendant evil of disease. The conclusion is that in music, in medicine, in all other things human as well as divine, both loves ought to be noted as far as may be, for they are both present.

The course of the season is also full of both principles; and when, as I was saying, the elements of hot and cold, moist and dry, attain the harmonious love of one another and blend in temperance and harmony, they bring to men, animals, and vegetables health and wealth, and do them no harm; whereas the wantonness and overbearingness of the other love affecting the seasons is a great injurer and destroyer, and is the source of pestilence, and brings many different sorts of diseases on animals and plants; for hoar-frost and hail and blight spring from the excesses and disorders of these elements of love, the knowledge of which in relation to the revolutions of the heavenly bodies and the seasons of the year is termed astronomy. Such is the great and mighty, or rather universal, force of all love. And that love, especially, which is concerned with the good, and which is perfected in company with temperance and justice, whether among gods or men, has the greatest power, and is the source of all our happiness and harmony and friendship with the gods which are above us, and with one another. I dare say that I have omitted several things which might be said in praise of Love, but this was not intentional, and you, Aristophanes, may now supply the omission or take some other line of commendation; as I perceive that you are cured of the hiccough.

Aristophanes professed to open another vein of discourse; he had a mind to praise Love in another way, not like that either of Pausanias or Eryximachus. Mankind, he said, judging by their neglect of him, have never, as I think, at all understood the power of Love. For if they had understood him they would surely have built noble temples and altars, and offered solemn sacrifices in his honor; but this is not done, and certainly ought to be done: for of all the gods he is the best friend of men, the helper and the healer of the ills which are the great obstruction to the happiness of the race. I shall rehearse to you his power, and you may repeat what I say to the rest of the world. And first let me treat of the nature and state of man; for the original human nature was not like the present, but different. In the first place, the sexes were originally three in number, not two as they are now; there was man, woman, and the union of the two, having a name corresponding to this double nature; this once had a real existence, but is now lost, and the name only is preserved as a term of reproach. In the second place, the primeval man was round and had four hands and four feet, back and sides forming a circle, one head with two faces, looking opposite ways, set on a round neck and precisely alike; also four ears, two privy members, and the remainder to correspond.

Terrible was their might and strength, and the thoughts of their hearts were great, and they made an attack upon the gods; and of them is told the tale of Otus and Ephialtes who, as Homer says, dared to scale heaven, and would have laid hands upon the gods. Doubt reigned in the councils of Zeus and of the gods. Should they kill them and annihilate the race with thunderbolts, as they had done the giants, then there would be an end of the sacrifice and worship which men offered to them; but, on the other hand, the gods could not suffer their insolence to be unrestrained. At last, after a good deal of reflection, Zeus discovered a way. He said: "I have a notion which will humble their pride and mend their manners; they shall continue to exist, but I will cut them in two and then they will be diminished in strength and increased in numbers; this will have the advantage of making them more profitable to us. They shall walk upright on two legs, and if they continue insolent and won't be quiet, I will split them again and they shall hop about on a single leg." He spoke and cut them in two, like a sorb-apple which is halved for pickling, or as you might divide an egg with a hair; and as he cut them one after another, he bade Apollo give the face and the half of the neck a turn in order that the man might contemplate the section of himself: this would teach him a lesson of humility. He was also to heal their wounds and compose their forms. Apollo twisted the face and pulled the skin all round over that which in our language is called the belly, like the purses which draw in, and he made one mouth at the centre, which he fastened in a knot (this is called the navel); he also moulded the breast and took out most of the wrinkles, much as a shoemaker might smooth out leather upon a last; he left a few, however, in the region of the belly and navel, as a memorial of the primeval change. After the division the two parts of man, each desiring his other half, came together, and threw their arms about one another, eager to grow into one, and would have perished from hunger without ever making an effort, because they did not like to do anything apart; and when one of the halves died and the other survived, the survivor sought another mate, whether the section of an entire man or of an entire woman, which had usurped the name of man and woman, and clung to that. And this was being the destruction of them, when Zeus in pity invented a new plan: he turned the parts of generation round in front, for this was not always their position, and they sowed the seed no longer as hitherto like grasshoppers in the ground, but in one another; and after the transposition the male generated in the female in order that by the mutual embraces of man and woman they might breed, and the race might continue; or if man came to man they might be satisfied, and rest and go their ways to the business of life: so ancient is the desire of one another which is implanted in us, reuniting our original nature, making one of two, and healing the state of man. Each of us when separated is but the indenture of a man, having one side only like a flat fish, and he is always looking for his other half. Men who are a section of that double nature which was once called Androgynous are lascivious; adulterers are generally of this breed, and also adulterous and lascivious women: the women who are a section of the woman don't care for men, but have female attachments; the female companions are of this sort. But the men who are a section of the male follow the male, and while they are young, being a piece of the man, they hang about him and embrace him, and they are themselves the best of boys and youths, because they have the most manly nature. Some indeed assert that they are shameless, but this is not true; for they do not act thus from any want of shame, but because they are valiant and manly, and have a manly countenance, and they embrace that which is like them. And these when they grow up are our statesmen, and these only, which is a great proof of the truth of what I am saying. And when they reach manhood they are lovers of youth, and are not naturally inclined to marry or beget children, which they do, if at all, only in obedience to the law, but they are satisfied if they may be allowed to live unwedded; and such a nature is prone to love and ready to return love, always embracing that which is akin to him. And when one of them finds his other half, whether he be a lover of youth or a lover of another sort, the pair are lost in an amazement of love and friendship and intimacy, and one will not be out of the other's sight, as I may say, even for a moment: these are they who pass their lives with one another; yet they could not explain what they desire of one another.

For the intense yearning which each of them has towards the other does not appear to be the desire of intercourse, but of something else which the soul desires and can not tell, and of which she has only a dark and doubtful presentiment. And the reason is that human nature was originally one and we were a whole, and the desire and pursuit of the whole is called love. There was a time, I say, when the two were one, but now because of this wickedness of men God has dispersed us, as the Arcadians were dispersed into villages by the Lacedaemonians. And if we are not obedient to the gods there is a danger that we shall be split up again and go about in basso-relievo, like the figures having only half a nose which are sculptured on columns, and that we shall be like tallies. Wherefore let us exhort all men to piety, that we may avoid the evil and obtain the good, of which Love is the lord and leader; and let no one oppose him—he is the enemy of the gods who opposes him. For if we are friends of God and reconciled to him we shall find our own true loves, which rarely happens in this world. This, Eryximachus, is my discourse of love, which, although different from yours, I must beg you to leave unassailed by the shafts of your ridicule, in order that each may have his turn; each, or rather either, for Agathon and Socrates are the only ones left.

Indeed, I am not going to attack you, said Eryximachus, for I thought your speech charming, and did I not know that Agathon and Socrates are masters in the art of love, I should be really afraid that they would have nothing to say, after all the world of things which have been said already. But, for all that, I am not without hopes.

Socrates said: You did your part well, Eryximachus; but if you were as I am now, or rather as I shall be when Agathon has spoken, you would, indeed, be in a great strait.

You want to cast a spell over me, Socrates, said Agathon, in the hope that I may be disconcerted, thinking of the anticipation which the theatre has of my fine speech.

I should be strangely forgetful, Agathon, replied Socrates, of the courage and magnanimity which you showed when your own compositions were about to be exhibited, coming upon the stage with the actors and facing the whole theatre altogether undismayed, if I thought that your nerves could be fluttered at a small party of friends.

Here Phaedrus interrupted them, saying: Don't answer him, my dear Agathon; for if he can only get a partner with whom he can talk, especially a good-looking one, he will no longer care about the completion of our plan. Now I love to hear him talk; but just at present I must not forget the encomium on Love which I ought to receive from him and every one. When you and he have paid tribute to the god, then you may talk.

Very good, Phaedrus, said Agathon; I see no reason why I should not proceed with my speech, as I shall have other opportunities of conversing with Socrates. Let me say first how I ought to speak, and then speak.

The previous speakers, instead of praising the god Love, or unfolding his nature, appear to have congratulated mankind on the benefits which he confers upon them. But I would rather praise the god first, and then speak of his gifts; this is always the right way of praising everything. May I express unblamed then, that of all the blessed gods he is the blessedest and the best? And also the fairest, which I prove in this way: for, in the first place, Phaedrus, he is the youngest, and of his youth he is himself the witness, fleeing out of the way of age, which is swift enough surely, swifter than most of us like: yet he can not be overtaken by him; he is not a bird of that feather; youth and love live and move together—like to like, as the proverb says. There are many things which Phaedrus said about Love in which I agree with him; but I can not agree that he is older than Iapetus and Kronos—that is not the truth; as I maintain, he is the youngest of the gods, and youthful ever. The ancient things of which Hesiod and Parmenides speak, if they were done at all, were done of necessity and not of love; had love been in those days, there would have been no chaining or mutilation of the gods, or other violence, but peace and sweetness, as there is now in heaven, since the rule of Love began. Love is young and also tender.

But I must now speak of his virtue: his greatest glory is that he can neither do nor suffer wrong from any god or any man; for he suffers not by force if he suffers, for force comes not near him, neither does he act by force. For all serve him of their own free will, and where there is love as well as obedience, there, as the laws which are the lords of the city say, is justice. And not only is he just but exceedingly temperate, for Temperance is the acknowledged ruler of the pleasures and desires, and no pleasure ever masters Love; he is their master and they are his servants; and if he conquers them he must be temperate indeed. As to courage, even the God of War is no match for him; he is the captive and Love is the lord, for love, the love of Aphrodite, masters him, as the tale runs; and the master is stronger than the servant. And if he conquers the bravest of all he must be himself the bravest. Of his courage and justice and temperance I have spoken; but I have yet to speak of his wisdom, and I must try to do my best, according to the measure of my ability. For in the first place he is a poet (and here, like Eryximachus, I magnify my art), and he is also the source of poesy in others, which he could not be if he were not himself a poet. And at the touch of him every one becomes a poet, even though he had no music in him before; this also is a proof that Love is a good poet and accomplished in all the musical arts; for no one can give to another that which he has not himself, or teach that of which he has no knowledge. Who will deny that the creation of the animals is his doing? Are they not all the works of his wisdom, born and begotten of him? And as to the artists, do we not know that he only of them whom love inspires has the light of fame?—he whom love touches not walks in darkness.

Therefore, Phaedrus, I say of love that he is the fairest and best in himself, and the cause of what is fairest and best in all other things. And I have a mind to say of him in verse that he is the god who

"Gives peace on earth and calms the stormy deep,
Who stills the waves and bids the sufferer sleep."

He makes men to be of one mind at a banquet such as this, fulfilling them with affection and emptying them of disaffection. In sacrifices, banquets, dances, he is our lord—supplying kindness and banishing unkindness, giving friendship and forgiving enmity, the joy of the good, the wonder of the wise, the amazement of the gods; desired by those who have no part in him, and precious to those who have the better part in him; parent of delicacy, luxury, desire, fondness, softness, grace; careful of the good, uncareful of the evil. In every word, work, wish, fear—pilot, helper, defender, savior; glory of gods and men, leader best and brightest: in whose footsteps let every man follow, chanting a hymn and joining in that fair strain with which love charms the souls of gods and men. Such is the discourse, Phaedrus, half playful, yet having a certain measure of seriousness, which, according to my ability, I dedicate to the god.

When Agathon had done speaking, Aristodemus said that there was a general cheer; the fair youth was thought to have spoken in a manner worthy of himself, and of the god. And Socrates, looking at Eryximachus, said: Tell me, son of Acumenus, was I not a prophet? Did I not anticipate that Agathon would make a wonderful oration, and that I should be in a strait?

I think, said Eryximachus, that you were right in the first anticipation, but not in the second.

Socrates then proceeded as follows:—In the magnificent discourse which you have uttered, I think that you were right, my dear Agathon, in saying that you would begin with the nature of love and then afterwards speak of his works—that is a way of beginning which I very much approve. And as you have spoken thus eloquently of the nature of love, will you answer me a further question?—Is love the love of something or of nothing? And here I must explain myself: I do not want you to say that love is the love of a father or the love of a mother—that would be ridiculous; but to answer as you would, if I asked is a father a father of something? to which you would find no difficulty in replying, of a son or daughter: and that would be right.

Very true, said Agathon.

Then now, said Socrates, let us recapitulate the argument. First, is not love of something, and of something too which is wanting to a man?

Yes, he replied.

Remember further what you said in your speech, or if you do not remember I will remind you: you said that the love of the beautiful disposes the empire of the gods, for that of deformed things there is no love—did you not say something like that?

Yes, said Agathon.

Yes, my friend, and the remark is a just one. And if this is true, love is the love of beauty and not of deformity?

He assented.

And the admission has been already made that love is of that which a man wants and has not?

True, he said.

Then love wants and has not beauty?

Certainly, he replied.

And would you call that beautiful which wants and does not possess beauty?

Certainly not.

Then would you still say that love is beautiful?

Agathon replied: I fear that I did not understand what I was saying.

Nay, Agathon, replied Socrates; but I should like to ask you one more question:—Is not the good also the beautiful?

Yes.

Then in wanting the beautiful, love wants also the good?

I can not refute you, Socrates, said Agathon. And let us suppose that what you say is true.

Say rather, dear Agathon, that you can not refute the truth; for Socrates is easily refuted.

And now I will take my leave of you, and rehearse the tale of love which I heard once upon a time from Diotima of Mantineia, who was a wise woman in this and many other branches of knowledge. She was the same who deferred the plague of Athens ten years by a sacrifice, and was my instructress in the art of love. In the attempt which I am about to make I shall pursue Agathon's method, and begin with his admissions, which are nearly if not quite the same which I made to the wise woman when she questioned me: this will be the easiest way, and I shall take both parts myself as well as I can. For, like Agathon, she spoke first of the being and nature of love, and then of his works. And I said to her in nearly the same words which he used to me, that love was a mighty god, and likewise fair; and she proved to me as I proved to him that, in my way of speaking about him, love was neither fair nor good. "What do you mean, Diotima," I said, "is love then evil and foul?"

"Hush," she cried; "is that to be deemed foul which is not fair?" "Certainly," I said. "And is that which is not wise, ignorant? do you not see that there is a mean between wisdom and ignorance?" "And what is this?" I said. "Right opinion," she replied; "which, as you know, being incapable of giving a reason, is not knowledge (for how could knowledge be devoid of reason? nor again, ignorance, for neither can ignorance attain the truth), but is clearly something which is a mean between ignorance and wisdom." "Quite true," I replied. "Do not then insist," she said, "that what is not fair is of necessity foul, or what is not good evil; or infer that because love is not fair and good he is therefore foul and evil; for he is in a mean between them." "Well," I said, "love is surely admitted by all to be a great god." "By those who know or by those who don't know?" "By all." "And how, Socrates," she said with a smile, "can love be acknowledged to be a great god by those who say that he is not a god at all?" "And who are they?" I said. "You and I are two of them," she replied. "How can that be?" I said. "That is very intelligible," she replied; "as you yourself would acknowledge that the gods are happy and fair—of course you would—would you dare to say that any god was not?" "Certainly not," I replied. "And you mean by the happy, those who are the possessors of things good or fair?" "Yes." "And you admitted that love, because he was in want, desires those good and fair things of which he is in want?" "Yes, I admitted that." "But how can he be a god who has no share in the good or the fair?" "That is not to be supposed." "Then you see that you also deny the deity of love."

"What then is love?" I asked. "Is he mortal?" "No." "What then?" "As in the former instance, he is neither mortal nor immortal, but in a mean between them." "What is he then, Diotima?" "He is a great spirit, and like all that is spiritual he is intermediate between the divine and the mortal." "And what is the nature of this spiritual power?" I said. "This is the power," she said, "which interprets and conveys to the gods the prayers and sacrifices of men, and to men the commands and rewards of the gods; and this power spans the chasm which divides them, and in this all is bound together, and through this the arts of the prophet and the priest, their sacrifices and mysteries and charms, and all prophecy and incantation, find their way. For God mingles not with man; and through this power all the intercourse and speech of God with man, whether awake or asleep, is carried on. The wisdom which understands this is spiritual; all other wisdom, such as that of arts or handicrafts, is mean and vulgar. Now these spirits or intermediate powers are many and divine, and one of them is love." "And who," I said, "was his father, and who his mother?" "The tale," she said, "will take time; nevertheless I will tell you. On the birthday of Aphrodite there was a feast of the gods, at which the god Poros or Plenty, who is the son of Metis or Discretion, was one of the guests. When the feast was over, Penia or Poverty, as the manner was, came about the doors to beg. Now Plenty, who was the worse for nectar (there was no wine in those days), came into the garden of Zeus and fell into a heavy sleep; and Poverty, considering her own straitened circumstances, plotted to have him for a husband, and accordingly she lay down at his side and conceived Love, who partly because he is naturally a lover of the beautiful, and because Aphrodite is herself beautiful, and also because he was born on Aphrodite's birthday is her follower and attendant. And as his parentage is, so also are his fortunes. In the first place he is always poor, and anything but tender and fair, as the many imagine him; and he is hard-featured and squalid, and has no shoes, nor a house to dwell in; on the bare earth exposed he lies under the open heaven, in the streets, or at the doors of houses, taking his rest; and like his mother he is always in distress. Like his father too, whom he also partly resembles, he is always plotting against the fair and good; he is bold, enterprising, strong, a hunter of men, always at some intrigue or other, keen in the pursuit of wisdom, and never wanting resources; a philosopher at all times, terrible as an enchanter, sorcerer, sophist; for as he is neither mortal nor immortal, he is alive and flourishing at one moment when he is in plenty, and dead at another moment, and again alive by reason of his father's nature. But that which is always flowing in is always flowing out, and so he is never in want and never in wealth, and he is also in a mean between ignorance and knowledge. The truth of the matter is just this: No god is a philosopher or seeker after wisdom, for he is wise already; nor does any one else who is wise seek after wisdom. Neither do the ignorant seek after wisdom. For herein is the evil of ignorance, that he who is neither good nor wise is nevertheless satisfied: he feels no want, and has therefore no desire."

"But who then, Diotima," I said, "are the lovers of wisdom, if they are neither the wise nor the foolish?" "A child may answer that question," she replied; "they are those who, like love, are in a mean between the two. For wisdom is a most beautiful thing, and love is of the beautiful; and therefore love is also a philosopher or lover of wisdom, and being a lover of wisdom is in a mean between the wise and the ignorant. And this again is a quality which Love inherits from his parents; for his father is wealthy and wise, and his mother poor and foolish. Such, my dear Socrates, is the nature of the spirit Love. The error in your conception of him was very natural, and as I imagine from what you say, has arisen out of a confusion of love and the beloved—this made you think that love was all beautiful. For the beloved is the truly beautiful, delicate, and perfect and blessed; but the principle of love is of another nature, and is such as I have described."

I said: "O thou stranger woman, thou sayest well, and now, assuming love to be such as you say, what is the use of him?" "That, Socrates," she replied, "I will proceed to unfold: of his nature and birth I have already spoken; and you acknowledge that love is of the beautiful. But some one will say: Of the beautiful in what, Socrates and Diotima—or rather let me put the question more clearly, and ask: When a man loves the beautiful, why does he love?" I answered her, "That the beautiful may be his." "Still," she said, "the answer suggests a further question, which is this: What is given by the possession of beauty?" "That," I replied, "is a question to which I have no answer ready." "Then," she said, "let me put the word 'good' in the place of the beautiful, and repeat the question: What does he who loves the good desire?" "The possession of the good," I said. "And what does he gain who possesses the good?" "Happiness," I replied; "there is no difficulty in answering that."

"Yes," she said, "the happy are made happy by the acquisition of good things. Nor is there any need to ask why a man desires happiness; the answer is already final." "That is true," I said. "And is this wish and this desire common to all? and do all men always desire their own good, or only some men?—what think you?" "All men," I replied; "the desire is common to all." "But all men, Socrates," she rejoined, "are not said to love, but only some of them; and you say that all men are always loving the same things." "I myself wonder," I said, "why that is." "There is nothing to wonder at," she replied; "the reason is that one part of love is separated off and receives the name of the whole, but the other parts have other names." "Give an example," I said. She answered me as follows: "There is poetry, which, as you know, is complex and manifold. And all creation or passage of non-being into being is poetry or making, and the processes of all art are creative; and the masters of arts are all poets." "Very true." "Still," she said, "you know that they are not called poets, but have other names; the generic term 'poetry' is confined to that specific art which is separated off from the rest of poetry, and is concerned with music and metre; and this is what is called poetry, and they who possess this kind of poetry are called poets." "Very true," I said. "And the same holds of love. For you may say generally that all desire of good and happiness is due to the great and subtle power of love; but those who, having their affections set upon him, are yet diverted into the paths of money-making or gymnastic philosophy, are not called lovers—the name of the genus is reserved for those whose devotion takes one form only—they alone are said to love, or to be lovers." "In that," I said, "I am of opinion that you are right." "Yes," she said, "and you hear people say that lovers are seeking for the half of themselves; but I say that they are seeking neither for the half, nor for the whole, unless the half or the whole be also a good.

And they will cut off their own hands and feet and cast them away, if they are evil; for they love them not because they are their own, but because they are good, and dislike them not because they are another's, but because they are evil. There is nothing which men love but the good. Do you think that there is?" "Indeed," I answered, "I should say not." "Then," she said, "the conclusion of the whole matter is, that men love the good." "Yes," I said. "To which may be added that they love the possession of the good?" "Yes, that may be added." "And not only the possession, but the everlasting possession of the good?" "That may be added too." "Then, love," she said, "may be described generally as the love of the everlasting possession of the good?" "That is most true," I said.

"Then if this be the nature of love, can you tell me further," she said, "what is the manner of the pursuit? what are they doing who show all this eagerness and heat which is called love? Answer me that." "Nay, Diotima," I said, "if I had known I should not have wondered at your wisdom, or have come to you to learn." "Well," she said, "I will teach you;—love is only birth in beauty, whether of body or soul." "The oracle requires an explanation," I said; "I don't understand you." "I will make my meaning clearer," she replied. "I mean to say, that all men are bringing to the birth in their bodies and in their souls. There is a certain age at which human nature is desirous of procreation; and this procreation must be in beauty and not in deformity: and this is the mystery of man and woman, which is a divine thing, for conception and generation are a principle of immortality in the mortal creature. And in the inharmonical they can never be. But the deformed is always inharmonical with the divine, and the beautiful harmonious. Beauty, then, is the destiny or goddess of parturition who presides at birth, and therefore when approaching beauty the conceiving power is propitious, and diffuse, and benign, and begets and bears fruit: on the appearance of foulness she frowns and contracts in pain, and is averted and morose, and shrinks up, and not without a pang refrains from conception. And this is the reason why, when the hour of conception arrives, and the teeming nature is full, there is such a flutter and ecstasy about beauty whose approach is the alleviation of pain. For love, Socrates, is not, as you imagine, the love of the beautiful only." "What then?" "The love of generation and birth in beauty." "Yes," I said. "Yes, indeed," she replied. "But why of birth?" I said. "Because to the mortal, birth is a sort of eternity and immortality," she replied; "and as has been already admitted, all men will necessarily desire immortality together with good, if love is of the everlasting possession of the good."

And this she taught me at various times when she spoke of love. And on another occasion she said to me, "What is the reason, Socrates, of this love, and the attendant desire? See you not how all animals, birds as well as beasts, in their desire of procreation, are in agony when they take the infection of love;—this begins with the desire of union, to which is added the care of offspring, on behalf of whom the weakest are ready to battle against the strongest even to the uttermost, and to die for them, and will let themselves be tormented with hunger or suffer anything in order to maintain their offspring. Man may be supposed to do this from reason; but why should animals have these passionate feelings? Can you tell me why?" Again I replied, that I did not know. She said to me: "And do you expect ever to become a master in the art of love, if you do not know this?" "But that," I said, "Diotima, is the reason why I come to you, because, as I have told you already, I am aware that I want a teacher; and I wish that you would explain to me this and the other mysteries of love." "Marvel not at this," she said, "if you believe that love is of the immortal, as we have already admitted; for here again, and on the same principle too, the mortal nature is seeking as far as is possible to be everlasting and immortal: and this is only to be attained by generation, because the new is always left in the place of the old. For even in the same individual there is succession and not absolute unity: a man is called the same; but yet in the short interval which elapses between youth and age, and in which every animal is said to have life and identity, he is undergoing a perpetual process of loss and reparation—hair, flesh, bones, blood, and the whole body are always changing. And this is true not only of the body, but also of the soul, whose habits, tempers, opinions, desires, pleasures, pains, fears, never remain the same in any one of us, but are always coming and going. And what is yet more surprising is, that this is also true of knowledge; and not only does knowledge in general come and go, so that in this respect we are never the same; but particular knowledge also experiences a like change. For what is implied in the word 'recollection,' but the departure of knowledge, which is ever being forgotten and is renewed and preserved by recollection, appearing to be the same although in reality new, according to that law of succession by which all mortal things are preserved, not by absolute sameness of existence, but by substitution, the old worn-out mortality leaving another new and similar one behind—unlike the immortal in this, which is always the same and not another? And in this way, Socrates, the mortal body, or mortal anything, partakes of immortality; but the immortal in another way. Marvel not then at the love which all men have of their offspring; for that universal love and interest is for the sake of immortality."

When I heard this, I was astonished, and said: "Is this really true, O thou wise Diotima?" And she answered with all the authority of a Sophist: "Of that, Socrates, you may be assured;—think only of the ambition of men, and you will marvel at their senselessness, unless you consider how they are stirred by the love of an immortality of fame. They are ready to run risks greater far than they would have run for their children, and to spend money and undergo any amount of toil, and even to die for the sake of leaving behind them a name which shall be eternal. Do you imagine that Alcestis would have died on behalf of Admetus, or Achilles after Patroclus, or your own Codrus in order to preserve the kingdom for his sons, if they had not imagined that the memory of their virtues, which is still retained among us, would be immortal? Nay," she said, "for I am persuaded that all men do all things for the sake of the glorious fame of immortal virtue, and the better they are the more they desire this; for they are ravished with the desire of the immortal.

"Men whose bodies only are creative, betake themselves to women and beget children—this is the character of their love; their offspring, as they hope, will preserve their memory and give them the blessedness and immortality which they desire in the future. But creative souls— for there are men who are more creative in their souls than in their bodies —conceive that which is proper for the soul to conceive or retain. And what are these conceptions?—wisdom and virtue in general. And such creators are all poets and other artists who may be said to have invention. But the greatest and fairest sort of wisdom by far is that which is concerned with the ordering of states and families, and which is called temperance and justice. And he who in youth has the seed of these implanted in him and is himself inspired, when he comes to maturity desires to beget and generate. And he wanders about seeking beauty that he may beget offspring—for in deformity he will beget nothing—and embraces the beautiful rather than the deformed; and when he finds a fair and noble and well-nurtured soul, and there is union of the two in one person, he gladly embraces him, and to such a one he is full of fair speech about virtue and the nature and pursuits of a good man; and he tries to educate him; and at the touch and presence of the beautiful he brings forth the beautiful which he conceived long before, and the beautiful is ever present with him and in his memory even when absent, and in company they tend that which he brings forth, and they are bound together by a far nearer tie and have a closer friendship than those who beget mortal children, for the children who are their common offspring are fairer and more immortal. Who, when he thinks of Homer and Hesiod and other great poets, would not rather have their children than any ordinary human ones? Who would not emulate them in the creation of children such as theirs, which have preserved their memory and given them everlasting glory? Or who would not have such children as Lycurgus left behind to be the saviors, not only of Lacedaemon, but of Hellas, as one may say? There is Solon, too, who is the revered father of Athenian laws; and many others there are in many other places, both among

Hellenes and barbarians. All of them have done many noble works, and have been the parents of virtue of every kind, and many temples have been raised in honor of their children, which were never raised in honor of the mortal children of any one.

"These are the lesser mysteries of love, into which even you, Socrates, may enter; to the greater and more hidden ones which are the crown of these, and to which, if you pursue them in a right spirit, they will lead, I know not whether you will be able to attain. But I will do my utmost to inform you, and do you follow if you can. For he who would proceed rightly in this matter should begin in youth to turn to beautiful forms; and first, if his instructor guide him rightly, he should learn to love one such form only—out of that he should create fair thoughts; and soon he would himself perceive that the beauty of one form is truly related to the beauty of another; and then if beauty in general is his pursuit, how foolish would he be not to recognize that the beauty in every form is one and the same! And when he perceives this he will abate his violent love of the one, which he will despise and deem a small thing, and will become a lover of all beautiful forms; this will lead him on to consider that the beauty of the mind is more honorable than the beauty of the outward form. So that if a virtuous soul have but a little comeliness, he will be content to love and tend him, and will search out and bring to the birth thoughts which may improve the young, until his beloved is compelled to contemplate and see the beauty of institutions and laws, and understand that all is of one kindred, and that personal beauty is only ,a trifle; and after laws and institutions he will lead him on to the sciences, that he may see their beauty, being not like a servant in love with the beauty of one youth or man or institution, himself a slave mean and calculating, but looking at the abundance of beauty and drawing towards the sea of beauty, and creating and beholding many fair and noble thoughts and notions in boundless love of wisdom; until at length he grows and waxes strong, and at last the vision is revealed to him of a single science, which is the science of beauty everywhere. To this I will proceed; please to give me your very best attention.

"For he who has been instructed thus far in the things of love, and who has learned to see the beautiful in due order and succession, when he comes toward the end will suddenly perceive a nature of wondrous beauty—and this, Socrates, is that final cause of all our former toils, which in the first place is everlasting—not growing and decaying, or waxing and waning; in the next place not fair in one point of view and foul in another, or at one time or in one relation or at one place fair, at another time or in another relation or at another place foul, as if fair to some and foul to others, or in the likeness of a face or hands or any other part of the bodily frame, or in any form of speech or knowledge, nor existing in any other being; as for example, an animal, whether in earth or heaven, but beauty only, absolute, separate, simple, and everlasting, which without diminution and without increase, or any change, is imparted to the ever-growing and perishing beauties of all other things. He who under the influence of true love rising upward from these begins to see that beauty, is not far from the end. And the true order of going or being led by another to the things of love, is to use the beauties of earth as steps along which he mounts upwards for the sake of that other beauty, going from one to two, and from two to all fair forms, and from fair forms to fair actions, and from fair actions to fair notions, until from fair notions he arrives at the notion of absolute beauty, and at last knows what the essence of beauty is. This, my dear Socrates," said the stranger of Mantineia, "is that life above all others which man should live, in the contemplation of beauty absolute; a beauty which if you once beheld, you would see not to be after the measure of gold, and garments, and fair boys and youths, which when you now behold you are in fond amazement, and you and many a one are content to live seeing only and conversing with them without meat or drink, if that were possible—you only want to be with them and to look at them. But what if man had eyes to see the true beauty—the divine beauty, I mean, pure and clear and unalloyed, not clogged with the pollutions of mortality, and all the colors and vanities of human life—thither looking, and holding converse with the true beauty divine and simple, and bringing into being and educating true creations of virtue and not idols only? Do you not see that in that communion only, beholding beauty with the eye of the mind, he will be enabled to bring forth, not images of beauty, but realities; for he has hold not of an image but of a reality, and bringing forth and educating true virtue to become the friend of God and be immortal, if mortal man may. Would that be an ignoble life?"

Such, Phaedrus—and I speak not only to you, but to all men—were the words of Diotima; and I am persuaded of their truth. And being persuaded of them, I try to persuade others, that in the attainment of this end human nature will not easily find a better helper than love. And therefore, also, I say that every man ought to honor him as I myself honor him, and walk in his ways, and exhort others to do the same, even as I praise the power and spirit of love according to the measure of my ability now and ever.

The words which I have spoken, you, Phaedrus, may call an encomium of love, or anything else which you please.

PHAEDRUS

Phaedrus. I always wonder at you, Socrates; for when you are in the country, you really are like a stranger who is being led about by a guide. Do you ever cross the border? I rather think that you never venture even outside the gates.

Socrates. Very true, my good friend; and I hope that you will excuse me when you hear the reason, which is, that I am a lover of knowledge, and the men who dwell in the city are my teachers, and not the trees, or the country. Though I do, indeed, believe that you have found a spell with which to draw me out of the city into the country, as hungry cows are led by shaking before them a bait of leaves or fruit. For only hold up the bait of discourse, and you may lead me all round Attica, and over the wide world. And now having arrived, I intend to lie down, and do you choose any posture in which you can read best. Begin.

Phaedrus. Listen. "You know my views of our common interest, and I do not think that I ought to fail in the object of my suit, because I am not your lover: for the kindnesses of lovers are afterwards regretted by them when their passion ceases, but non-lovers have no time of repentance, because they are free and not subject to necessity, and they confer their benefits as far as they are able, in the way which is most conducive to their own interest. Then again, lovers remember how they have neglected their interests, for the sake of their loves; they consider the benefits which they have conferred on them; and when to these they add the troubles which they have endured, they think that they have long ago paid all that is due to them. But the non-lover has no such tormenting recollections; he has never neglected his affairs or quarrelled with his relations; he has no troubles to reckon up, or excuses to allege; for all has gone smoothly with him. What remains, then, but that he should freely do what will gratify the beloved? But you will say that the lover is more to be esteemed, because his love is thought to be greater; for he is willing to say and do what is hateful to other men, in order to please his beloved: well, that, if true, is only a proof that he will prefer any future love to his present, and will injure his old love at the pleasure of the new. And how can a man reasonably sacrifice himself to one who is possessed with a malady which no experienced person would attempt to cure, for the patient himself admits that he is not in his right mind, and acknowledges that he is wrong in his mind, but is unable, as he says, to control himself. How, if he came to his right mind, could he imagine that the desires were good which he conceived when in his wrong mind? Then again, there are many more non-lovers than lovers; and, therefore, you will have a larger choice, and are far more likely to find among them a compatible friend. And if you fear common opinion, and would avoid publicity and reproach, the lover, who is always thinking that other men are as emulous of him as he is of them, will be sure to boast of his successes, and make a show of them openly in the pride of his heart;—he wants others to know that his labor has not been lost; but the non-lover is more his own master, and is desirous of solid good, and not of the vainglory of men. Again, the lover may be generally seen and known following the beloved (this is his regular occupation), and when they are observed to exchange two words they are supposed to meet about some affair of love, either past or future; but when non-lovers meet, no one asks the reason why, because people know that talking is natural, whether friendship or mere pleasure is the motive. And, again, if you fear the fickleness of friendship, consider that in any other case a quarrel might be a mutual calamity; but now, when you have given up what is most precious to you, you will be the great loser, and therefore, you will have reason in being more afraid of the lover, for his vexations are many, and he is always fancying that everything is against him. And for this reason he debars his beloved from society; he will not have you intimate with the wealthy, lest they should exceed him in wealth, or with men of education, lest they should be his superiors in knowledge; and he is equally afraid of the power of any other good. He would persuade you to have nothing to do with them, in order that he may have you all to himself, and if, out of regard to your own interest, you have more sense than to comply with this desire, a quarrel will ensue. But those who are non-lovers, and whose success in love is the reward of their superiority, will not be jealous of the companions of their beloved, but will rather hate those who refuse to be his companions, thinking that their refusal is a mark of contempt, and that he would be benefited by having companions; more love than hatred may be expected to come of that. Many lovers also have loved the person of a youth before they knew his character, or were acquainted with his domestic relations; so that when their passion has passed away, there is no knowing whether they will continue to be his friends; whereas, in the case of non-lovers who were always friends, the friendship is not lessened by sensual delights; but the recollection of these remains with them, and is an earnest of good things to come. Further, I say that you are likely to be improved by me, whereas the lover will spoil you. For they praise your words and actions in a bad way; partly, they are afraid of offending you, and partly, their judgment is weakened by their passion: for lovers are singular beings when disappointed in love—they deem that painful which is not painful to others, and when successful they can not help praising that which ought not to give them pleasure; so that the beloved is a far more appropriate object of pity than of envy. But if you listen to me, in the first place, I, in my intercourse with you, shall not regard present enjoyment, but future advantage, being not conquered by love, but conquering myself; nor for small causes taking violent offences, but even when the cause is great, slowly laying up little wrath—unintentional offences I shall forgive, and intentional ones I shall try to prevent; and these are the marks of a friendship which will last. But if you think that only a lover can be a firm friend, you ought to consider that, if this were true, we should set small value on sons, or fathers, or mothers; nor should we ever have loyal friends, for our love of them arises not from passion, but from other associations. Further, if we ought to confer favors on those who are the most eager suitors, we ought to confer them not on the most virtuous, but on the most needy; for they are the persons who will be most relieved, and will therefore be the most grateful; and, in general, when you make a feast, invite not your friend, but the beggar and the empty soul, for they will love you, and attend you, and come about your doors, and will be the best pleased, and the most grateful, and will invoke blessings on your head. But, perhaps, you will say that you ought not to give to the most importunate, but to those who are best able to reward you; nor to the lover only, but to those who are worthy of love; nor to those who will enjoy the charm of your youth, but to those who will share their goods with you in age; nor to those who, having succeeded, will glory in their success to others, but to those who will be modest and hold their peace; nor to those who care about you for a moment only, but to those who will continue your friends for life; nor to those who, when their passion is over, will pick a quarrel with you, but rather to those who, when the bloom of youth is over, will show their own virtue. Remember what I have said; and consider this also, that friends admonish the lover under the idea that his way of life is bad, but no one of his kindred ever yet censured the non-lover, or thought that he was ill-advised about his own interests.

"Perhaps you will ask me whether I propose that you should indulge every non-lover. To which I reply that not even the lover would advise you to indulge all lovers, for the favor is less in the just estimation of the receiver and more difficult to hide from the world. Now love ought to be for the advantage of both parties and for the injury of neither.

"I believe that I have said enough; but if there is anything more which you desire or which needs to be supplied, ask and I will answer."

Now, Socrates, what do you think? Is not the discourse excellent, especially the language?

Socrates. Yes indeed, admirable; the effect on me was ravishing. And this I owe to you, Phaedrus, for I observed you while reading to be in an ecstasy, and thinking that you are more experienced in these matters than I am, I followed your example, and, like you, became inspired with a divine frenzy.

Phaedrus. Only go on and you may do as you please.

Socrates. Come, O ye Muses, melodious as ye are called, whether you have received this name from the character of your strains, or because the Melians are a musical race, help, O help me in the tale which my good friend desires me to rehearse, for the good of his friend whom he always deemed wise and will now deem wiser than ever.

Once upon a time there was a fair boy, or, more properly speaking, a youth; he was very fair and had a great many lovers; and there was one special cunning one, who had persuaded the youth that he did not love him, but he really loved him all the same; and one day as he was paying his addresses to him, he used this very argument—that he ought to accept the non-lover rather than the lover; and his words were as follows:—

"All good counsel begins in the same way; a man should know what he is advising about, or his counsel will come to nought. But people imagine that they know about the nature of things, when they don't know about them, and, not agreeing at the beginning, they end, as might be expected, in contradicting one another and themselves. Now you and I must not be guilty of the error which we condemn in others; but as our question is whether the lover or non-lover is to be preferred, let us first of all agree in defining the nature and power of love, and then, keeping our eyes upon this and to this appealing, let us further inquire whether love brings advantage or disadvantage.

"Every one sees that love is a desire, and we know also that non-lovers desire the beautiful and good. Now in what way is the lover to be distinguished from the non-lover? Let us note that in every one of us there are two guiding and ruling principles which lead us whither they will; one is the natural desire of pleasure, the other is an acquired opinion which is in search of the best; and these two are sometimes in harmony and then again at war, and sometimes the one, sometimes the other conquers. When opinion conquers, and by the help of reason leads us to the best, the conquering principle is called temperance; but when desire, which is devoid of reason, rules in us and drags us to pleasure, that power of misrule is called excess. Now excess has many names, and many members, and many forms, and any of these forms when marked gives a name to the bearer of the name, neither honorable nor desirable. The desire of eating, which gets the better of the higher reason and the other desires, is called gluttony, and he who is possessed by this is called a glutton; the tyrannical desire of drink, which inclines the possessor of the desire to drink, has a name which is only too obvious; and the same may be said of the whole family of desires and their names, whichever of them happens to be dominant. And now I think that you will perceive the drift of my discourse; but as every spoken word is in a manner plainer than the unspoken, I had better say further that the irrational desire which overcomes the tendency of opinion towards right, and is led away to the enjoyment of beauty, and especially of personal beauty, by the desires which are her kindred—that desire, I say, the conqueror and leader of the rest, and waxing strong from having this very power, is called the power of love."

And now, dear Phaedrus, I shall pause for an instant to ask whether you do not think me, as I appear to myself, inspired?

Phaedrus. Yes, Socrates, you seem to have a very unusual flow of words.

Socrates. Listen to me, then, in silence; for surely the place is holy; so that you must not wonder, if, as I proceed, I appear to be in a divine fury, for already I am getting into dithyrambics.

Phaedrus. That is quite true.

Socrates. And that I attribute to you. But hear what follows, and perhaps the fit may be averted; all is in their hands above. And now I will go on talking to my youth. Listen:—

Thus, my friend, we have declared and determined the nature of love. Keeping this in view, let us now inquire what advantage or disadvantage is likely to ensue from the lover or the non-lover to him who accepts their advances.

He who is the victim of his passions and the slave of pleasure will of course desire to make his beloved as agreeable to himself as possible. Now to him who is not in his right senses that is agreeable which is not opposed to him, but that which is equal or superior is hateful to him, and therefore the lover will not brook any superiority or equality on the part of his beloved; he is always employed in reducing him to inferiority. And the ignorant is the inferior of the wise, the coward of the brave, the slow of speech of the speaker, the dull of the clever. These are the sort of natural and inherent defects in the mind of the beloved which enhance the delight of the lover, and there are acquired defects which he must produce in him, or he will be deprived of his fleeting joy. And therefore he can not help being jealous, and will debar him from the advantages of society which would make a man of him, and especially from that society which would have given him wisdom. That is to say, he will be compelled to banish from him divine philosophy, in his excessive fear lest he should come to be despised in his eyes; and there is no greater injury which he can inflict on him than this. Moreover, he will contrive that he shall be wholly ignorant, and in everything dependent on himself; he is to be the delight of his lover's heart, and a curse to himself. Verily, a lover is a profitable guardian and associate for him in all that relates to his mind.

Let us next see how his master, whose law of life is pleasure and not good, will keep and train the body of his servant. Will he not choose a beloved who is delicate rather than sturdy and strong? One brought up in shady bowers and not in the bright sun, not practised in manly exercises or dried by perspiration, but knowing only a soft and luxurious diet, instead of the hues of health having only the colors of paint and ornament, and the rest of a piece?—such a life as any one can imagine and which I need not detail at length. But I may sum up all that I have to say in a word, and pass on. Such a person in war, or in any of the great exigencies in life, will be the anxiety of his friends and also of his lover, and certainly not the terror of his enemies; which nobody can deny.

And now let us tell what advantage or disadvantage the beloved will receive from the guardianship and society of his lover in the matter of his possessions; that is the next point to consider. All men will see, and the lover above all men, that his own first wish is to deprive his beloved of his dearest and best and most sacred possessions, father, mother, kindred, friends, all who he thinks may be hinderers or reprovers of their sweet converse; he will even cast a jealous eye upon his gold and silver or other property, because these make him a less easy and manageable prey, and hence he is of necessity displeased at the possession of them and rejoices at their loss; and he would like him to be wifeless, childless, homeless, as well; and the longer the better, for the longer he is all this, the longer he will enjoy him.

There are some sort of animals, such as flatterers, which are dangerous and mischievous enough, and yet nature has mingled a temporary pleasure and grace in their composition. You may say that a courtesan is hurtful, and disapprove of such creatures and their practices, and yet for the time they are very pleasant. But the lover is not only mischievous to his love, he is also extremely unpleasant to live with. Equals, as the proverb says, delight in equals; equality of years inclines them to the same pleasures, and similarity begets friendship, and yet you may have more than enough even of this, and compulsion is always said to be grievous. Now the lover is not only unlike his beloved, but he forces himself upon him. For he is old and his love is young, and neither day nor night will he leave him if he can help; and necessity and the sting of desire drive him on, and allure him with the pleasure which he receives from seeing, hearing, touching, perceiving him. And therefore he is delighted to fasten upon him and to minister to him. But what pleasure or consolation can the beloved be receiving all this time? Must he not feel the extremity of disgust when he looks at an old withered face and the remainder to match, which even in a description is not agreeable, and quite detestable when you are forced into daily contact with them; moreover he is jealously watched and guarded against everything and everybody, and has to hear misplaced and exaggerated praises of himself, and censures as inappropriate, which are quite intolerable when the man is sober, and, besides being intolerable, are published all over the world in all their shamelessness and wearisomeness when he is drunk.

And not only while his love continues is he mischievous and unpleasant, but when his love ceases he becomes a perfidious enemy of him on whom he showered his oaths and prayers and promises, and yet could hardly prevail upon him to tolerate the tedium of his company even from motives of interest. The time of payment arrives, and now he is the servant of another master; instead of love and infatuation, wisdom and temperance are his bosom's lords; the man has changed, but the beloved is not aware of this; he asks for a return and recalls to his recollection former acts and words, for he fancies that he is talking to the same person, and the other, being ashamed and not having the courage to tell him that he has changed, and not knowing how to make good his promises, has now grown virtuous and temperate; he does not want to do as he did or to be as he was before. Therefore he runs away and can but end a defaulter; quick as the spinning of a teetotum, he changes pursuit into flight, and the other is compelled to follow him with passion and imprecation, not knowing that he ought never from the first to have accepted a demented lover instead of a sensible non-lover; and that in making such a choice he was yielding to a faithless, morose, envious, disagreeable being, hurtful to his estate, hurtful to his bodily constitution, and still more hurtful to the cultivation of his mind, which is and ever will be the most honorable possession both of gods and men. Consider this, fair youth, and know that in the friendship of the lover there is no real kindness; he has an appetite and wants to feed upon you.

"As wolves love lambs so lovers love their loves."

But, as I said before, I am speaking in verse, and therefore I had better make an end; that is enough.

Phaedrus. I thought that you were only half-way and were going to make a similar speech about all the advantages of accepting the non-lover. Why don't you go on?

Socrates. Know then, fair youth, that the former discourse was that of a finely-scented gentleman, who is all myrrh and fragrance, named Phaedrus, the son of Vain Man. And this is the recantation of Stesichorus the pious, who comes from the town of Desire, and is to the following effect: That was a lie in which I said that the beloved ought to accept the non-lover and reject the lover, because the one is sane, and the other mad. For that might have been truly said if madness were simply an evil; but there is also a madness which is the special gift of heaven, and the source of the chiefest blessings among men. For prophecy is a madness, and the prophetess at Delphi and the priestesses of Dodona, when out of their senses, have conferred great benefits on Hellas, both in public and private life, but when in their senses few or none. And I might also tell you how the Sibyl and other persons, who have had the gift of prophecy, have told the future of many a one and guided them aright; but that is obvious, and would be tedious.

There will be more reason in appealing to the ancient inventors of names, who, if they had thought madness a disgrace or dishonor, would never have called prophecy, which is the noblest of arts, by the very same name as madness, thus inseparably connecting them; but they must have thought that there was an inspired madness which was no disgrace. And this is confirmed by the name which they gave to the rational investigation of futurity, whether made by the help of birds or other signs; this as supplying from the reasoning faculty insight and information to human thought, but the word has been lately altered and made sonorous by the modern introduction of the letter Omega, and in proportion as prophecy is higher and more perfect than divination both in name and reality, in the same proportion as the ancients testify, is madness superior to a sane mind, for the one is only of human, but the other of divine origin. Again, where plagues and mightiest woes have bred in a race, owing to some ancient wrath, there madness, lifting up her voice and flying to prayers and rites, has come to the rescue of those who are in need; and he who has part in this gift, and is truly possessed and duly out of his mind, is by the use of purifications and mysteries made whole and delivered from evil, future as well as present, and has a release from the calamity which afflicts him. There is also a third kind of madness, which is a possession of the Muses; this enters into a delicate and virgin soul, and there inspiring frenzy, awakens lyric and all other numbers; with these adorning the myriad actions of ancient heroes for the instruction of posterity. But he who, not being inspired and having no touch of madness in his soul, comes to the door and thinks that he will get into the temple by the help of art—he, I say, and his poetry are not admitted; the sane man is nowhere at all when he enters into rivalry with the madman.

I might tell of many other noble deeds which have sprung from inspired madness. And therefore, let no one frighten or flutter us by saying that temperate love is preferable to mad love, but let him further show, if he would carry off the palm, that love is not sent by the gods for any good to lover or beloved. And we, on our part, will prove in answer to him that the madness of love is the greatest of heaven's blessings, and the proof shall be one which the wise will receive, and the witling disbelieve. And, first of all, let us inquire what is the truth about the affections and actions of the soul, divine as well as human. And thus we begin our proof:

The soul is immortal, for that is immortal which is ever in motion; but that which moves and is moved by another, in ceasing to move ceases also to live. Therefore, only that which is self-moving, never failing of self, never ceases to move, and is the fountain and beginning of motion to all that moves besides. Now, the beginning is unbegotten, for that which is begotten has a beginning; but the beginning has no beginning, for if a beginning were begotten of something, that would have no beginning. But that which is unbegotten must also be indestructible; for if beginning were destroyed, there could be no beginning out of anything, nor anything out of a beginning; and all things must have a beginning. And therefore the self-moving is the beginning of motion; and this can neither be destroyed nor begotten, for in that case the whole heavens and all generation would collapse and stand still, and never again have motion or birth. But if the self-moving is immortal, he who affirms that self-motion is the very idea and essence of the soul will not be put to confusion. For the body which is moved from without is soulless; but that which is moved from within has a soul, and this is involved in the nature of the soul. But if the soul be truly affirmed to be the self-moving, then must she also be without beginning, and immortal. Enough of the soul's immortality.

Her form is a theme of divine and large discourse; human language may, however, speak of this briefly, and in a figure. Let our figure be of a composite nature—a pair of winged horses and a charioteer. Now the winged horses and the charioteer of the gods are all of them noble, and of noble breed, while ours are mixed; and we have a charioteer who drives them in a pair, and one of them is noble and of noble origin, and the other is ignoble and of ignoble origin; and, as might be expected, there is a great deal of trouble in managing them. I will endeavor to explain to you in what way the mortal differs from the immortal creature. The soul or animate being has the care of the inanimate, and traverses the whole heaven in divers forms appearing;—when perfect and fully winged she soars upward, and is the ruler of the universe; while the imperfect soul loses her feathers, and drooping in her flight at last settles on the solid ground—there, finding a home, she receives an earthly frame which appears to be self-moved, but is really moved by her power; and this composition of soul and body is called a living and mortal creature. For no such union can be reasonably believed, or at all proved to be other than mortal; although fancy may imagine a god whom, not having seen nor surely known, we invent—such a one, an immortal creature having a body, and having also a soul which have been united in all time. Let that, however, be as God wills, and be spoken of acceptably to him. But the reason why the soul loses her feathers should be explained, and is as follows:

The wing is intended to soar aloft and carry that which gravitates downwards into the upper region, which is the dwelling of the gods; and this is that element of the body which is most akin to the divine. Now the divine is beauty, wisdom, goodness, and the like; and by these the wing of the soul is nourished, and grows apace; but when fed upon evil and foulness, and the like, wastes and falls away. Zeus, the mighty lord holding the reins of a winged chariot, leads the way in heaven, ordering all and caring for all; and there follows him the heavenly array of gods and demi-gods, divided into eleven bands; for only Hestia is left at home in the house of heaven; but the rest of the twelve greater deities march in their appointed order. And they see in the interior of heaven many blessed sights; and there are ways to and fro, along which the happy gods are passing, each one fulfilling his own work; and any one may follow who pleases, for jealousy has no place in the heavenly choir. This is within the heaven. But when they go to feast and festival, then they move right up the steep ascent, and mount the top of the dome of heaven. Now the chariots of the gods, self-balanced, upward glide in obedience to the rein; but the others have a difficulty, for the steed who has evil in him, if he has not been properly trained by the charioteer, gravitates and inclines and sinks towards the earth:—and this is the hour of agony and extremest conflict of the soul. For the immortal souls, when they are at the end of their course, go out and stand upon the back of heaven, and the revolution of the spheres carries them round, and they behold the world beyond. Now of the heaven which is above the heavens, no earthly poet has sung or ever will sing in a worthy manner. But I must tell, for I am bound to speak truly when speaking of the truth. The colorless and formless and in-tangible essence is visible to the mind, which is the only lord of the soul. Circling around this in the region above the heavens is the place of true knowledge. And as the divine intelligence, and that of every other soul which is rightly nourished, is fed upon mind and pure knowledge, such an intelligent soul is glad at once more beholding being; and feeding on the sight of truth is replenished, until the revolution of the worlds brings her round again to the same place. During the revolution she beholds justice, temperance, and knowledge absolute, not in the form of generation or of relation, which men call existence, but knowledge absolute in exist-ence absolute; and beholding other existences in like manner, and feeding upon them, she passes down into the interior of the heavens and returns home, and there the charioteer, putting up his horses at the stall, gives them ambrosia to eat and nectar to drink.

This is the life of the gods; but of other souls, that which follows God best and is likest to him lifts the head of the charioteer into the outer world, and is carried round in the revolution, troubled indeed by the steeds, and beholding true being, but hardly; another rises and falls, and sees, and again fails to see by reason of the unruliness of the steeds. The rest of the souls are also longing after the upper world and they all follow, but not being strong enough they sink into the gulf, as they are carried round, plunging, treading on one another, striving to be first; and there is confusion and the extremity of effort, and many of them are lamed or have their wings broken through the ill-driving of the charioteers; and all of them after a fruitless toil go away without being initiated into the mysteries of being, and are nursed with the food of opinion. The reason of their great desire to behold the plain of truth is that the food which is suited to the highest part of the soul comes out of that meadow; and the wing on which the soul soars is nourished with this. And there is a law of the goddess Retribution, that the soul which attains any vision of truth in company with the god is preserved from harm until the next period, and he who always attains is always unharmed. But when she is unable to follow, and fails to behold the vision of truth, and through some ill-hap sinks beneath the double load of forgetfulness and vice, and her feathers fall from her and she drops to earth, then the law ordains that this soul shall in the first generation pass, not into that of any other animal, but only of man; and the soul which has seen most of truth shall come to the birth as a philosopher, or artist, or musician, or lover; that which has seen truth in the second degree shall be a righteous king or warrior or lord; the soul which is of the third class shall be a politician, or economist, or trader; the fourth shall be a lover of gymnastic toils, or a physician; the fifth a prophet or hierophant; to the sixth a poet or imitator will be appropriate; to the seventh the life of an artisan or husbandman; to the eighth that of a sophist or demagogue; to the ninth that of a tyrant;—all these are states of probation, in which he who lives righteously improves, and he who lives unrighteously deteriorates his lot.

Ten thousand years must elapse before the soul can return to the place from whence she came, for she can not grow her wings in less; only the soul of a philosopher, guileless and true, or the soul of a lover, who is not without philosophy, may acquire wings in the third recurring period of a thousand years: and if they choose this life three times in succession, then they have their wings given them, and go away at the end of three thousand years. But the others receive judgment when they have completed their first life, and after the judgment they go, some of them to the houses of correction which are under the earth, and are punished; others to some place in heaven whither they are lightly borne by justice, and there they live in a manner worthy of the life which they led here when in the form of men. And at the end of the first thousand years the good souls and also the evil souls both come to cast lots and choose their second life, and they may take any that they like. And then the soul of the man may pass into the life of a beast, or from the beast again into the man. But the soul of him who has never seen the truth will not pass into the human form, for man ought to have intelligence, as they say, "secundum speciem," proceeding from many particulars of sense to one conception of reason; and this is the recollection of those things which our soul once saw when in company with God—when looking down from above on that which we now call being and upwards towards the true being. And therefore the mind of the philosopher alone has wings; and this is just, for he is always, according to the measure of his abilities, clinging in recollection to those things in which God abides, and in beholding which He is what he is. And he who employs aright these memories is ever being initiated into perfect mysteries and alone becomes truly perfect. But, as he forgets earthly interests and is rapt in the divine, the vulgar deem him mad, and rebuke him; they do not see that he is inspired.

Thus far I have been speaking of the fourth and last kind of madness, which is imputed to him who, when he sees the beauty of earth, is transported with the recollection of the true beauty; he would like to fly away, but he can not; he is like a bird fluttering and looking upward and careless of the world below; and he is therefore esteemed mad. And I have shown that this is of all inspirations the noblest and best, and comes of the best, and that he who has part or lot in this madness is called a lover of the beautiful. For as has been already said, every soul of man has in the way of nature beheld true being; this was the condition of her passing into the form of man. But all men do not easily recall the things of the other world; they may have seen them for a short time only, or they may have been unfortunate when they fell to earth, and may have lost the memory of the holy things which they saw there through some evil and corrupting association. Few there are who retain the remembrance of them sufficiently; and they, when they behold any image of that other world, are rapt in amazement; but they are ignorant of what this means, because they have no clear perceptions. For there is no light in the earthly copies of justice or temperance or any of the higher qualities which are precious to souls: they are seen but through a glass dimly; and there are few who, going to the images, behold in them the realities, and they only with difficulty. They might have seen beauty shining in brightness, when, with the happy band following in the train of Zeus, as we philosophers did, or with other gods as others did, they saw a vision and were initiated into most blessed mysteries, which we celebrated in our state of innocence; and having no feeling of evils as yet to come; beholding apparitions innocent and simple and calm and happy as in a mystery; shining in pure light, pure ourselves and not yet enshrined in that living tomb which we carry about, now that we are imprisoned in the body, as in an oyster-shell. Let me linger thus long over the memory of scenes which have passed away.

But of beauty, I repeat again that we saw her there shining in company with the celestial forms; and coming to earth we find her here too, shining in clearness through the clearest aperture of sense. For sight is the keenest of our bodily senses; though not by that is wisdom seen, for her loveliness would have been transporting if there had been a visible image of her, and this is true of the loveliness of the other ideas as well. But beauty only has this portion, that she is at once the loveliest and also the most apparent. Now he who has not been lately initiated, or who has become corrupted, is not easily carried out of this world to the sight of absolute beauty in the other; he looks only at that which has the name of beauty in this world, and instead of being awed at the sight of her, like a brutish beast he rushes on to enjoy and beget; he takes wantonness to his bosom, and is not afraid or ashamed of pursuing pleasure in violation of nature. But he whose initiation is recent, and who has been the spectator of many glories in the other world, is amazed when he sees any one having a godlike face or form, which is the expression or imitation of divine beauty; and at first a shudder runs through him, and some "misgiving" of a former world steals over him; then, looking upon the face of his beloved as of a god, he reverences him, and if he were not afraid of being thought a downright madman, he would sacrifice to his beloved as to the image of a god; then as he gazes on him there is a sort of reaction, and the shudder naturally passes into an unusual heat and perspiration; for, as he receives the effluence of beauty through the eyes, the wing moistens and he warms. And as he warms, the parts out of which the wing grew, and which had been hitherto closed and rigid and had prevented the wing from shooting forth are melted, and as nourishment streams upon him, the lower end of the wing begins to swell and grow from the root upwards, extending under the whole soul—for once the whole was winged. Now during this process the whole soul is in a state of effervescence and irritation, like the state of irritation and pain in the gums at the time of cutting teeth; in like manner the soul when beginning to grow wings has inflammation and pains and ticklings, and when looking at the beauty of youth she receives the sensible warm traction of particles which flow towards her, therefore called attraction, and is refreshed and warmed by them, and then she ceases from her pain with joy. But when she is separated and her moisture fails, then the orifices of the passages out of which the wing shoots dry up and close, and intercept the germ of the wing; which, being shut up within in company with desire, pricks the aperture which is nearest, until at length the entire soul is pierced and maddened and pained, and at the recollection of beauty is again delighted. And from both of them together the soul is oppressed at the strangeness of her condition, and is in a great strait and excitement, and in her madness can neither sleep by night nor abide in her place by day. And wherever she thinks that she will behold the beautiful one, thither in her desire she runs. And when she has seen him, and drunk rivers of desire, her constraint is loosened, and she is refreshed, and has no more pangs and pains; and this is the sweetest of all pleasures at the time, and is the reason why the soul of the lover never forsakes his beautiful one, whom he esteems above all; he has forgotten his mother and brethren and companions, and he thinks nothing of the neglect and loss of his property; and as to the rules and proprieties of life, on which he formerly prided himself, he now despises them, and is ready to sleep and serve, wherever he is allowed, as near as he can to his beautiful one who is not only the object of his worship, but the only physician who can heal him in his extreme agony. And this state, my dear imaginary youth, is by men called love, and among the gods has a name which you, in your simplicity, may be inclined to mock; there are two lines in honor of love in the Homeric Apocrypha in which the name occurs. One of them is rather outrageous, and is not quite metrical; they are as follows:—

> "Mortals call him Eros (love),
> But the immortals call him Pteros (fluttering dove),
> Because fluttering of wings is a necessity to him."

You may believe this or not as you like. At any rate the loves of lovers and their causes are such as I have described.

Now the lover who is the attendant of Zeus is better able to bear the winged god, and can endure a heavier burden; but the attendants and companions of Ares, when under the influence of love, if they fancy that they have been at all wronged, are ready to kill and put an end to themselves and their beloved. And in like manner he who follows in the train of any other god honors him, and imitates him as far as he is able while the impression lasts; and this is his way of life and the manner of his behavior to his beloved and to every other in the first period of his earthly existence. Every one chooses the object of his affections according to his character, and this he makes his god, and fashions and adorns as a sort of image which he is to fall down and worship. The followers of Zeus desire that their beloved should have a soul like him; and, therefore, they seek some philosophical and imperial nature, and when they have found him and loved him, they do all they can to create such a nature in him, and if they have no experience hitherto, they learn of any one who can teach them, and themselves follow in the same way. And they have the less difficulty in finding the nature of their own god in themselves, because they have been compelled to gaze intensely on him; their recollection clings to him, and they become possessed by him, and receive his character and ways, as far as man can participate in God. These they attribute to the beloved, and they love him all the more, and if they draw inspiration from Zeus, like the Bacchic Nymphs, they pour this out upon him in order to make him as like their god as possible. But those who are the followers of Hera seek a royal love, and when they have found him they do the same with him; and in like manner the followers of Apollo, and of every other god walking in the ways of their god, seek a love who is to be like their god, and when they have found him, they themselves imitate their god, and persuade their love to do the same, and bring him into harmony with the form and ways of the god as far as they can; for they have no feelings of envy or mean enmity towards their beloved, but they do their utmost to create in him the greatest likeness of themselves and the god whom they honor. And the desire of the lover, if effected, and the initiation of which I speak into the mysteries of true love, is thus fair and blissful to the beloved when he is chosen by the lover who is driven mad by love. Now the beloved or chosen one is taken captive in the following manner:—

As I said at the beginning of this tale, I divided each soul into three parts, two of them having the forms of horses and the third that of a charioteer; and one of the horses was good and the other bad, but I have not yet explained the virtue and vice of either, and to that I will now proceed. The well-conditioned horse is erect and well-formed; he has a lofty neck and an aquiline nose, and his color is white, and he has dark eyes and is a lover of honor and modesty and temperance, and the follower of true glory; he needs not the touch of the whip, but is guided by word and admonition only. Whereas the other is a large misshapen animal, put together anyhow; he has a strong short neck; he is flat-faced and of a dark color, grey-eyed and bloodshot, the mate of insolence and pride, shag-eared, deaf, hardly yielding to blow or spur. Now when the charioteer beholds the vision of love, and has his whole soul warmed with sense, and is full of tickling and desire, the obedient steed, then as always under the government of shame, refrains himself from leaping on the beloved; but the other, instead of heeding the blows of the whip, prances away and gives all manner of trouble to his companion and to the charioteer, and urges them on toward the beloved and reminds them of the joys of love. They at first indignantly oppose him and will not be urged on to do terrible and unlawful deeds; but at last, when there is no end of evil, they yield and suffer themselves to be led on to do as he bids them. And now they are at the spot and behold the flashing beauty of the beloved. But when the charioteer sees that, his memory is carried to the true beauty, and he beholds her in company with Modesty set in her holy place. And when he sees her he is afraid and falls back in adoration, and in falling is compelled to pull back the reins, which he does with such force as to bring both the steeds on their haunches, the one willing and unresisting, the unruly one very unwilling; and when they have gone back a little, the one is overflowing with shame and wonder, and pours forth rivers of perspiration over the entire soul; the other, when the pain is over which the bridle and the fall had given him, having with difficulty taken breath, is full of wrath and reproaches, which he heaps upon the charioteer and his fellow-steed, as though from want of courage and manhood they had been false to their agreement and guilty of desertion. And, when they again decline, he forces them on, and will scarce yield to their request that he would wait until another time. Returning at the appointed hour, they

make as if they had forgotten, and he reminds them, fighting and neigh-
ing and dragging them, until at length he, on the same thoughts intent,
forces them to draw near. And when they are near he stoops his head and
puts up his tail, and takes the bit in his mouth and pulls shamelessly. Then
the charioteer is worse off than ever; he drops at the very start, and with
still greater violence draws the bit out of the teeth of the wild steed and
covers his abusive tongue and jaws with blood, and forces his legs and
haunches to the ground and punishes him sorely. And when this has happened several times and the villain has ceased from his wanton way, he is
tamed and humbled, and follows the will of the charioteer, and when he
sees the beautiful one he is ready to die of fear. And from that time forward the soul of the lover follows the beloved in modesty and holy fear.

And so the beloved who, like a god, has received every true and loyal
service from his lover, not in pretence but in reality, being also himself of
a nature friendly to his admirer, if in former days he has blushed to own
his passion and turned away his lover, because his youthful companions
or others slanderously told him that he would be disgraced, now as years
advance, at the appointed age and time is led to receive him into communion. For fate which has ordained that there shall be no friendship
among the evil has also ordained that there shall ever be friendship among
the good. And when he has received him into communion and intimacy,
then the beloved is amazed at the good will of the lover; he recognizes
that the inspired friend is worth all other friendship or kinships, which
have nothing of friendship in them in comparison. And as he continues to
feel this and approaches and embraces him, in gymnastic exercises and at
other times of meeting, then does the fountain of that stream, which Zeus
when he was in love with Ganymede called desire, overflow upon the
lover, and some enters into his soul, and some when he is filled flows out
again, and as a breeze or an echo leaps from the smooth rocks and re-
bounds to them again, so does the stream of beauty, passing the eyes which
are the natural doors and windows of the soul, return again to the beautiful one; there arriving and fluttering the passages of the wings, and water-
ing them and inclining them to grow, and filling the soul of the beloved
also with love. And thus he loves, but he knows not what; he does not
understand and can not explain his own state; he appears to have caught
the infection of another's eye; the lover is his mirror in whom he is beholding himself, but he is not aware of this. When he is with the lover,
both cease from their pain, but when he is away then he longs as he is
longed for, and has love's image, love for love (Anteros) lodging in his
breast, which he calls and deems not love but friendship only, and his
desire is as the desire of the other, but weaker; he wants to see him, touch
him, kiss, embrace him, and not long afterwards his desire is accomplished. Now, when they meet, the wanton steed of the lover has a word

to say to the charioteer; he would like to have a little pleasure as a return for many pains, but the wanton steed of the beloved says not a word, for he is bursting with passion which he understands not, but he throws his arms round the lover and embraces him as his dearest friend; and, when they are side by side, he is not in a state in which he can refuse the lover anything, if he ask him, while his fellow-steed and the charioteer oppose him with shame and reason. After this their happiness depends upon their self-control; if the better elements of the mind which lead to order and philosophy prevail, then they pass their life in this world in happiness and harmony—masters of themselves and orderly—enslaving the vicious and emancipating the virtuous elements; and when the end comes, being light and ready to fly away, they conquer in one of the three heavenly or truly Olympian victories; nor can human discipline or divine inspiration confer any greater blessing on man than this. If, on the other hand, they leave philosophy and lead the lower life of ambition, then, probably in the dark or in some other careless hour, the two wanton animals take the two souls when off their guard and bring them together, and they accomplish that desire of their hearts which to the many is bliss; and this having once enjoyed they continue to enjoy, yet rarely because they have not the approval of the whole soul. They too are dear, but not so dear to one another as the others, either at the time of their love or afterwards. They consider that they have given and taken from each other the most sacred pledges, and they may not break them and fall into enmity. At last they pass out of the body, unwinged, but eager to soar, and thus obtain no mean reward of love and madness. For those who have once begun the heavenward pilgrimage may not go down again to darkness and the journey beneath the earth, but they live in light always; happy companions in their pilgrimage, and when the time comes at which they receive their wings they have the same plumage because of their love.

Thus great are the heavenly blessings which the friendship of a lover will confer on you, my youth. Whereas the attachment of the non-lover which is just a vulgar compound of temperance and niggardly earthly ways and motives, will breed meanness—praised by the vulgar as virtue in your inmost soul; will send you bowling round the earth during a period of nine thousand years, and leave you a fool in the world below.

And thus, dear Eros, I have made and paid my recantation, as well as I could and as fairly as I could; the poetical figures I was compelled to use, because Phaedrus would have them. And now forgive the past and accept the present, and be gracious and merciful to me, and do not deprive me of sight or take from me the art of love, but grant that I may be yet more esteemed in the eyes of the fair. And if Phaedrus or I myself said anything objectionable in our first speeches, blame Lysias, who is the father of the brat, and let us have no more of his progeny; bid him study philosophy, like his brother Polemarchus; and then his lover Phaedrus will no longer halt between two, but dedicate himself wholly to love and philosophical discourses.

GORGIAS

O MY FRIEND! I want you to see that the noble and the good may possibly be something different from saving and being saved, and that he who is truly a man ought not to care about living a certain time:—he knows, as women say, that none can escape the day of destiny, and therefore he is not fond of life; he leaves all that with God, and considers in what way he can best spend his appointed term;—whether by assimilating himself to that constitution under which he lives, as you at this moment have to consider, how you may become as like as possible to the Athenian people, if you intended to be dear to them, and to have power in the state; whereas I want you to think and see whether this is for the interest of either of us;—I would not have us risk that which is dearest on the acquisition of this power, like the Thessalian enchantresses, who, as they say, bring down the moon from heaven at the risk of their own perdition.

EUTHYDEMUS

Crito. I have often told you, Socrates, that I am in a constant difficulty about my two sons. What am I to do with them? There is no hurry about the younger one, who is only a child; but the other, Critobulus, is getting on, and needs some one who will improve him. I can not help thinking, when I hear you talk, that there is a sort of madness in many of our anxieties about our children:—in the first place, about marrying a wife of good family to be the mother of them, and then about heaping up money for them—and yet taking no care about their education. But then again, when I contemplate any of those who pretend to educate others, I am amazed. They all seem to me to be such outrageous beings, if I am to confess the truth: so that I do not know how I can advise the youth to study philosophy.

Socrates. Dear Crito, do you not know that in every profession the inferior sort are numerous and good for nothing, and the good are few and beyond all price: for example, are not gymnastic and rhetoric and money-making and the art of the general, noble arts?

Crito. Certainly they are, in my judgment.

Socrates. Well, and do you not see that in each of these arts the many are ridiculous performers?

Crito. Yes, indeed, that is very true.

Socrates. And will you on this account shun all these pursuits yourself and refuse to allow them to your son?

Crito. That would not be reasonable, Socrates.

Socrates. Do you then be reasonable, Crito, and do not mind whether the teachers of philosophy are good or bad, but think only of philosophy herself. Try and examine her well and truly, and if she be evil seek to turn away all men from her, and not your sons only; but if she be what I believe that she is, then follow her and serve her, you and your house, as the saying is, and be of good cheer.

PARMENIDES

SOCRATES SAID: What do you mean, Zeno? Is your argument that the existence of many necessarily involves like and unlike, and that this is impossible, for neither can the like be unlike, nor the unlike like; is that your position? Just that, said Zeno. And if the unlike can not be like, or the like unlike, then neither can the many exist, for that would involve an impossibility. Is the design of your argument throughout to disprove the existence of the many? and is each of your treatises intended to furnish a separate proof of this, there being as many proofs in all as you have composed arguments, of the non-existence of the many? Is that your meaning, or have I misunderstood you?

No, said Zeno; you have quite understood the general drift of the treatise.

I see, Parmenides, said Socrates, that Zeno is your second self in his writings too; he puts what you say in another way, and half deceives us into believing that he is saying what is new. For you, in your compositions, say that the all is one, and of this you adduce excellent proofs; and he, on the other hand, says that the many is naught, and gives many great and convincing evidences of this. To deceive the world, as you have done, by saying the same thing in different ways, one of you affirming and the other denying the many, is a strain of art beyond the reach of most of us.

Yes, Socrates, said Zeno. But although you are as keen as a Spartan hound in pursuing the track, you do not quite apprehend the true motive of the performance, which is not really such an artificial piece of work as you imagine; there was no intention of concealment effecting any grand result—that was a mere accident. For the truth is, that these writings of mine were meant to protect the arguments of Parmenides against those who ridicule him, and urge the many ridiculous and contradictory results which were supposed to follow from the assertion of the one. My answer is addressed to the partisans of the many, and intended to show that greater or more ridiculous consequences follow from their hypothesis of the existence of the many if carried out, than from the hypothesis of the existence of the one. A love of controversy led me to write the book in the days of my youth, and some one stole the writings, and I had therefore no choice about the publication of them; the motive, however, of writing, was not the ambition of an old man, but the pugnacity of a young one. This you do not seem to see, Socrates; though in other respects, as I was saying, your notion is a very just one.

That I understand, said Socrates, and quite accept your account. But tell me, Zeno, do you not further think that there is an idea of likeness in the abstract, and another idea of unlikeness, which is the opposite of likeness, and that in these two, you and I and all other things to which we apply the term many, participate; and that the things which participate in likeness are in that degree and manner like; and that those which participate in unlikeness are in that degree unlike, or both like and unlike in the degree in which they participate in both? And all things may partake of both opposites, and be like and unlike to themselves, by reason of this participation. Even in that there is nothing wonderful. But if a person could prove the absolute like to become unlike, or the absolute unlike to become like, that, in my opinion, would be a real wonder; not, however, if the things which partake of the ideas experience likeness and unlikeness—there is nothing extraordinary in this. Nor, again, if a person were to show that all is one by partaking of one, and that the same is many by partaking of many, would that be very wonderful? But if he were to show me that the absolute many was one, or the absolute one many, I should be truly amazed. And I should say the same of other things. I should be surprised to hear that the genera and species had opposite qualities in themselves; but if a person wanted to prove of me that I was many and also one, there would be no marvel in that. When he wanted to show that I was many he would say that I have a right and a left side, and a front and a back, and an upper and a lower half, for I can not deny that I partake of multitude; when, on the other hand, he wants to prove that I am one, he will say, that we who are here assembled are seven, and that I am one and partake of the one, and in saying both he speaks truly. Or if a person shows that the same wood and stones and the like, being many are also one, we admit that he shows the existence of the one and many, but he does not show that the many are one or the one many; he is uttering not a wonder but a truism. If, however, as I was suggesting just now, we were to make an abstraction, I mean of like, unlike, one, many, rest, motion, and similar ideas, and then to show that these in their abstract form admit of admixture and separation, I should greatly wonder at that. This part of the argument appears to be treated by you, Zeno, in a very spirited manner; nevertheless, as I was saying, I should be far more amazed if any one found in the ideas themselves which are conceptions, the same puzzle and entanglement which you have shown to exist in visible objects.

Socrates, he said, I admire the bent of your mind towards philosophy; tell me now, was this your own distinction between abstract ideas and the things which partake of them? and do you think that there is an idea of likeness apart from the likeness which we possess, or of the one and many, or of the other notions of which Zeno has been speaking?

I think that there are such abstract ideas, said Socrates.

Parmenides proceeded. And would you also make abstract ideas of the just and the beautiful and the good, and of all that class of notions?

Yes, he said, I should.

And would you make an abstract idea of man distinct from us and from all other human creatures, or of fire and water?

I am often undecided, Parmenides, as to whether I ought to include them or not.

And would you feel equally undecided, Socrates, about things the mention of which may provoke a smile?—I mean such things as hair, mud, dirt, or anything else that is foul and base; would you suppose that each of these has an idea distinct from the phenomena with which we come into contact, or not?

Certainly not, said Socrates; visible things like these are such as they appear to us, and I am afraid that there would be an absurdity in assuming any idea of them, although I sometimes get disturbed, and begin to think that there is nothing without an idea; but then again, when I have taken up this position, I run away, because I am afraid that I may fall into a bottomless pit of nonsense, and perish; and I return to the ideas of which I was just now speaking, and busy myself with them.

Yes, Socrates, said Parmenides; that is because you are still young; the time will come when philosophy will have a firmer grasp of you, if I am not mistaken, and then you will not despise even the meanest things; at your age, you are too much disposed to look to the opinions of men. But I should like to know whether you mean that there are certain forms or ideas of which all other things partake, and from which they are named; that similars, for example, become similar, because they partake of similarity; and great things become great, because they partake of greatness; and that just and beautiful things become just and beautiful, because they partake of justice and beauty?

Yes, certainly, said Socrates, that is my meaning.

And does not each individual partake either of the whole of the idea or of a part of the idea? Is any third way possible?

Impossible, he said.

Then do you think that the whole idea is one, and yet being one exists in each one of many?

Why not, Parmenides? said Socrates.

Because one and the same existing as a whole in many separate individuals, will thus be in a state of separation from itself.

Nay, replied the other; the idea may be like the day which is one and the same in many places, and yet continuous with itself; in this way each idea may be one and the same in all.

I like your way, Socrates, of dividing one into many; and if I were to spread out a sail and cover a number of men, that, as I suppose, in your way of speaking, would be one and a whole in or on many—that will be the sort of thing which you mean?

I am not sure.

And would you say that the whole sail is over each man, or a part only?

A part only.

Then, Socrates, the ideas themselves will be divisible, and the individuals will have a part only and not the whole existing in them?

That seems to be true.

Then would you like to say, Socrates, that the one idea is really divisible and yet remains one?

Certainly not, he said.

Suppose that you divide greatness, and that of many great things each one is great by having a portion of greatness less than absolute greatness—is that conceivable?

No.

Or will each equal part, by taking some portion of equality less than absolute equality, be equal to some other?

Impossible.

Or suppose one of us to have a portion of smallness; this is but a part of the small, and therefore the small is greater; and while the absolute small is greater, that to which the part of the small is added, will be smaller and not greater than before.

That is impossible, he said.

Then in what way, Socrates, will all things participate in the ideas, if they are unable to participate in them either as parts or wholes?

Indeed, he said, that is a question which is not easily determined.

Well, said Parmenides, and what do you say of another question?

What is that?

I imagine that the way in which you are led to assume the existence of ideas is as follows:—You see a number of great objects, and there seems to you to be one and the same idea of greatness pervading them all; and hence you conceive of a single greatness.

That is true, said Socrates.

And if you go on and allow your mind in like manner to contemplate the idea of greatness and these other greatnesses, and to compare them, will not another idea of greatness arise, which will appear to be the source of them all?

That is true.

Then another abstraction of greatness will appear over and above absolute greatness, and the individuals which partake of it; and then another, which will be the source of that, and then others, and so on; and there will be no longer a single idea of each kind, but an infinite number of them.

But may not the ideas, asked Socrates, be cognitions only, and have no proper existence except in our minds, Parmenides? For in that case there may be single ideas, which do not involve the consequences which were just now mentioned.

And can there be individual cognitions which are cognitions of nothing?

That is impossible, he said.

The cognition must be of something?

Yes.

Of something that is or is not?

Of something that is.

Must it not be of the unity, or single nature, which the cognition recognizes as attaching to all?

Yes.

And will not this unity, which is always the same in all, be the idea?

From that, again, there is no escape.

Then, said Parmenides, if you say that other things participate in the ideas, must you not say that everything is made up of thoughts or cognitions, and that all things think; or will you say that being thoughts they are without thought?

But that, said Socrates, is irrational. The more probable view, Parmenides, of these ideas is, that they are patterns fixed in nature, and that other things are like them, and resemblances of them; and that what is meant by the participation of other things in the ideas, is really assimilation to them.

But if, said he, the individual is like the idea, must not the idea also be like the individual, in as far as the individual is a resemblance of the idea? That which is like, can not be conceived of as other than the like of like.

Impossible.

And when two things are alike, must they not partake of the same idea?

They must.

And will not that of which the two partake, and which makes them alike, be the absolute idea [of likeness]?

Certainly.

Then the idea can not be like the individual, or the individual like the idea; for if they are alike, some further idea of likeness will always arise, and if that be like anything else, another and another; and new ideas will never cease being created, if the idea resembles that which partakes of it?

Quite true.

The theory, then, that other things participate in the ideas by resemblance, has to be given up, and some other mode of participation devised?

That is true.

Do you see then, Socrates, how great is the difficulty of affirming self-existent ideas?

Yes, indeed.

THEAETETUS

1. Socrates, a Midwife and the Son of a Midwife

Socrates. Such are the midwives, whose work is a very important one, but not so important as mine; for women do not bring into the world at one time real children, and at another time idols which are with difficulty distinguished from them; if they did, then the discernment of the true and false birth would be the crowning achievement of the art of midwifery—you would think that?

Theaetetus. Yes, I certainly should.

Socrates. Well, my art of midwifery is in most respects like theirs; but the difference lies in this—that I attend men and not women, and I practise on their souls when they are in labor, and not on their bodies; and the triumph of my art is in examining whether the thought which the mind of the young man is bringing to the birth is a false idol or a noble and true creation. And like the midwives, I am barren, and the reproach which is often made against me, that I ask questions of others and have not the wit to answer them myself, is very just; the reason is, that the god compels me to be a midwife, but forbids me to bring forth. And therefore I am not myself wise, nor have I anything which is the invention or offspring of my own soul, but the way is this:—Some of those who converse with me, at first appear to be absolutely dull, yet afterwards, as our acquaintance ripens, if the god is gracious to them, they all of them make astonishing progress; and this not only in their own opinion but in that of others. There is clear proof that they have never learned anything

of me, but they have acquired and discovered many noble things of themselves, although the god and I help to deliver them.

And the proof is, that many of them in their ignorance, attributing all
to themselves and despising me, either of their own accord or at the insti-
gation of others, have gone away sooner than they ought; and the result
has been that they have produced abortions by reason of their evil com-
munications, or have lost the children of which I delivered them by an
ill bringing up, deeming lies and shadows of more value than the truth;
and they have at last ended by seeing themselves, as others see them, to
be great fools. Aristides, the son of Lysimachus, is one of this sort, and
there are many others. The truants often return to me and beg that I
would converse with them again—they are ready to go down on their
knees—and then, if my familiar allows, which is not always the case, I
receive them, and they begin to grow again. Dire are the pangs which my
art is able to arouse and to allay in those who have intercourse with me,
just like the pangs of women in childbirth; night and day they are full of
perplexity and travail which is even worse than that of the women. So
much for them. And there are others, Theaetetus, who come to me appar-
ently having nothing in them; and as I know that they have no need of
my art, I coax them into another union, and by the grace of God I can
generally tell who is likely to do them good. Many of them I have given
away to Prodicus, and some to other inspired sages.

I tell you this long story, friend Theaetetus, because I suspect, as
indeed you seem to think yourself, that you are in labor—great with some
conception. Come then to me, who am a midwife and the son of a midwife, and try to answer the question which I will ask you. And if I abstract
and expose your first-born, because I discover upon inspection that the
conception which you have formed is a vain shadow, do not quarrel with
me on that account, as the manner of women is when their first children
are taken from them. For I have actually known some who were ready to
bite me when I deprived them of a darling folly; they did not perceive
that I acted from good will, not knowing that no god is the enemy of
man (that was not within the range of their ideas); neither am I their
enemy in all this, but religion will never allow me to admit falsehood, or
to stifle the truth. Once more, then, Theaetetus, I repeat my old question,
"What is knowledge?" and do not say that you can not tell; but quit yourself like a man, and by the help of God you will be able to tell.

2. The Lawyer and the Philosopher

Socrates. Here is a new question offering, Theodorus, which is likely
to be still longer than the last.

Theodorus. Well, Socrates, we have plenty of leisure.

Socrates. That is true, and your remark recalls to my mind an observation which I have often made, that those who have passed their days in the pursuit of philosophy are ridiculously at fault when they have to appear and plead in court. How natural is this!

Theodorus. What do you mean?

Socrates. I mean to say, that those who from their youth upwards have been knocking about in the courts and such like places, compared with those who have received a philosophical education, are slaves, and the others are freemen.

Theodorus. In what is the difference seen?

Socrates. In the leisure of which you were speaking, and which a freeman can always command; he has his talk out in peace, and, like ourselves, wanders at will from one subject to another, and from a second to a third, if his fancy prefers a new one, caring not whether his words are many or few; his only aim is to attain the truth. But the lawyer is always in a hurry; there is the water of the clepsydra driving him on, and not allowing him to expatiate at will; and there is his adversary standing over him, enforcing his rights; the affidavit, which in their phraseology is termed the brief, is recited; and from this he must not deviate. He is a servant, and is disputing about a fellow-servant before his master, who is seated, and has the cause in his hands; the trial is never about some indifferent matter, but always concerns himself; and often he has to run for his life. The consequence has been, that he has become keen and shrewd; he has learned how to flatter his master in word and indulge him in deed; but his soul is small and unrighteous. His slavish condition has deprived him of growth and uprightness and independence; dangers and fears, which were too much for his truth and honesty, came upon him in early years, when the tenderness of youth was unequal to them, and he has been driven into crooked ways; from the first he has practised deception and retaliation, and has become stunted and warped. And so he has passed out of youth into manhood, having no soundness in him; and is now, as he thinks, a master in wisdom. Such is the lawyer, Theodorus. Will you have the companion picture of the philosopher, who is of our brotherhood; or shall we return to the argument? Do not let us abuse the freedom of digression which we claim.

Theodorus. Nay, Socrates, let us finish what we were about; for you truly said that we belong to a brotherhood which is free, and are not the servants of the argument; but the argument is our servant, and must wait our leisure. Where is the judge or spectator who has a right to censure or control us, as he might the poets?

Socrates. Then, as this is your wish, I will describe the leaders; for there is no use in talking about the inferior sort. In the first place, the lords of philosophy have never, from their youth upwards, known their way to the agora, or the dicastery, or the council, or any other political assembly; they neither see nor hear the laws or votes of the state written or spoken; the eagerness of political societies in the attainment of offices—clubs, and banquets, and revels, and singing-maidens, do not enter even into their dreams. Whether any event has turned out well or ill in the city, what disgrace may have descended to any one from his ancestors, male or female, are matters of which the philosopher no more knows than he can tell, as they say, how many pints are contained in the ocean. Neither is he conscious of his ignorance. For he does not hold aloof in order that he may gain a reputation; but the truth is, that the outer form of him only is in the city; his mind, disdaining the littlenesses and nothingnesses of human things, is "flying all abroad," as Pindar says, measuring with line and rule the things which are under and on the earth and above the heaven, interrogating the whole nature of each and all, but not condescending to anything which is within reach.

Theodorus. What do you mean, Socrates?

Socrates. I will illustrate my meaning, Theodorus, by the jest which the clever, witty Thracian handmaid made about Thales, when he fell into a well as he was looking up at the stars. She said, that he was so eager to know what was going on in heaven, that he could not see what was before his feet. This is a jest which is equally applicable to all philosophers. For the philosopher is wholly unacquainted with his next door neighbor; he is ignorant, not only of what he is doing, but whether he is or is not a human creature; he is searching into the essence of man, and is unwearied in discovering what belongs to such a nature to do or suffer different from any other;—I think that you understand me, Theodorus?

Theodorus. I do, and what you say is true.

Socrates. And thus, my friend, on every occasion, private as well as public, as I said at first, when he appears in a law-court, or in any place in which he has to speak of things which are at his feet and before his eyes, he is the jest, not only of Thracian handmaids but of the general herd, tumbling into wells and every sort of disaster through his inexperience. He looks such an awkward creature, and conveys the impression that he is stupid. When he is reviled, he has nothing personal to say in answer to the civilities of his adversaries, for he knows no scandals of any one, and they do not interest him; and therefore he is laughed at for his sheepishness; and when others are being praised and glorified, he can not help laughing very sincerely in the simplicity of his heart; and this again makes him look like a fool. When he hears a tyrant or king eulogized, he fancies that he is listening to the praises of some keeper of cattle—a swineherd, or shepherd, or cowherd, who is being praised for the quantity of milk which he squeezes from them; and he remarks that the creature whom they tend, and out of whom they squeeze the wealth, is of a less tractable and more insidious nature. Then, again, he observes that the great man is of necessity as ill-mannered and uneducated as any shepherd —for he has no leisure, and he is surrounded by a wall, which is his mountain-pen. Hearing of enormous landed proprietors of ten thousand acres and more, our philosopher deems this to be a trifle, because he has been accustomed to think of the whole earth; and when they sing the praises of family, and say that some one is a gentleman because he has had seven generations of wealthy ancestors, he thinks that their sentiments only betray the dulness and narrowness of vision of those who utter them, and who are not educated enough to look at the whole, nor to consider that every man has had thousands and thousands of progenitors, and among them have been rich and poor, kings and slaves, Hellenes and barbarians, many times over. And when some one boasts of a catalogue of twenty-five ancestors, and goes back to Heracles, the son of Amphitryon, he can not understand his poverty of ideas. Why is he unable to calculate that Amphitryon had a twenty-fifth ancestor, who might have been anybody, and was such as fortune made him, and he had a fiftieth, and so on? He is amused at the notion that he can not do a sum, and thinks that a little arithmetic would have got rid of his senseless vanity. Now, in all these cases our philosopher is derided by the vulgar, partly because he is above them, and also because he is ignorant of what is before him, and always at a loss.

Theodorus. That is very true, Socrates.

Socrates. But, O my friend, when he draws the other into upper air, and gets him out of his pleas and rejoinders into the contemplation of justice and injustice in their own nature and in their difference from one another and from all other things; or from the commonplaces about the happiness of kings to the consideration of government, and of human happiness and misery in general—what they are, and how a man should seek after the one and avoid the other—when that narrow, keen, little legal mind is called to account about all this, he gives the philosopher his revenge; for dizzied by the height at which he is hanging, and from which he looks into space, which is a strange experience to him, he being dismayed, and lost, and stammering out broken words, is laughed at, not by Thracian handmaidens or any other uneducated persons, for they have no eye for the situation, but by every man who has not been brought up as a slave. Such are the two characters, Theodorus: the one of the philosopher or gentleman, who may be excused for appearing simple and useless when he has to perform some menial office, such as packing up a bag, or flavoring a sauce or fawning speech; the other, of the man who is able to do every kind of service smartly and neatly, but knows not how to wear his cloak like a gentleman; still less does he acquire the music of speech, or hymn the true life which is lived by immortals or men blessed of heaven.

Theodorus. If you could only persuade everybody, Socrates, as you do me, of the truth of your words, there would be more peace and fewer evils among men.

Socrates. Evils, Theodorus, can never perish; for there must always remain something which is antagonist to good. Of necessity, they hover around this mortal sphere and the earthly nature, having no place among the gods in heaven. Wherefore, also, we ought to fly away thither, and to fly thither is to become like God, as far as this is possible; and to become like him, is to become holy and just and wise. But, O my friend, you can not easily convince mankind that they should pursue virtue or avoid vice, not for the reasons which the many give, in order, forsooth, that a man may seem to be good;—this is what they are always repeating, and this, in my judgment, is an old wives' fable. Let them hear the truth: In God is no unrighteousness at all—he is altogether righteous; and there is nothing more like him than he of us, who is the most righteous. And the true wisdom of men, and their nothingness and cowardice, are nearly concerned with this. For to know this is true wisdom and manhood, and the ignorance of this is too plainly folly and vice. All other kinds of wisdom or cunning, which seem only, such as the wisdom of politicians, or the wisdom of the arts, are coarse and vulgar. The unrighteous man, or the sayer and doer of unholy things, had far better not yield to the illusion that his roguery is cleverness; for men glory in their shame—they fancy that they hear others saying of them, "these are not mere good-for-nothing persons, burdens of the earth, but such as men should be who mean to dwell safely in a state." Let us tell them that they are all the more truly what they do not know that they are; for they do not know the penalty of injustice, which above all things they ought to know—not stripes and death, as they suppose, which evildoers often escape, but a penalty which can not be escaped.

Theodorus. What is that?

Socrates. There are two patterns set before them in nature: the one, blessed and divine, the other godless and wretched; and they do not see, in their utter folly and infatuation, that they are growing like the one and unlike the other, by reason of their evil deeds; and the penalty is, that they lead a life answering to the pattern which they resemble. And if we tell them, that unless they depart from their cunning, the place of innocence will not receive them after death; and that here on earth, they will live ever in the likeness of their own evil selves, and with evil friends—when they hear this they in their superior cunning will seem to be listening to fools.

Theodorus. Very true, Socrates.

Socrates. Too true, my friend, as I well know; there is, however, one peculiarity in their case: when they begin to reason in private about their dislike of philosophy, if they have the courage to hear the argument out, and do not run away, they grow at last strangely discontented with themselves; their rhetoric fades away, and they seem to be no better than children. These, however, are digressions from which we must now desist, or they will overflow, and drown our original argument; to which, if you please, we will now return.

Theodorus. For my part, Socrates, I would rather have the digressions, for at my age I find them easier to follow; but if you wish, let us go back to the argument.

PHILEBUS

Protarchus. Considering, Socrates, how many we are, and that all of us are young men, is there not a danger that we and Philebus may conspire and attack you, if you speak evil of us? Yet we understand; and if there is any better way or manner of quietly escaping out of all this turmoil and perplexity, and arriving at the truth, we hope that you will guide us into that way, and we will do our best to follow, for the inquiry in which we are engaged, Socrates, is not a small one.

Socrates. Not a small one, my boys, as Philebus calls you, and there neither is nor ever will be a better than my own favorite way, which has nevertheless already often deserted me in the hour of need.

Protarchus. Tell us what that is.

Socrates. One which may be easily explained, but is by no means easy of application, and is the parent of all the discoveries of the art.

Protarchus. Say only what.

Socrates. A gift of heaven, which, as I conceive, the gods tossed into the world by the hands of some Prometheus, together with a blaze of fire; and the ancients, who were our betters and nearer the gods than we are, handed down the tradition, that all things which are supposed to exist draw their existence from the one and many, and have the finite and infinite in them as a part of their nature: seeing, then, that such is the order of the world, we too ought in all our investigations to assume that there is one idea of everything; this unity we shall be sure to find, and having found, we may next proceed to look for two, if there be two, or, if not, then for three or some other number, subdividing each of these units, until at last the original one is seen, not only as one and many and infinite, but also in some definite number; the infinite must not be suffered to approach the many until the entire number of the species intermediate between unity and infinity has been found out,—then, and not till then, we may rest from division, and all the remaining individuals may be allowed to pass into infinity.

This, as I was saying, is the way of considering and learning and teaching one another, which the gods have handed down to us. But the wise men of our time are either too quick or too slow in conceiving plurality in unity. Having no method, they make their one and many anyhow, and from unity pass at once to infinity, without thinking of the intermediate steps. And this, I repeat, is what makes the difference between the mere art of disputation and true dialectic.

TIMAEUS

THERE IS a corresponding inquiry concerning the modes in which the mind and the body are to be treated, and by what means they are preserved, on which I may and ought to enter; for it is more our duty to speak of the good than of the evil. Everything that is good is fair, and the fair is not without measure, and the animal who is fair may be supposed to have measure. Now we perceive lesser symmetries and comprehend them, but about the highest and greatest we have no understanding; for with a view to health and disease, and virtue and vice, there is no symmetry or want of symmetry greater than that of the soul to the body; and this we do not perceive, or ever reflect that when a weaker or lesser frame is the vehicle of a great and mighty soul, or conversely, when they are united in the opposite way, then the whole animal is not fair, for it is defective in the most important of all symmetries; but the fair mind in the fair body will be the fairest and loveliest of all sights to him who has the seeing eye. Just as a body which has a leg too long, or some other disproportion, is an unpleasant sight, and also, when undergoing toil, has many sufferings, and makes violent efforts, and often stumbles through awkwardness, and is the cause of infinite evil to its own self—in like manner we should conceive of the double nature which we call the living being; and when in this compound there is an impassioned soul more powerful than the body, that soul, I say, convulses and disorders the whole inner nature of man; and when too eager in the pursuit of knowledge, causes wasting; or again, when teaching or disputing in private or in public, and strifes and controversies arise, inflames and dissolves the composite frame of man and introduces rheums; and the nature of this is not understood by most professors of medicine, who ascribe the phenomenon to the opposite of the real cause. And once more, when a body large and too much for the soul is united to a small and weak intelligence, seeing that there are two desires natural to man,—one of food for the sake of the body, and one of wisdom for the sake of the diviner part of us—then, I say, the motions of the stronger principle, getting the better and increasing their own power, but making the soul dull, and stupid, and forgetful, engender ignorance, which is the greatest of diseases.

There is one protection against both:—that we should not move the body without the soul or the soul without the body, and thus they will aid one another, and be healthy and well balanced. And therefore the mathematician or any one else who devotes himself to some intellectual pursuit must allow his body to have motion also, and practise gymnastic; and he who would train the limbs of the body, should impart to them the motions of the soul, and should practise music and all philosophy, if he would be called truly fair and truly good.

And in like manner should the parts be treated, and the principle of the whole similarly applied to them; for as the body is heated and also cooled within by the elements which enter in, and is again dried up and moistened by external things, and experiences these and the like affections from both kinds of motions, the result is that the body if given up to motion when in a state of quiescence is overmastered and destroyed; but if any one, in imitation of that which we call the foster-mother and nurse of the universe, will not allow the body to be at rest, but is always producing motions and shakings, which constantly react upon the natural motions both within and without, and by shaking moderately the affections and parts which wander about the body, brings them into order and affinity with one another according to the theory of the universe which we were maintaining, he will not allow enemy placed by the side of enemy to create wars and disorders in the body, but he will place friend by the side of friend, producing health.

Now of all motions that is the best which is produced in a thing by itself, for it is most akin to the motion of the intelligent and the motion of the universe; but that motion which is caused by others is not so good, and worst of all is that which moves the parts of the body, when prostrate and at rest, in parts only and by external means; wherefore also that is the best of the purifications and adjustments of the body which is effected by gymnastic; next is that which is effected by carrying the body, as in sailing or any other mode of conveyance which is not fatiguing; the third sort of motion may be of use in a case of extreme necessity, but in any other will be adopted by no man of sense: I mean the purgative treatment of physicians; for diseases which are not attended by great dangers should not be irritated by purgatives, for every form of disease is in a manner akin to the living being—for the combination out of which they were formed has an appointed term of life and of existence. And the whole race and every animal has his appointed natural time, apart from violent casualties; for the triangles are originally framed with power to live for a certain time, beyond which no man can prolong his life. And this holds also of the nature of diseases, for if any one regardless of their appointed time would destroy nature by purgatives, he only increases and multiplies them. Wherefore we ought always to manage them by regimen, as far as a man can spare the time, and not provoke a disagreeable enemy by medical treatment.

Let this much be said of the general nature of man, and of the body which is a part of him, and of the manner in which a man may govern himself and be governed best, and live most according to reason: and we must begin by providing that the governing principle shall be the fairest and best possible for the purpose of government. But to discuss such a subject accurately would be a sufficiently long business of itself. As a mere supplement or sequel of what has preceded, it may be summed up as follows. As I have often said, that there are three kinds of soul located within us, each of them having their own proper motions—so I must now say in the fewest words possible, that the one part, if remaining inactive and ceasing from the natural motion, must necessarily become very weak, but when trained and exercised then very strong. Wherefore we should take care that the three parts of the soul are exercised in proportion to one another.

Concerning the highest part of the human soul, we should consider that God gave this as a genius to each one, which was to dwell at the extremity of the body, and to raise us like plants, not of an earthly but of a heavenly growth, from earth to our kindred which is in heaven. And this is most true; for the divine power suspended the head and root of us from that place where the generation of the soul first began, and thus made erect the whole body. He, therefore, who is always occupied with the cravings of desire and ambition, and is eagerly striving after them, must have all his opinions mortal, and, as far as man can be, must be all of him mortal, because he has cherished his mortal part. But he who has been earnest in the love of knowledge and true wisdom, and has been trained to think that these are the immortal and divine things of a man, if he attain truth, must of necessity, as far as human nature is capable of attaining immortality, be all immortal, as he is ever serving the divine power; and having the genius residing in him in the most perfect order, he must be pre-eminently happy.

Now there is only one way in which one being can serve another, and this is by giving him his proper nourishment and motion. And the motions which are akin to the divine principle within us are the thoughts and revolutions of the universe. These each man should follow, and correct those corrupted courses of the head which are concerned with generation, and by learning the harmonies and revolutions of the whole, should assimilate the perceiver to the thing perceived, according to his original nature, and by thus assimilating them, attain that final perfection of life, which the gods set before mankind as best, both for the present and the future.

CRITIAS

THERE WERE many special laws which the several kings had inscribed about the temples, but the most important was the following:—That they were not to take up arms against one another, and they were all to come to the rescue if any one in any city attempted to overthrow the royal house; like their ancestors, they were to deliberate in common about war and other matters, giving the supremacy to the family of Atlas. And the king was not to have the power of life and death over any of his kinsmen unless he had the assent of the majority of the ten kings.

Such was the vast power which the god settled in the lost island of Atlantis; and this he afterwards directed against our land on the following pretext, as traditions tell: For many generations, as long as the divine nature lasted in them, they were obedient to the laws, and well-affectioned towards the gods, who were their kinsmen; for they possessed true and in every way great spirits, practising gentleness and wisdom in the various chances of life, and in their intercourse with one another. They despised everything but virtue, not caring for their present state of life, and thinking lightly of the possession of gold and other property, which seemed only a burden to them; neither were they intoxicated by luxury; nor did wealth deprive them of their self-control; but they were sober, and saw clearly that all these goods are increased by virtuous friendship with one another, and that by excessive zeal for them, and honor of them, the good of them is lost and friendship perishes with them. By such reflections and by the continuance in them of a divine nature, all that which we have described waxed and increased in them; but when this divine portion began to fade away in them, and became diluted too often and with too much of the mortal admixture, and the human nature got the upper hand, then they, being unable to bear their fortune, became unseemly, and to him who had an eye to see, they began to appear base, and had lost the fairest of their precious gifts; but to those who had no eye to see the true happiness, they still appeared glorious and blessed at the very time when they were filled with unrighteous avarice and power. Zeus, the god of gods, who rules with law, and is able to see into such things, perceiving that an honorable race was in a most wretched state, and wanting to inflict punishment on them, that they might be chastened and improve, collected all the gods into his most holy habitation, which being placed in the centre of the world, sees all things that partake of generation.

NICOMACHEAN ETHICS

by

ARISTOTLE

CONTENTS

Nicomachean Ethics

ARISTOTLE

384–322 B.C.

ARISTOTLE, like Plato, was endowed with an intellect of incredible versatility. He made substantial contributions to almost every field of human thought, including politics, drama, poetry, physics, medicine, psychology, history, logic, astronomy, ethics, natural history, mathematics, rhetoric, biology, and the fine arts. In at least one of these fields—logic—his genius has never been surpassed.

The son of Nicomachus, court physician to Amyntas II, king of Macedon, Aristotle was born at Stagira, a small village on the Strymonic Gulf. His mother, Phaestis, was a descendant of one of the "Pilgrim Fathers" who migrated from Chalcis to establish the Greek colony at Stagira. This lineage gave Aristotle a position of great prestige both at court and in the community at large.

Nicomachus instructed his son in the art of healing and created in him an interest in medicine and biology. This interest grew into a love for the sciences in general. Later on, his experimentation in science led him to speculation in philosophy. From a dissecter of the human body he developed into a dissecter of the anatomy of the world.

When he was eighteen years old, he left his native Stagira for Athens, the center of Greek cultural and political life. Here he became acquainted with Plato and enrolled himself as a student in the Academy. He remained with the "Master" for about twenty years, quarreling with him and idolizing him and absorbing his philosophy and gradually building up a philosophy of his own.

Upon the death of Plato, Aristotle left Athens and spent several years traveling. In the course of his travels he met an old friend and classmate, Hermias, who was now king of a large territory in Asia Minor. The king gave Aristotle his daughter, Pythias, in marriage, together with a generous dowry. The philosopher could now build his theoretical castles in the air upon a practical foundation of gold.

In 343 Aristotle accepted an invitation from King Philip of Macedon to teach "sweetness and wisdom" to the savage young Prince Alexander, then a boy of thirteen. The relationship between the brilliant philosopher and the turbulent Alexander was more enlightening to the teacher than it was to the pupil. After three years of patient instruction, Aristotle learned that a young man intent upon aggression will never listen to reason. When King Philip died, Alexander plunged into his conquests and Aristotle returned to Athens.

Here he established his celebrated school at the Lyceum, a gymnasium near the temple of Apollo Lyceus. He delivered his lectures to his students informally—conversing with them as they strolled among the trees and flowers of the garden. This practice is believed to have given the name *peripatetic* to the followers of Aristotle's school. In addition to his teaching, Aristotle wrote on almost every subject, and collected a library that was one of the wonders of the world.

But neither his philosophy nor his library availed to save him from the danger of a violent death. At first it was Alexander who threatened to kill him. He had already killed another philosopher, Callisthenes, the nephew of Aristotle.

This danger to Aristotle's life was removed when Alexander died after a drunken debauch. But now a similar danger threatened Aristotle from another source. The Athenians, having been conquered by Alexander, accused his former teacher of being a spy. Mindful of the fate of Socrates, whom the Athenians had put to death, Aristotle decided to leave the city before it was too late.

He retired to Chalcis, the seat of his ancient ancestors, where he died in 322.

Aristotle's philosophy is, in this volume, represented by his *Nicomachean Ethics*—so named in honor of his son, Nicomachus the Younger. The book on *Ethics,* though complete in itself, is the first half of a longer treatise on "the philosophy of human affairs." The second half of this longer treatise is the *Politics,* a condensation of which is included in the volume of this series dealing with the subject of Government.

The question which Aristotle poses in the *Ethics* is: What is the highest good? His answer to the question is that the highest good is the life of reason. It is the purpose of man's conduct, maintains Aristotle, to establish upon the basis of reason a life of happiness for all mankind. And how is this happiness to be attained? Through the practice of the *golden mean*—that is, the middle course between the two extremes of ignoble conduct. The happy man, the virtuous man, is he who preserves this golden mean. He is the man who steers midway between the two shoals that threaten on either side to wreck human happiness. In every act, in every thought, in every emotion, a man may be *overdoing* his duty, or *underdoing* it, or *doing it just right*. For example, when a man shares his goods with other people, he may be *extravagant,* and thus overdo it, or *stingy,* and thus underdo it, or *liberal,* and so do it just right. In the regulation of his appetites, a man may be *gluttonous,* or *abstemious,* or *moderate.* In every case, the *rational* course of life is the *middle* course of life, and the rational man is the man who does nothing too much or too little, but who does everything in moderation. The virtuous man will be neither supernormal nor subnormal, but justly and reasonably normal. He will act "at the right times, with reference to the right objects, toward the right people, with the right motive and in the right way. . . . He will not expose himself needlessly to danger but will be ready in great crises to give his life if necessary. He will take joy in doing favors to other men, but he will feel shame in having favors done to him by other men. For it is a mark of superiority to confer a kindness, but of inferiority to receive it. . . . The virtuous man, the *superior* man, will be altruistic because he will be wise. . . . He will not speak evil of others, even of his enemies, unless it be to themselves. . . . He will never feel malice, and he will always forget injuries. . . . In short, he will be a good friend to others because he will be his own best friend."

This is the ideal man as pictured in the *Ethics* of Aristotle. His life of unselfish moderation is in reality a life of *enlightened* selfishness. For man is not an *individual* self, but a *social* self. Every good deed is a profitable investment. It is bound, sooner or later, to be returned with interest. The golden mean produces a trust fund of spiritual capital that will ultimately make for the enrichment of all mankind.

NICOMACHEAN ETHICS

Book One

EVERY ART, and every science reduced to a teachable form, and in like manner every action and moral choice, aims, it is thought, at some good: for which reason a common and by no means a bad description of the Chief Good is, "that which all things aim at."

Now there plainly is a difference in the Ends proposed: for in some cases they are acts of working, and in others certain works or tangible results beyond and beside the acts of working: and where there are certain Ends beyond and beside the actions, the works are in their nature better than the acts of working. Again, since actions and arts and sciences are many, the Ends likewise come to be many.

And whatever of such actions, arts, or sciences range under some one faculty, in all such, the Ends of the master-arts are more choiceworthy than those ranging under them, because it is with a view to the former that the latter are pursued.

Since then of all things which may be done there is some one End which we desire for its own sake, and with a view to which we desire everything else; and since we do not choose in all instances with a further End in view, this plainly must be the Chief Good, i.e., the best thing of all.

And now, resuming the statement with which we commenced, since all knowledge and moral choice grasps at good of some kind or another, what is the highest of all the goods which are the objects of action?

So far as name goes, there is a pretty general agreement: for HAPPINESS both the multitude and the refined few call it, and "living well" and "doing well" they conceive to be the same with "being happy;" but about the Nature of this Happiness, men dispute, and the multitude do not in their account of it agree with the wise.

Now of the Chief Good (i.e., of Happiness) men seem to form their notions from the different modes of life, as we might naturally expect: the many and most low conceive it to be pleasure, and hence they are content with the life of sensual enjoyment. For there are three lines of life which stand out prominently to view: that just mentioned, and the life in society, and, thirdly, the life of contemplation.

In the next place, since good is predicated in as many ways as there are modes of existence, it manifestly cannot be something common and universal and one in all: else it would not have been predicated in all the categories, but in one only.

And now let us revert to the Good of which we are in search: what can it be? for manifestly it is different in different actions and arts: for it is different in the healing art and in the art military, and similarly in the rest. What then is the Chief Good in each? Is it not "that for the sake of which the other things are done"? and this in the healing art is health, and in the art military victory, and in that of house-building a house, and in any other thing something else; in short, in every action and moral choice the End, because in all cases men do everything else with a view to this. So that if there is some one End of all things which are and may be done, this must be the Good proposed by doing, or if more than one, then these.

Now since the ends are plainly many, and of these we choose some with a view to others, it is clear that all are not final: but the Chief Good is manifestly something final; and so, if there is some one only which is final, this must be the object of our search: but if several, then the most final of them will be it.

Now that which is an object of pursuit in itself we call more final than that which is so with a view to something else; that again which is never an object of choice with a view to something else than those which are so both in themselves and with a view to this ulterior object: and so by the term "absolutely final" we denote that which is an object of choice always in itself, and never with a view to any other.

And of this nature Happiness is mostly thought to be, for this we choose always for its own sake, and never with a view to anything further: whereas honour, pleasure, intellect, in fact every excellence we choose for their own sakes, it is true, but we choose them also with a view to happiness, conceiving that through their instrumentality we shall be happy: but no man chooses happiness with a view to them, nor in fact with a view to any other thing whatsoever.

So then Happiness is manifestly something final and self-sufficient, being the end of all things which are and may be done.

But, it may be, to call Happiness the Chief Good is a mere truism, and what is wanted is some clearer account of its real nature. Now this object may be easily attained, when we have discovered what is the work of man; for as in the case of flute-player, statuary, or artisan of any kind, or, more generally, all who have any work or course of action, their Chief Good and Excellence is thought to reside in their work, so it would seem to be with man, if there is any work belonging to him.

Now there is a common division of goods into three classes; one being called external, the other two those of the soul and body respectively, and those belonging to the soul we call most properly and specially good. Well, in our definition we assume that the actions and workings of the soul constitute Happiness, and these of course belong to the soul. And so our account is a good one, at least according to this opinion, which is of ancient date, and accepted by those who profess philosophy. Rightly too are certain actions and workings said to be the end, for thus it is brought into the number of the goods of the soul instead of the external. Agreeing also with our definition is the common notion that the happy man lives well and does well, for it has been stated by us to be pretty much a kind of living well and doing well.

But further, the points required in Happiness are found in combination in our account of it.

For some think it is virtue, others practical wisdom, others a kind of scientific philosophy; others that it is these, or else some one of them, in combination with pleasure, or at least not independently of it; while others again take in external prosperity.

Still it is quite plain that it does require the addition of external goods, as we have said: because without appliances it is impossible, or at all events not easy, to do noble actions: for friends, money, and political influence are in a manner instruments whereby many things are done. He is not at all capable of Happiness who is very ugly, or is ill-born, or solitary and childless; and still less perhaps supposing him to have very bad children or friends, or to have lost good ones by death. As we have said already, the addition of prosperity of this kind does seem necessary to complete the idea of Happiness; hence some rank good fortune, and others virtue, with Happiness.

And hence too a question is raised, whether it is a thing that can be learned, or acquired by habituation or discipline of some other kind, or whether it comes in the way of divine dispensation, or even in the way of chance.

Now to be sure, if anything else is a gift of the gods to men, it is probable that Happiness is a gift of theirs too, and specially because of all human goods it is the highest. But this, it may be, is a question belonging more properly to an investigation different from ours: and it is quite clear that on the supposition of its not being sent from the gods direct, but coming to us by reason of virtue and learning of a certain kind, or discipline, it is yet one of the most godlike things; because the prize and End of virtue is manifestly somewhat most excellent, nay divine and blessed.

It will also on this supposition be widely participated, for it may through learning and diligence of a certain kind exist in all who have not been maimed for virtue.

And if it is better we should be happy thus than as a result of chance, this is in itself an argument that the case is so; because those things which are in the way of nature, and in like manner of art, and of every cause, and specially the best cause, are by nature in the best way possible: to leave then to chance what is greatest and most noble would be very much out of harmony with all these facts.

Having determined these points, let us examine, with respect to Happiness, whether it belongs to the class of things praiseworthy or things precious; for to that of faculties it evidently does not.

Now it is plain that everything which is a subject of praise is praised for being of a certain kind and bearing a certain relation to something else: for instance, the just, and the valiant, and generally the good man, and virtue itself, we praise because of the actions and the results: and the strong man, and the quick runner, and so forth, we praise for being of a certain nature and bearing a certain relation to something good and excellent. Now if it is to such objects that praise belongs, it is evident that what is applicable to the best objects is not praise, but something higher and better: which is plain matter of fact, for not only do we call the gods blessed and happy, but of men also we pronounce those blessed who most nearly resemble the gods. And in like manner in respect of goods; no man thinks of praising Happiness as he does the principle of justice, but calls it blessed, as being somewhat more godlike and more excellent.

Moreover, since Happiness is a kind of working of the soul in the way of perfect Excellence, we must inquire concerning Excellence: for so probably shall we have a clearer view concerning Happiness; and again, he who is really a statesman is generally thought to have spent most pains on this, for he wishes to make the citizens good and obedient to the laws.

Well, we are to inquire concerning Excellence, i.e., Human Excellence of course, because it was the Chief Good of Man and the Happiness of Man that we were inquiring of just now.

By Human Excellence we mean not that of man's body but that of his soul; for we call Happiness a working of the Soul.

Now the Excellence of this manifestly is not peculiar to the human species but common to others: for this part and this faculty is thought to work most in time of sleep, and the good and bad man are least distinguishable while asleep; whence it is a common saying that during one half of life there is no difference between the happy and the wretched; and this accords with our anticipations, for sleep is an inactivity of the soul, in so far as it is denominated good or bad, except that in some wise some of its movements find their way through the veil and so the good come to have better dreams than ordinary men. But enough of this: we must forego any further mention of the nutritive part, since it is not naturally capable of the Excellence which is peculiarly human.

And there seems to be another Irrational Nature of the Soul, which yet in a way partakes of Reason. For in the man who controls his appetites, and in him who resolves to do so and fails, we praise the Reason or Rational part of the Soul, because it exhorts aright and to the best course: but clearly there is in them, beside the Reason, some other natural principle which fights with and strains against the Reason.

But of Reason this too does evidently partake, as we have said: for instance, in the man of self-control it obeys Reason: and perhaps in the man of perfected self-mastery, or the brave man, it is yet more obedient; in them it agrees entirely with the Reason.

So then the Irrational is plainly twofold: the one part, the merely vegetative, has no share of Reason, but that of desire, or appetition generally, does partake of it in a sense, in so far as it is obedient to it and capable of submitting to its rule.

Now that the Irrational is in some way persuaded by the Reason, admonition, and every act of rebuke and exhortation indicate. If then we are to say that this also has Reason, then the Rational, as well as the Irrational, will be twofold, the one supremely and in itself, the other paying it a kind of filial regard.

The Excellence of Man then is divided in accordance with this difference: we make two classes, calling the one Intellectual, and the other Moral; pure science, intelligence, and practical wisdom—Intellectual: liberality, and perfected self-mastery—Moral: in speaking of a man's Moral character, we do not say he is a scientific or intelligent but a meek man, or one of perfected self-mastery: and we praise the man of science in right of his mental state; and of these such as are praiseworthy we call Excellences.

Book Two

WELL: human Excellence is of two kinds, intellectual and Moral: now the Intellectual springs originally, and is increased subsequently, from teaching, and needs therefore experience and time; whereas the Moral comes from custom, and so the Greek term denoting it is but a slight deflection from the term denoting custom in that language.

From this fact it is plain that not one of the Moral Virtues comes to be in us merely by nature: because of such things as exist by nature, none can be changed by custom: a stone, for instance, by nature gravitating downwards, could never by custom be brought to ascend, not even if one were to try and accustom it by throwing it up ten thousand times; nor could fire again be brought to descend, nor in fact could anything whose nature is in one way be brought by custom to be in another. The

Virtues then come to be in us neither by nature, nor in despite of nature, but we are furnished by nature with a capacity for receiving them, and are perfected in them through custom.

Again, in whatever cases we get things by nature, we get the faculties first and perform the acts of working afterwards; an illustration of which is afforded by the case of our bodily senses, for it was not from having often seen or heard that we got these senses, but just the reverse: we had them and so exercised them, but did not have them because we had exercised them.

Again, every Virtue is either produced or destroyed from and by the very same circumstances. So too then is it with the Virtues: for by acting in the various relations in which we are thrown with our fellow men, we come to be, some just, some unjust: and by acting in dangerous positions and being habituated to feel fear or confidence, we come to be, some brave, others cowards.

Similarly is it also with respect to the occasions of lust and anger: for some men come to be perfected in self-mastery and mild, others destitute of all self-control and passionate; the one class by behaving in one way under them, the other by behaving in another. Or, in one word, the habits are produced from the acts of working like to them: and so what we have to do is to give a certain character to these particular acts, because the habits formed correspond to the differences of these.

So then, whether we are accustomed this way or that straight from childhood, makes not a small but an important difference, or rather I would say it makes all the difference.

Now, that we are to act in accordance with Right Reason is a general maxim, and may for the present be taken for granted: we will speak of it hereafter, and say both what Right Reason is, and what are its relations to the other virtues.

But let this point be first thoroughly understood between us, that all which can be said on moral action must be said in outline, as it were, and not exactly: for as we remarked at the commencement, such reasoning only must be required as the nature of the subject-matter admits of, and matters of moral action and expediency have no fixedness any more than matters of health. And if the subject in its general maxims is such, still less in its application to particular cases is exactness attainable: because these fall not under any art or system of rules, but it must be left in each instance to the individual agents to look to the exigencies of the particular case, as it is in the art of healing, or that of navigating a ship. Still, though the present subject is confessedly such, we must try and do what we can for it.

First then this must be noted, that it is the nature of such things to be spoiled by defect and excess; as we see in the case of health and strength, for excessive training impairs the strength as well as deficient: meat and drink, in like manner, in too great or too small quantities, impair the health: while in due proportion they cause, increase, and preserve it.

Thus it is therefore with the habits of perfected Self-Mastery and Courage and the rest of the Virtues: for the man who flies from and fears all things, and never stands up against anything, comes to be a coward; and he who fears nothing, but goes at everything, comes to be rash. In like manner too, he that tastes of every pleasure and abstains from none comes to lose all self-control; while he who avoids all, as do the dull and clownish, comes as it were to lose his faculties of perception: that is to say, the habits of perfected Self-Mastery and Courage are spoiled by the excess and defect, but by the mean state are preserved.

And for a test of the formation of the habits we must take the pleasure or pain which succeeds the acts; for he is perfected in Self-Mastery who not only abstains from the bodily pleasures but is glad to do so; whereas he who abstains but is sorry to do it has not Self-Mastery: he again is brave who stands up against danger, either with positive pleasure or at least without any pain; whereas he who does it with pain is not brave.

For Moral Virtue has for its object-matter pleasures and pains, because by reason of pleasure we do what is bad, and by reason of pain decline doing what is right. Again: since Virtues have to do with actions and feelings, and on every feeling and every action pleasure and pain follow, here again is another proof that Virtue has for its object-matter pleasure and pain. Virtue then is assumed to be that habit which is such, in relation to pleasures and pains, as to effect the best results, and Vice the contrary.

The following considerations may also serve to set this in a clear light. There are principally three things moving us to choice and three to avoidance, the honourable, the expedient, the pleasant; and their three contraries, the dishonourable, the hurtful, and the painful: now the good man is apt to go right, and the bad man wrong, with respect to all these of course, but most specially with respect to pleasure: because not only is this common to him with all animals but also it is a concomitant of all those things which move to choice, since both the honourable and the expedient give an impression of pleasure.

Let us then be understood to have stated that Virtue has for its object-matter pleasures and pains, and that it is either increased or marred by the same circumstances by which it is originally generated, and that it exerts itself on the same circumstances out of which it was generated.

Next, we must examine what Virtue is. Well, since the things which come to be in the mind are, in all, of three kinds, Feelings, Capacities, States, Virtue of course must belong to one of the three classes.

Now Feelings neither the virtues nor vices are, because in right of the Feelings we are not denominated either good or bad, but in right of the virtues and vices we are.

Again, in right of the Feelings we are neither praised nor blamed. And for these same reasons they are not Capacities, for we are not called good or bad merely because we are able to feel, nor are we praised or blamed.

Since then the virtues are neither Feelings nor Capacities, it remains that they must be States.

Now what the genus of Virtue is has been said; but we must not merely speak of it thus, that it is a state, but say also what kind of a state it is.

Virtue then is "a state apt to exercise deliberate choice, being in the relative mean, determined by reason, and as the man of practical wisdom would determine." It is a middle state between two faulty ones, in the way of excess on one side and of defect on the other: and it is so moreover, because the faulty states on one side fall short of, and those on the other exceed, what is right, both in the case of the feelings and the actions; but Virtue finds, and when found adopts, the mean.

And so, viewing it in respect of its essence and definition, Virtue is a mean state; but in reference to the chief good and to excellence it is the highest state possible.

Now that Moral Virtue is a mean state, and how it is so, and that it lies between two faulty states, one in the way of excess and another in the way of defect, and that it is so because it has an aptitude to aim at the mean both in feelings and actions, all this has been set forth fully and sufficiently.

And so it is hard to be good: for surely hard it is in each instance to find the mean, just as to find the mean point or centre of a circle is not what any man can do, but only he who knows how: just so to be angry, to give money, and be expensive, is what any man can do, and easy: but to do these to the right person, in due proportion, at the right time, with a right object, and in the right manner, this is not as before what any man can do, nor is it easy; and for this cause goodness is rare, and praiseworthy, and noble.

Book Three

Now since Virtue is concerned with the regulation of feelings and actions, and praise and blame arise upon such as are voluntary, while for the involuntary allowance is made, and sometimes compassion is excited, it is perhaps a necessary task for those who are investigating the nature of Virtue to draw out the distinction between what is voluntary and what involuntary; and it is certainly useful for legislators, with respect to the assigning of honours and punishments.

Involuntary actions then are thought to be of two kinds, being done either on compulsion, or by reason of ignorance.

An action is, properly speaking, compulsory, when the origination is external to the agent, being such that in it the agent contributes nothing; as if a wind were to convey you anywhere, or men having power over your person.

But when actions are done, either from fear of greater evils, or from some honourable motive, as, for instance, if you were ordered to commit some base act by a despot who had your parents or children in his power, and they were to be saved upon your compliance or die upon your refusal, in such cases there is room for a question whether the actions are voluntary or involuntary.

The truth is, such actions are of a mixed kind, but are most like voluntary actions; for they are choiceworthy at the time when they are being done, and the end or object of the action must be taken with reference to the actual occasion. Further, we must denominate an action voluntary or involuntary at the time of doing it: now in the given case the man acts voluntarily, because the originating of the motion of his limbs in such actions rests with himself; and where the origination is in himself it rests with himself to do or not to do.

Such actions then are voluntary, though in the abstract perhaps involuntary because no one would choose any of such things in and by itself.

What kind of actions then are to be called compulsory? may we say, simply and abstractedly whenever the cause is external and the agent contributes nothing; and that where the acts are in themselves such as one would not wish but choiceworthy at the present time and in preference to such and such things, and where the origination rests with the agent, the actions are in themselves involuntary but at the given time and in preference to such and such things voluntary; and they are more like voluntary than involuntary, because the actions consist of little details, and these are voluntary.

So then that seems to be compulsory "whose origination is from without, the party compelled contributing nothing."

Now every action of which ignorance is the cause is not involuntary, but that only is involuntary which is attended with pain and remorse; for clearly the man who has done anything by reason of ignorance, but is not annoyed at his own action, cannot be said to have done it *with* his will because he did not know he was doing it, nor again *against* his will because he is not sorry for it.

Now since all involuntary action is either upon compulsion or by reason of ignorance, Voluntary Action would seem to be "that whose origination is in the agent, he being aware of the particular details in which the action consists."

Having thus drawn out the distinction between voluntary and involuntary action our next step is to examine into the nature of Moral Choice, because this seems most intimately connected with Virtue and to be a more decisive test of moral character than a man's acts are.

Now Moral Choice is plainly voluntary, but the two are not co-extensive, voluntary being the more comprehensive term; for first, children and all other animals share in voluntary action but not in Moral Choice; and next, sudden actions we call voluntary but do not ascribe them to Moral Choice.

May we not say, then, it is "that voluntary which has passed through a stage of previous deliberation"? because Moral Choice is attended with reasoning and intellectual process. The etymology of its Greek name seems to give a hint of it, being when analysed "chosen in preference to somewhat else."

Wish has for its object-matter the End, but there are two opinions respecting it; some thinking that its object is real good, others whatever impresses the mind with a notion of good.

Now those who maintain that the object of Wish is real good are beset by this difficulty, that what is wished for by him who chooses wrongly is not really an object of Wish. Those who maintain, on the contrary, that that which impresses the mind with a notion of good is properly the object of Wish, have to meet this difficulty, that there is nothing naturally an object of Wish but to each individual whatever seems good to him; now different people have different notions, and it may chance contrary ones.

Now since the End is the object of Wish, and the means to the End of Deliberation and Moral Choice, the actions regarding these matters must be in the way of Moral Choice, i.e., voluntary: but the acts of working out the virtues are such actions, and therefore Virtue is in our power.

And so too is Vice: because wherever it is in our power to do it is also in our power to forbear doing, and vice versa: therefore if the doing is in our power, so too is the forbearing, and vice versa.

But if it is in our power to do and to forbear doing what is creditable or the contrary, and these respectively constitute the being good or bad, then the being good or vicious characters is in our power.

If then, as is commonly said, the Virtues are voluntary, the Vices must be voluntary also, because the cases are exactly similar.

Well now, we have stated generally respecting the Moral Virtues, the genus, that they are mean states, and that they are habits, and how they are formed, and that they are of themselves calculated to act upon the circumstances out of which they were formed, and that they are in our own power and voluntary, and are to be done so as right Reason may direct.

First, then, of Courage. Now that it is a mean state, in respect of fear and boldness, has been already said: further, the objects of our fears are obviously things fearful or, in a general way of statement, evils; which accounts for the common definition of fear, viz. "expectation of evil."

Of course we fear evils of all kinds: disgrace, for instance, poverty, disease, desolateness, death; but not all these seem to be the object-matter of the Brave man, because there are things which to fear is right and noble, and not to fear is base; disgrace, for example, since he who fears this is a good man and has a sense of honour, and he who does not fear it is shameless. But poverty, perhaps, or disease, and in fact whatever does not proceed from viciousness, nor is attributable to his own fault, a man ought not to fear: still, being fearless in respect of these would not constitute a man Brave in the proper sense of the term.

And, again, a man is not a coward for fearing insult to his wife or children, or envy, or any such thing; nor is he a Brave man for being bold when going to be scourged.

What kind of fearful things then do constitute the object-matter of the Brave man? first of all, must they not be the greatest, since no man is more apt to withstand what is dreadful? Now the object of the greatest dread is death, because it is the end of all things, and the dead man is thought to be capable neither of good nor evil. Still it would seem that the Brave man has not for his object-matter even death in every circumstance; on the sea, for example, or in sickness: in what circumstances then? must it not be in the most honourable? now such is death in war, because it is death in the greatest and most honourable danger; and this is confirmed by the honours awarded in communities, and by monarchs.

He then may be most properly denominated Brave who is fearless in respect of honourable death and such sudden emergencies as threaten death; now such specially are those which arise in the course of war.

Again, fearful is a term of relation, the same thing not being so to all, and there is according to common parlance somewhat so fearful as to be beyond human endurance: this of course would be fearful to every man of sense, but those objects which are level to the capacity of man differ in magnitude and admit of degrees, so too the objects of confidence or boldness.

Now the Brave man cannot be frighted from his propriety. Fear such things indeed he will, but he will stand up against them as he ought and as right reason may direct, with a view to what is honourable, because this is the end of the virtue.

Now it is possible to fear these things too much, or too little, or again to fear what is not really fearful as if it were such. So the errors come to be either that a man fears when he ought not to fear at all, or that he fears in an improper way, or at a wrong time, and so forth; and so too in respect of things inspiring confidence. He is Brave then who withstands, and fears, and is bold, in respect of right objects, from a right motive, in right manner, and at right times: since the Brave man suffers or acts as he ought and as right reason may direct.

Now the end of every separate act of working is that which accords with the habit, and so to the Brave man Courage; which is honourable; therefore such is also the End, since the character of each is determined by the End.

So honour is the motive from which the Brave man withstands things fearful and performs the acts which accord with Courage.

It must be remarked, however, that though Courage has for its object-matter boldness and fear it has not both equally so, but objects of fear much more than the former; for he that under pressure of these is undisturbed and stands related to them as he ought is better entitled to the name of Brave than he who is properly affected towards objects of confidence. So then men are termed Brave for withstanding painful things.

It follows that Courage involves pain and is justly praised, since it is a harder matter to withstand things that are painful than to abstain from such as are pleasant.

It must not be thought but that the End and object of Courage is pleasant, but it is obscured by the surrounding circumstances: which happens also in the gymnastic games; to the boxers the End is pleasant with a view to which they act, I mean the crown and the honours; but the receiving the blows they do is painful and annoying to flesh and blood, and so is all the labour they have to undergo; and, as these drawbacks are many, the object in view being small appears to have no pleasantness in it.

Next let us speak of Perfected Self-Mastery, which seems to claim the next place to Courage, since these two are the Excellences of the Irrational part of the Soul. It is a mean state, having for its object-matter Pleasures. The state of utter absence of self-control has plainly the same object-matter; the next thing then is to determine what kind of Pleasures.

Let Pleasures then be understood to be divided into mental and bodily: instances of the former being love of honour or of learning: it being plain that each man takes pleasure in that of these two objects which he has a tendency to like, his body being no way affected but rather his intellect. Now men are not called perfectly self-mastering or wholly destitute of self-control in respect of pleasures of this class: nor in fact in respect of any which are not bodily; those for example who love to tell long stories, and are prosy, and spend their days about mere chance matters, we call gossips but not wholly destitute of self-control, nor again those who are pained at the loss of money or friends.

It is bodily Pleasures then which are the object-matter of Perfected Self-Mastery, but not even all these indifferently: I mean, that they who take pleasure in objects perceived by the Sight, as colours, and forms, and painting, are not denominated men of Perfected Self-Mastery, or wholly destitute of self-control; and yet it would seem that one may take pleasure even in such objects, as one ought to do, or excessively, or too little.

Book Four

WE WILL next speak of Liberality. Now this is thought to be the mean state, having for its object-matter Wealth: I mean, the Liberal man is praised not in the circumstances of war, nor in those which constitute the character of perfected self-mastery, nor again in judicial decisions, but in respect of giving and receiving Wealth, chiefly the former. By the term Wealth I mean "all those things whose worth is measured by money."

Now the states of excess and defect in regard of Wealth are respectively Prodigality and Stinginess: the latter of these terms we attach invariably to those who are over-careful about Wealth, but the former we apply sometimes with a complex notion; that is to say, we give the name to those who fail of self-control and spend money on the unrestrained gratification of their passions; and this is why they are thought to be most base, because they have many vices at once.

Now Liberality is a term of relation to a man's means, for the Liberalness depends not on the amount of what is given but on the moral state of the giver which gives in proportion to his means. There is then no reason why he should not be the more Liberal man who gives the less amount, if he has less to give out of.

Again, they are thought to be more Liberal who have inherited, not acquired for themselves, their means; because, in the first place, they have never experienced want, and next, all people love most their own works, just as parents do and poets.

Next in order would seem to come a dissertation on Magnificence, this being thought to be, like liberality, a virtue having for its object-matter Wealth; but it does not, like that, extend to all transactions in respect of Wealth, but only applies to such as are expensive, and in these circumstances it exceeds liberality in respect of magnitude, because it is fitting expense on a large scale: this term is of course relative: I mean, the expenditure of equipping and commanding a trireme is not the same as that of giving a public spectacle: "fitting" of course also is relative to the individual, and the matter wherein and upon which he has to spend. And a man is not denominated Magnificent for spending as he should do in small or ordinary things, as, for instance,

"Oft to the wandering beggar did I give,"

but for doing so in great matters: that is to say, the Magnificent man is liberal, but the liberal is not thereby Magnificent. The falling short of such a state is called Meanness, the exceeding it Vulgar Profusion, Want of Taste, and so on; which are faulty, not because they are on an excessive scale in respect of right objects, but because they show off in improper objects, and in improper manner: of these we will speak presently. The Magnificent man is like a man of skill, because he can see what is fitting, and can spend largely in good taste; for, as we said at the commencement, the confirmed habit is determined by the separate acts of working, and by its object-matter.

So the Magnificent man must be also a liberal man, because the liberal man will also spend what he ought, and in right manner: but it is the Great, that is to say the large, scale which is distinctive of the Magnificent man, the object-matter of liberality being the same, and without spending more money than another man he will make the work more magnificent. I mean, the excellence of a possession and of a work is not the same: as a piece of property that thing is most valuable which is worth most, gold for instance; but as a work that which is great and beautiful, because the contemplation of such an object is admirable, and so is that which is Magnificent. So the excellence of a work is Magnificence on a large scale.

The man who is in the state of excess, called one of Vulgar Profusion, is in excess because he spends improperly. I mean in cases requiring small expenditure he lavishes much and shows off out of taste; giving his club a feast fit for a wedding-party, or if he has to furnish a chorus for a comedy, giving the actors purple to wear in the first scene, as did the Megarians. And all such things he will do, not with a view to that which is really honourable, but to display his wealth, and because he thinks he shall be admired for these things; and he will spend little where he ought to spend much, and much where he should spend little.

The Mean man will be deficient in every case, and even where he has spent the most he will spoil the whole effect for want of some trifle; he is procrastinating in all he does, and contrives how he may spend the least, and does even that with lamentations about the expense, and thinking that he does all things on a greater scale than he ought.

The very name of Great-mindedness implies that great things are its object-matter; and we will first settle what kind of things. It makes no difference, of course, whether we regard the moral state in the abstract or as exemplified in an individual.

Well then, he is thought to be Great-minded who values himself highly and at the same time justly, because he that does so without grounds is foolish, and no virtuous character is foolish or senseless. Well, the character I have described is Great-minded. The man who estimates himself lowly, and at the same time justly, is modest; but not Great-minded, since this latter quality implies greatness, just as beauty implies a large bodily conformation while small people are neat and well made but not beautiful.

The Small-minded man is deficient, both as regards himself and also as regards the estimation of the Great-minded: while the Vain man is in excess as regards himself, but does not get beyond the Great-minded man. Now the Great-minded man, being by the hypothesis worthy of the greatest things, must be of the highest excellence, since the better a man is the more is he worth, and he who is best is worth the most: it follows, then, that to be truly Great-minded a man must be good, and whatever is great in each virtue would seem to belong to the Great-minded. It would no way correspond with the character of the Great-minded to flee, spreading his hands all abroad; nor to injure any one; for with what object in view will he do what is base, in whose eyes nothing is great? in short, if one were to go into particulars, the Great-minded man would show quite ludicrously unless he were a good man: he would not be in fact deserving of honour if he were a bad man, honour being the prize of virtue and given to the good.

This virtue, then, of Great-mindedness seems to be a kind of ornament of all the other virtues, in that it makes them better and cannot be without them; and for this reason it is a hard matter to be really and truly Great-minded; for it cannot be without thorough goodness and nobleness of character.

The virtue of Great-mindedness has for its object great Honour, and there seems to be a virtue having Honour also for its object, which may seem to bear to Great-mindedness the same relation that Liberality does to Magnificence: that is, both these virtues stand aloof from what is great but dispose us as we ought to be disposed towards moderate and small matters. Further: as in giving and receiving of wealth there is a mean state, an excess, and a defect, so likewise in grasping after Honour there is the more or less than is right, and also the doing so from right sources and in right manner.

Book Five

Now the points for our inquiry in respect of Justice and Injustice are, what kind of actions are their object-matter, and what kind of a mean state Justice is, and between what points the abstract principle of it, i.e., the Just, is a mean. And our inquiry shall be, if you please, conducted in the same method as we have observed in the foregoing parts of this treatise.

We see then that all men mean by the term Justice a moral state such that in consequence of it men have the capacity of doing what is just, and actually do it, and wish it: similarly also with respect to Injustice, a moral state such that in consequence of it men do unjustly and wish what is unjust: let us also be content then with these as a groundwork sketched out.

But the object of our inquiry is Justice, in the sense in which it is a part of Virtue, and likewise with respect to particular Injustice. And of the existence of this last the following consideration is a proof: there are many vices by practising which a man acts unjustly, of course, but does not grasp at more than his share of good; if, for instance, by reason of cowardice he throws away his shield, or by reason of ill-temper he uses abusive language, or by reason of stinginess does not give a friend pecuniary assistance; but whenever he does a grasping action, it is often in the way of none of these vices, certainly not in all of them, still in the way of some vice or other, and in the way of Injustice. There is then some kind of Injustice distinct from that co-extensive with Vice and related to it as a part to a whole, and some "Unjust" related to that which is co-extensive with violation of the law as a part to a whole.

The Unjust has been divided into the unlawful and the unequal, and the Just accordingly into the lawful and the equal: the aforementioned Injustice is in the way of the unlawful. And as the unequal and the more are not the same, but differing as part to whole, so the Unjust and the Injustice we are now in search of are not the same with, but other than, those before mentioned, the one being the parts, the other the wholes; for this particular Injustice is a part of the Injustice co-extensive with Vice, and likewise this Justice of the Justice co-extensive with Virtue. So that what we have now to speak of is the particular Justice and Injustice, and likewise the particular Just and Unjust.

Here then let us dismiss any further consideration of the Justice ranking as co-extensive with Virtue. It is clear, too, that we must separate off the Just and the Unjust involved in these: because one may pretty well say that most lawful things are those which naturally result in action from Virtue in its fullest sense, because the law enjoins the living in accordance with each Virtue and forbids living in accordance with each Vice. And the producing causes of Virtue in all its bearings are those enactments which have been made respecting education for society.

The unjust man is unequal, and the abstract "Unjust" unequal: further, it is plain that there is some mean of the unequal, that is to say, the equal or exact half. If then the Unjust is unequal the Just is equal, which all must allow without further proof: and as the equal is a mean the Just must be also a mean. Now the equal implies two terms at least: it follows then that the Just is both a mean and equal, and these to certain persons; and, in so far as it is a mean, between certain things, and, so far as it is equal, between two, and in so far as it is just it is so to certain persons. The Just then must imply four terms at least, for those to which it is just are two, and the terms representing the things are two.

And there will be the same equality between the terms representing the persons, as between those representing the things: because as the latter are to one another so are the former: for if the persons are not equal they must not have equal shares; in fact this is the very source of all the quarrelling and wrangling in the world, when either they who are equal have and get awarded to them things not equal, or being not equal those things which are equal. Again, the necessity of this equality of ratios is shown by the common phrase "according to rate," for all agree that the Just in distributions ought to be according to some rate: but what that rate is to be, all do not agree; the democrats are for freedom, oligarchs for wealth, others for nobleness of birth, and the aristocratic party for virtue.

This then is the one species of the Just.

And the remaining one is the Corrective, which arises in voluntary as well as involuntary transactions. Now this Just has a different form from the aforementioned; for that which is concerned in distribution of common property is always according to the aforementioned proportion: I mean that, if the division is made out of common property, the shares will bear the same proportion to one another as the original contributions did: and the Unjust which is opposite to this Just is that which violates the proportionate.

And so the equal is a mean between the more and the less, which represent gain and loss in contrary ways: between which the equal was stated to be a mean, which equal we say is Just: and so the Corrective Just must be the mean between loss and gain. And this is the reason why, upon a dispute arising, men have recourse to the judge: going to the judge is in fact going to the Just, for the judge is meant to be the personification of the Just. And men seek a judge as one in the mean, which is expressed in a name given by some to judges under the notion that if they can hit on the mean they shall hit on the Just. The Just is then surely a mean, since the judge is also.

So it is the office of a judge to make things equal, and the line, as it were, having been unequally divided, he takes from the greater part that by which it exceeds the half, and adds this on to the less. And when the whole is divided into two exactly equal portions, then men say they have their own, when they have gotten the equal; and the equal is a mean between the greater and the less according to arithmetical equality.

Again, since a man may do unjust acts and not yet have formed a character of injustice, the question arises whether a man is unjust in each particular form of injustice, say a thief, or adulterer, or robber, by doing acts of a given character.

We may say, I think, that this will not of itself make any difference; a man may, for instance, have had connection with another's wife, knowing well with whom he was sinning, but he may have done it not of deliberate choice but from the impulse of passion: of course he acts unjustly, but he has not necessarily formed an unjust character: that is, he may have stolen yet not be a thief; or committed an act of adultery but still not be an adulterer, and so on in other cases which might be enumerated.

For the present we proceed to say that, the Justs and the Unjusts being what have been mentioned, a man is said to act unjustly or justly when he embodies these abstracts in voluntary actions, but when in involuntary, then he neither acts unjustly or justly except accidentally; I mean that the being just or unjust is really only accidental to the agents in such cases.

So both unjust and just actions are limited by the being voluntary or the contrary: for when an embodying of the Unjust is voluntary, then it is blamed and is at the same time also an unjust action: but, if voluntariness does not attach, there will be a thing which is in itself unjust but not yet an unjust action.

Now a question may be raised whether we have spoken with sufficient distinctness as to being unjustly dealt with, and dealing unjustly towards others.

First, whether the case is possible which Euripides has put, saying somewhat strangely,

> "My mother he hath slain; the tale is short,
> Either he willingly did slay her willing,
> Or else with her will but against his own."

I mean then, is it really possible for a person to be unjustly dealt with with his own consent, or must every case of being unjustly dealt with be against the will of the sufferer as every act of unjust dealing is voluntary?

And next, are cases of being unjustly dealt with to be ruled all one way as every act of unjust dealing is voluntary, or may we say that some cases are voluntary and some involuntary?

Similarly also as regards being justly dealt with: all just acting is voluntary, so that it is fair to suppose that the being dealt with unjustly or justly must be similarly opposed, as to being either voluntary or involuntary.

Now as for being justly dealt with, the position that every case of this is voluntary is a strange one, for some are certainly justly dealt with without their will. The fact is a man may also fairly raise this question, whether in every case he who has suffered what is unjust is therefore unjustly dealt with, or rather that the case is the same with suffering as it is with acting; namely, that in both it is possible to participate in what is just, but only accidentally. Clearly the case of what is unjust is similar: for doing things in themselves unjust is not identical with acting unjustly, nor is suffering them the same as being unjustly dealt with. So too of acting justly and being justly dealt with, since it is impossible to be unjustly dealt with unless some one else acts unjustly or to be justly dealt with unless some one else acts justly.

Now if acting unjustly is simply "hurting another voluntarily" and the man who fails of self-control voluntarily hurts himself, then this will be a case of being voluntarily dealt unjustly with, and it will be possible for a man to deal unjustly with himself. Or again, a man may, by reason of failing of self-control, receive hurt from another man acting voluntarily, and so here will be another case of being unjustly dealt with voluntarily.

The solution, I take it, is this: the definition of being unjustly dealt with is not correct, but we must add, to the hurting with the knowledge of the person hurt and the instrument and the manner of hurting him, the fact of its being against the wish of the man who is hurt.

With respect to being unjustly dealt with, then, it is clear that it is not voluntary.

We have next to speak of Equity and the Equitable, that is to say, of the relations of Equity to Justice and the Equitable to the Just; for when we look into the matter the two do not appear identical nor yet different in kind; and we sometimes commend the Equitable and the man who embodies it in his actions, so that by way of praise we commonly transfer the term also to other acts instead of the term good, thus showing that the more Equitable a thing is the better it is: at other times following a certain train of reasoning we arrive at a difficulty, in that the Equitable though distinct from the Just is yet praiseworthy; it seems to follow either that the Just is not good or the Equitable not Just, since they are by hypothesis different; or if both are good then they are identical.

This is a tolerably fair statement of the difficulty which on these grounds arises in respect of the Equitable; but, in fact, all these may be reconciled and really involve no contradiction: for the Equitable is Just, being also better than one form of Just, but is not better than the Just as though it were different from it in kind: Just and Equitable then are identical, and, both being good, the Equitable is the better of the two.

What causes the difficulty is this: the Equitable is Just, but not the Just which is in accordance with written law, being in fact a correction of that kind of Just. And the account of this is, that every law is necessarily universal while there are some things which it is not possible to speak of rightly in any universal or general statement. Where then there is a necessity for general statement, while a general statement cannot apply rightly to all cases, the law takes the generality of cases, being fully aware of the error thus involved; and rightly too notwithstanding, because the fault is not in the law, or in the framer of the law, but is inherent in the nature of the thing, because the matter of all action is necessarily such.

The answer to the second of the two questions indicated above, whether it is possible for a man to deal unjustly by himself, is obvious from what has been already stated.

In the first place, one class of Justs is those which are enforced by law in accordance with Virtue in the most extensive sense of the term: for instance, the law does not bid a man kill himself; and whatever it does not bid it forbids: well, whenever a man does hurt contrary to the law (unless by way of requital of hurt), voluntarily, i.e., knowing to whom he does it and wherewith, he acts Unjustly. Now he that from rage kills himself, voluntarily, does this in contravention of Right Reason, which the law does not permit. He therefore acts Unjustly: but towards whom? Towards the Community, not towards himself (because he suffers with his own consent, and no man can be Unjustly dealt with with his own consent), and on this principle the Community punishes him; that is, a certain infamy is attached to the suicide as to one who acts Unjustly towards the Community.

Next, a man cannot deal Unjustly by himself in the sense in which a man is Unjust who only does Unjust acts without being entirely bad (for the two things are different, because the Unjust man is in a way bad, as the coward is, not as though he were chargeable with badness in the full extent of the term, and so he does not act Unjustly in this sense), because if it were so then it would be possible for the same thing to have been taken away from and added to the same person: but this is really not possible, the Just and the Unjust always implying a plurality of persons.

Again, an Unjust action must be voluntary, done of deliberate purpose, and aggressive (for the man who hurts because he has first suffered and is merely requiting the same is not thought to act Unjustly), but here the man does to himself and suffers the same things at the same time.

Again, it would imply the possibility of being Unjustly dealt with with one's own consent.

And, besides all this, a man cannot act Unjustly without his act falling under some particular crime; now a man cannot seduce his own wife, commit a burglary on his own premises, or steal his own property.

Book Six

HAVING STATED in a former part of this treatise that men should choose the mean instead of either the excess or defect, and that the mean is according to the dictates of Right Reason, we will now proceed to explain this term.

For in all the habits which we have expressly mentioned, as likewise in all the others, there is, so to speak, a mark with his eye fixed on which the man who has Reason tightens or slacks his rope; and there is a certain limit of those mean states which we say are in accordance with Right Reason, and lie between excess on the one hand and defect on the other.

Now to speak thus is true enough but conveys no very definite meaning: as, in fact, in all other pursuits requiring attention and diligence on which skill and science are brought to bear; it is quite true of course to say that men are neither to labour nor relax too much or too little, but in moderation, and as Right Reason directs; yet if this were all a man had he would not be greatly the wiser; as, for instance, if in answer to the question, what are proper applications to the body, he were to be told, "Oh, of course, whatever the science of medicine, and in such manner as the physician, directs."

And so in respect of the mental states it is requisite not merely that this should be true which has been already stated, but further that it should be expressly laid down what Right Reason is, and what is the definition of it.

Now in our division of the Excellences of the Soul, we said there were two classes, the Moral and the Intellectual: the former we have already gone through; and we will now proceed to speak of the others, premising a few words respecting the Soul itself. It was stated before, you will remember, that the Soul consists of two parts, the Rational and Irrational: we must now make a similar division of the Rational.

Let it be understood then that there are two parts of the Soul possessed of Reason; one whereby we realise those existences whose causes cannot be otherwise than they are, and one whereby we realise those which can be otherwise than they are; and let us name the former, "that which is apt to know," the latter, "that which is apt to calculate."

There are in the Soul three functions on which depend moral action and truth: Sense, Intellect, Appetition, whether vague Desire or definite Will. Now of these Sense is the originating cause of no moral action, as is seen from the fact that brutes have Sense but are in no way partakers of moral action.

Intellect and Will are thus connected. What in the Intellectual operation is Affirmation and Negation in the Will is Pursuit and Avoidance. And so, since Moral Virtue is a State apt to exercise Moral Choice and Moral Choice is Will consequent on deliberation, the Reason must be true and the Will right, to constitute good Moral Choice, and what the Reason affirms the Will must pursue.

Now this Intellectual operation and this Truth is what bears upon Moral Action; of course truth and falsehood must be the good and the bad of that Intellectual Operation which is purely Speculative and concerned neither with action nor production, because this is manifestly the work of every Intellectual faculty, while of the faculty which is of a mixed Practical and Intellectual nature the work is that Truth which, as I have described above, corresponds to the right movement of the Will.

Now the starting-point of moral action is Moral Choice, Appetition, and Reason directed to a certain result: and thus Moral Choice is neither independent of intellect, i.e., intellectual operation, nor of a certain moral state: for right or wrong action cannot exist independently of operation of the Intellect and moral character.

But operation of the Intellect by itself moves nothing, only when directed to a certain result, i.e., exercised in Moral Action, and so Moral Choice is either Intellect put in a position of Will-ing, or Appetition subjected to an Intellectual Process. And such a Cause is Man.

But nothing which is done and past can be the object of Moral Choice; for instance, no man chooses to have sacked Troy; because, in fact, no one ever deliberates about what is past but only about that which is future and which may therefore be influenced, whereas what has been cannot not have been: and so Agathon is right in saying,

> "Of this alone is Deity bereft,
> To make undone whatever hath been done."

Thus then the Truth is the work of both the Intellectual Parts of the Soul; those states therefore are the Excellences of each in which each will best attain truth.

Commencing then from the point stated above we will now speak of these Excellences again. Let those faculties whereby the Soul attains truth in Affirmation or Negation be assumed to be in number five: viz., Art, Knowledge, Practical Wisdom, Science, Intuition.

What Knowledge is is plain from the following considerations, if one is to speak accurately instead of being led away by resemblances. We all conceive that what we strictly speaking *know* cannot be otherwise than it is, because as to those things which can be otherwise than they are we are uncertain whether they are or are not the moment they cease to be within the sphere of our actual observation.

So, then, whatever comes within the range of Knowledge is by necessity, and therefore eternal, and all eternal things are without beginning and indestructible.

Again, all Knowledge is thought to be capable of being taught, and what comes within its range capable of being learned. And all teaching is based upon previous knowledge (a statement you will find in the *Analytics* also); for there are two ways of teaching, by Syllogism and by Induction. In fact, Induction is the source of universal propositions, and Syllogism reasons from these universals. Syllogism then may reason from principles which cannot be themselves proved syllogistically; and therefore must be proved by Induction.

So Knowledge is "a state or mental faculty apt to demonstrate syllogistically," etc., as in the *Analytics:* because a man, strictly and properly speaking, *knows,* when he establishes his conclusion in a certain way and the principles are known to him: for if they are not better known to him than the conclusion such knowledge as he has will be merely accidental.

Now Knowledge is a conception concerning universals and Necessary matter, and there are of course certain First Principles in all trains of demonstrative reasoning. That faculty, then, which takes in the first principles of that which comes under the range of Knowledge cannot be either Knowledge, or Art, or Practical Wisdom: not Knowledge, because what is the object of Knowledge must be derived from demonstrative reasoning; not either of the other two, because they are exercised upon Contingent matter only. Nor can it be Science which takes in these, because the Scientific Man must in some cases depend on demonstrative Reasoning.

It comes then to this: since the faculties whereby we always attain truth and are never deceived when dealing with matter Necessary or even Contingent are Knowledge, Practical Wisdom, Science, and Intuition, and the faculty which takes in First Principles cannot be any of the three first, the last, namely, Intuition, must be it which performs this function.

We must inquire again also about Virtue: for it may be divided into Natural Virtue and Matured, which two bear to each other a relation similar to that which Practical Wisdom bears to Cleverness, one not of identity but resemblance. I speak of Natural Virtue, because men hold that each of the moral dispositions attach to us all somehow by nature:

we have dispositions towards justice, self-mastery, and courage, for instance, immediately from our birth: but still we seek Goodness in its highest sense as something distinct from these, and that these dispositions should attach to us in a somewhat different fashion. Children and brutes have these natural states, but then they are plainly hurtful unless combined with an intellectual element: at least thus much is matter of actual experience and observation, that as a strong body destitute of sight must, if set in motion, fall violently because it has not sight, so it is also in the case we are considering: but if it can get the intellectual element it then excels in acting. Just so the Natural State of Virtue, being like this strong body, will then be Virtue in the highest sense when it too is combined with the intellectual element.

So that, as in the case of the Opinionative faculty, there are two forms, Cleverness and Practical Wisdom; so also in the case of the Moral there are two, Natural Virtue and Matured; and of these the latter cannot be formed without Practical Wisdom.

This leads some to say that all the Virtues are merely intellectual Practical Wisdom, and Socrates was partly right in his inquiry and partly wrong: wrong in that he thought all the Virtues were merely intellectual Practical Wisdom, right in saying they were not independent of that faculty.

Book Seven

NEXT we must take a different point to start from, and observe that of what is to be avoided in respect of moral character there are three forms; Vice, Imperfect Self-Control, and Brutishness. Of the two former it is plain what the contraries are, for we call the one Virtue, the other Self-Control; and as answering to Brutishness it will be most suitable to assign Superhuman, i.e., heroical and godlike Virtue, as, in Homer, Priam says of Hector that "he was very excellent, nor was he like the offspring of mortal man, but of a god": and so, if, as is commonly said, men are raised to the position of gods by reason of very high excellence in Virtue, the state opposed to the Brutish will plainly be of this nature: because as brutes are not virtuous or vicious so neither are gods; but the state of these is something more precious than Virtue, of the former something different in kind from Vice.

And as, on the one hand, it is a rare thing for a man to be godlike, so the brutish man is rare; the character is found most among barbarians, and some cases of it are caused by disease or maiming; also such men as exceed in Vice all ordinary measures we therefore designate by this opprobrious term. Well, we must in a subsequent place make some mention of this disposition, and Vice has been spoken of before: for the present we must speak of Imperfect Self-Control and its kindred faults of Softness and Luxury, on the one hand, and of Self-Control and Endurance on the other; since we are to conceive of them, not as being the same states exactly as Virtue and Vice respectively, nor again as differing in kind.

Now we must examine first whether men of Imperfect Self-Control act with a knowledge of what is right or not: next, if with such knowledge, in what sense; and next, what are we to assume is the object-matter of the man of Imperfect Self-Control, and of the man of Self-Control; I mean, whether pleasure and pain of all kinds or certain definite ones; and as to Self-Control and Endurance, whether these are designations of the same character or different. And in like manner we must go into all questions which are connected with the present.

But the real starting point of the inquiry is, whether the two characters of Self-Control and Imperfect Self-Control are distinguished by their object-matter, or their respective relations to it. I mean, whether the man of Imperfect Self-Control is such simply by virtue of having such and such object-matter; or not, but by virtue of his being related to it in such and such a way, or by virtue of both: next, whether Self-Control and Imperfect Self-Control are unlimited in their object-matter: because he who is designated without any addition a man of Imperfect Self-Control is not unlimited in his object-matter, but has exactly the same as the man who has lost all Self-Control: nor is he so designated because of his relation to this object-matter merely, but because of his relation to it being such and such. For the man who has lost all Self-Control is led on with deliberate moral choice, holding that it is his line to pursue pleasure as it rises: while the man of Imperfect Self-Control does not think that he ought to pursue it, but does pursue it all the same.

Now as to the notion that it is True Opinion and not Knowledge in contravention of which men fail in Self-Control, it makes no difference to the point in question, because some of those who hold Opinions have no doubt about them but suppose themselves to have accurate Knowledge; if then it is urged that men holding Opinions will be more likely than men who have Knowledge to act in contravention of their conceptions, as having but a moderate belief in them, we reply, Knowledge will not differ in this respect from Opinion: because some men believe their own Opinions no less firmly than others do their positive Knowledge: Heraclitus is a case in point.

The next question to be discussed is whether there is a character to be designated by the term "of Imperfect Self-Control" simply, or whether all who are so are to be accounted such, in respect of some particular thing; and, if there is such a character, what is his object-matter.

Now that pleasures and pains are the object-matter of men of Self-Control and of Endurance, and also of men of Imperfect Self-Control and Softness, is plain.

Further, things which produce pleasure are either necessary, or objects of choice in themselves but yet admitting of excess. All bodily things which produce pleasure are necessary; and I call such those which relate to food and other grosser appetites, in short such bodily things as we assumed were the Object-matter of absence of Self-Control and of Perfected Self-Mastery.

The other class of objects are not necessary, but objects of choice in themselves: I mean, for instance, victory, honour, wealth, and suchlike good or pleasant things. And those who are excessive in their liking for such things contrary to the principle of Right Reason which is in their own breasts we do not designate men of Imperfect Self-Control simply, but with the addition of the thing wherein, as in respect of money, or gain, or honour, or anger, and not simply; because we consider them as different characters and only having that title in right of a kind of resemblance. And a proof of the real difference between these so designated with an addition and those simply so called is this, that Imperfect Self-Control is blamed, not as an error merely but also as being a vice, either wholly or partially; but none of these other cases is so blamed.

But of those who have for their object-matter the bodily enjoyments, which we say are also the object-matter of the man of Perfected Self-Mastery and the man who has lost all Self-Control, he that pursues excessive pleasures and too much avoids things which are painful, not from moral choice but in spite of his moral choice and intellectual conviction, is termed "a man of Imperfect Self-Control," not with the addition of any particular object-matter as we do in respect of want of control of anger, but simply.

Again, the man utterly destitute of Self-Control, as was observed before, is not given to remorse: for it is part of his character that he abides by his moral choice: but the man of Imperfect Self-Control is almost made up of remorse: and so the case is not as we determined it before, but the former is incurable and the latter may be cured: for depravity is like chronic diseases, dropsy and consumption, for instance, but Imperfect Self-Control is like acute disorders: the former being a continuous evil, the latter not so. And, in fact, Imperfect Self-Control and Confirmed Vice are different in kind: the latter being imperceptible to its victim, the former not so.

But, of the different forms of Imperfect Self-Control, those are better who are carried off their feet by a sudden access of temptation than they who have Reason but do not abide by it; these last being overcome by passion less in degree, and not wholly without premeditation as are the others: for the man of Imperfect Self-Control is like those who are soon intoxicated and by little wine and less than the common run of men.

Well then, that Imperfection of Self-Control is not Confirmed Viciousness is plain: and yet perhaps it is such in a way, because in one sense it is contrary to moral choice and in another the result of it: at all events, in respect of the actions, the case is much like what Demodocus said of the Miletians. "The people of Miletus are not fools, but they do just the kind of things that fools do"; and so they of Imperfect Self-Control are not unjust, but they do unjust acts.

And it is not possible for the same man to be at once a man of Practical Wisdom and of Imperfect Self-Control: because the character of Practical Wisdom includes, as we showed before, goodness of moral character. And again, it is not knowledge merely, but aptitude for action, which constitutes Practical Wisdom: and of this aptitude the man of Imperfect Self-Control is destitute. But there is no reason why the Clever man should not be of Imperfect Self-Control: and the reason why some men are occasionally thought to be men of Practical Wisdom, and yet of Imperfect Self-Control, is this, that Cleverness differs from Practical Wisdom in the way I stated in a former book, and is very near it so far as the intellectual element is concerned but differs in respect of the moral choice.

Nor is the man of Imperfect Self-Control like the man who both has and calls into exercise his knowledge, but like the man who, having it, is overpowered by sleep or wine.

Again, he acts voluntarily, but he is not a confirmed bad man, for his moral choice is good, so he is at all events only half bad. Nor is he unjust, because he does not act with deliberate intent: for of the two chief forms of the character, the one is not apt to abide by his deliberate resolutions, and the other, the man of constitutional strength of passion, is not apt to deliberate at all.

So in fact the man of Imperfect Self-Control is like a community which makes all proper enactments and has admirable laws, only does not act on them, verifying the scoff of Anaxandrides,

> "That State did will it, which cares nought for laws";

whereas the bad man is like one which acts upon its laws, but then unfortunately they are bad ones.

Book Eight

NEXT would seem properly to follow a dissertation on Friendship: because, in the first place, it is either itself a virtue or connected with virtue;

and next it is a thing most necessary for life, since no one would choose to live without friends though he should have all the other good things in the world: and, in fact, men who are rich or possessed of authority and influence are thought to have special need of friends: for where is the use of such prosperity if there be taken away the doing of kindnesses of which friends are the most usual and most commendable objects? Or how can it be kept or preserved without friends? because, the greater it is, so much the more slippery and hazardous: in poverty moreover and all other adversities men think friends to be their only refuge.

Furthermore, Friendship helps the young to keep from error: the old, in respect of attention and such deficiencies in action as their weakness makes them liable to; and those who are in their prime, in respect of noble deeds, because they are thus more able to devise plans and carry them out.

Again, it seems to be implanted in us by Nature: as, for instance, in the parent towards the offspring and the offspring towards the parent, and in those of the same tribe towards one another, and specially in men of the same nation; for which reason we commend those men who love their fellows: and one may see in the course of travel how close of kin and how friendly man is to man.

Furthermore, Friendship seems to be the bond of Social Communities, and legislators seem to be more anxious to secure it than Justice even. I mean, Unanimity is somewhat like to Friendship, and this they certainly aim at and specially drive out faction as being inimical.

As the motives to Friendship differ in kind so do the respective feelings and Friendships. The species then of Friendship are three, in number equal to the objects of it, since in the line of each there may be "mutual affection mutually known."

Now they who have Friendship for one another desire one another's good according to the motive of their Friendship; accordingly they whose motive is utility have no Friendship for one another really, but only in so far as some good arises to them from one another.

And they whose motive is pleasure are in like case: I mean, they have Friendship for men of easy pleasantry, not because they are of a given character but because they are pleasant to themselves. So then they whose motive to Friendship is utility love their friends for what is good to themselves; they whose motive is pleasure do so for what is pleasurable to themselves; that is to say, not in so far as the friend beloved *is* but in so far as he is useful or pleasurable. These Friendships then are a matter of result: since the object is not beloved in that he is the man he is but in that he furnishes advantage or pleasure as the case may be.

Such Friendships are of course very liable to dissolution if the parties do not continue alike: I mean, that the others cease to have any Friendship for them when they are no longer pleasurable or useful. Now it is the nature of utility not to be permanent but constantly varying: so, of course, when the motive which made them friends is vanished, the Friendship likewise dissolves; since it existed only relatively to those circumstances.

Friendship of this kind is thought to exist principally among the old, and in such of men in their prime and of the young as are given to the pursuit of profit. They that are such have no intimate intercourse with one another; for sometimes they are not even pleasurable to one another: nor, in fact, do they desire such intercourse unless their friends are profitable to them, because they are pleasurable only in so far as they have hopes of advantage. With these Friendships is commonly ranked that of hospitality.

Further; just as in respect of the different virtues some men are termed good in respect of a certain inward state, others in respect of acts of work-ing, so is it in respect of Friendship: I mean, they who live together take pleasure in, and impart good to, one another: but they who are asleep or are locally separated do not perform acts, but only are in such a state as to act in a friendly way if they acted at all: distance has in itself no direct effect upon Friendship, but only prevents the acting it out: yet, if the absence be protracted, it is thought to cause a forgetfulness even of the Friendship: and hence it has been said, "many and many a Friendship doth want of intercourse destroy."

Accordingly, neither the old nor the morose appear to be calculated for Friendship, because the pleasurableness in them is small, and no one can spend his days in company with that which is positively painful or even not pleasurable; since to avoid the painful and aim at the pleasurable is one of the most obvious tendencies of human nature. They who get on with one another very fairly, but are not in habits of intimacy, are rather like people having kindly feelings towards one another than friends; nothing being so characteristic of friends as the living with one another, because the neces-sitous desire assistance, and the happy companionship, they being the last persons in the world for solitary existence: but people cannot spend their time together unless they are mutually pleasurable and take pleasure in the same objects, a quality which is thought to appertain to the Friendship of companionship.

The connection then subsisting between the good is Friendship par excellence, as has already been frequently said: since that which is abstract-edly good or pleasant is thought to be an object of Friendship and choice-worthy, and to each individual whatever is such to him; and the good man to the good man for both these reasons.

But there is another form of Friendship, that, namely, in which the one party is superior to the other; as between father and son, elder and younger, husband and wife, ruler and ruled. These also differ one from another: I mean, the Friendship between parents and children is not the same as between ruler and the ruled, nor has the father the same towards the son as the son towards the father, nor the husband towards the wife as she towards him; because the work, and therefore the excellence, of each of these is different, and different therefore are the causes of their feeling Friendship; distinct and different therefore are their feelings and states of Friendship.

And the same results do not accrue to each from the other, nor in fact ought they to be looked for: but, when children render to their parents what they ought to the authors of their being, and parents to their sons what they ought to their offspring, the Friendship between such parties will be permanent and equitable.

Further, the feeling of Friendship should be in a due proportion in all Friendships which are between superior and inferior; I mean, the better man, or the more profitable, and so forth, should be the object of a stronger feeling than he himself entertains, because when the feeling of Friendship comes to be after a certain rate then equality in a certain sense is produced, which is thought to be a requisite in Friendship.

And that equality is thus requisite is plainly shown by the occurrence of a great difference of goodness or badness, or prosperity, or something else: for in this case, people are not any longer friends, nay they do not even feel that they ought to be. The clearest illustration is perhaps the case of the gods, because they are most superior in all good things. It is obvious too, in the case of kings, for they who are greatly their inferiors do not feel entitled to be friends to them; nor do people very insignificant to be friends to those of very high excellence or wisdom. Of course, in such cases it is out of the question to attempt to define up to what point they may continue friends: for you may remove many points of agreement and the Friendship last nevertheless; but when one of the parties is very far separated, it cannot continue any longer.

Now of course all Friendship is based upon Communion, as has been already stated: but one would be inclined to separate off from the rest the Friendship of Kindred, and that of Companions: whereas those of men of the same city, or tribe, or crew, and all such, are more peculiarly, it would seem, based upon Communion, inasmuch as they plainly exist in right of some agreement expressed or implied: among these one may rank also the Friendship of Hospitality.

The Friendship of Kindred is likewise of many kinds, and appears in all its varieties to depend on the Parental: parents, I mean, love their children as being a part of themselves, children love their parents as being themselves somewhat derived from them. But parents know their offspring more than these know that they are from the parents, and the source is more closely bound to that which is produced than that which is produced is to that which formed it: of course, whatever is derived from one's self is proper to that from which it is so derived: but the source to it is in no degree proper, or in an inferior degree at least.

Then again the greater length of time comes in: the parents love their offspring from the first moment of their being, but their offspring them only after a lapse of time when they have attained intelligence or instinct. These considerations serve also to show why mothers have greater strength of affection than fathers.

There are then, as was stated at the commencement of this book, three kinds of Friendship, and in each there may be friends on a footing of equality and friends in the relation of superior and inferior; we find, I mean, that people who are alike in goodness become friends, and better with worse, and so also pleasant people; again, because of advantage people are friends, either balancing exactly their mutual profitableness or differing from one another herein. Well then, those who are equal should in right of this equality be equalised also by the degree of their Friendship and the other points, and those who are on a footing of inequality by rendering Friendship in proportion to the superiority of the other party.

Quarrels arise also in those Friendships in which the parties are unequal because each party thinks himself entitled to the greater share, and of course, when this happens, the Friendship is broken up.

The man who is better than the other thinks that having the greater share pertains to him of right, for that more is always awarded to the good man: and similarly the man who is more profitable to another than that other to him: "one who is useless," they say, "ought not to share equally, for it comes to a tax, and not a Friendship, unless the fruits of the Friendship are reaped in proportion to the works done": their notion being that, as in a money partnership, they who contribute more receive more, so should it be in Friendship likewise.

On the other hand, the needy man and the less virtuous advance the opposite claim: they urge that "it is the very business of a good friend to help those who are in need, else what is the use of having a good or powerful friend if one is not to reap the advantage at all?"

Now each seems to advance a right claim and to be entitled to get more out of the connection than the other, only *not more of the same thing:* but the superior man should receive more respect, the needy man more profit: respect being the reward of goodness and beneficence, profit being the aid of need.

Book Nine

WELL, in all the Friendships the parties to which are dissimilar it is the proportionate which equalises and preserves the Friendship, as has been already stated: I mean, in the Social Friendship the cobbler, for instance, gets an equivalent for his shoes after a certain rate; and the weaver, and all others in like manner. Now in this case a common measure has been provided in money, and to this accordingly all things are referred and by this are measured: but in the Friendship of Love the complaint is sometimes from the lover that, though he loves exceedingly, his love is not requited; he having perhaps all the time nothing that can be the object of Friendship: again, oftentimes from the object of love that he who as a suitor promised any and every thing now performs nothing. These cases occur because the Friendship of the lover for the beloved object is based upon pleasure, that of the other for him upon utility, and in one of the parties the requisite quality is not found: for, as these are respectively the grounds of the Friendship, the Friendship comes to be broken up because the motives to it cease to exist: the parties loved not one another but qualities in one another which are not permanent, and so neither are the Friendships: whereas the Friendship based upon the moral character of the parties, being independent and disinterested, is permanent, as we have already stated.

Quarrels arise also when the parties realise different results and not those which they desire; for the not attaining one's special object is all one, in this case, with getting nothing at all: as in the well-known case where a man made promises to a musician, rising in proportion to the excellence of his music; but when, the next morning, the musician claimed the performance of his promises, he said that he had given him pleasure for pleasure: of course, if each party had intended this, it would have been all right: but if the one desires amusement and the other gain, and the one gets his object but the other not, the dealing cannot be fair: because a man fixes his mind upon what he happens to want, and will give so and so for that specific thing.

Now the friendly feelings which are exhibited towards our friends, and by which Friendships are characterised, seem to have sprung out of those which we entertain towards ourselves.

I mean, people define a friend to be "one who intends and does what is good to another for that other's sake"; or "one who wishes his friend to be and to live for that friend's own sake." Others again, "one who lives with another and chooses the same objects," or "one who sympathises with his friend in his sorrows and in his joys."

Well, by some one of these marks people generally characterise Friendship: and each of these the good man has towards himself, and all others have them in so far as they suppose themselves to be good.

For he is at unity in himself, and with every part of his soul he desires the same objects; and he wishes for himself both what is, and what he believes to be, good; and he does it; and for the sake of himself, inasmuch as he does it for the sake of his Intellectual Principle which is generally thought to be a man's Self. Again, he wishes himself, and specially this Principle whereby he is an intelligent being, to live and be preserved in life, because existence is a good to him that is a good man.

But it is to himself that each individual wishes what is good, and no man, conceiving the possibility of his becoming other than he now is, chooses that that New Self should have all things indiscriminately: a god, for instance, has at the present moment the Chief Good, but he has it in right of being whatever he actually now is: and the Intelligent Principle must be judged to be each man's Self, or at least eminently so [though other Principles help, of course, to constitute him the man he is].

Benefactors are commonly held to have more Friendship for the objects of their kindness than these for them: and the fact is made a subject of discussion and inquiry, as being contrary to reasonable expectation.

The account of the matter which satisfies most persons is that the one are debtors and the others creditors: and therefore that, as in the case of actual loans the debtors wish their creditors out of the way while the creditors are anxious for the preservation of their debtors, so those who have done kindnesses desire the continued existence of the people they have done them to, under the notion of getting a return of their good offices, while these are not particularly anxious about requital.

Epicharmus, I suspect, would very probably say that they who give this solution judge from their own baseness; yet it certainly is like human nature, for the generality of men have short memories on these points, and aim rather at receiving than conferring benefits.

But the real cause, it would seem, rests upon nature, and the case is not parallel to that of creditors; because in this there is no affection to the persons, but merely a wish for their preservation with a view to the return: whereas, in point of fact, they who have done kindnesses feel friendship and love for those to whom they have done them, even though they neither are, nor can by possibility hereafter be, in a position to serve their benefactors.

A question is raised also respecting the Happy man, whether he will want Friends, or no?

Some say that they who are blessed and independent have no need

of Friends, for they already have all that is good, and so, as being independent, want nothing further: whereas the notion of a friend's office is
to be as it were a second Self and procure for a man what he cannot get
by himself: hence the saying,

"When Fortune gives us good, what need we Friends?"

On the other hand, it looks absurd, while we are assigning to the
Happy man all other good things, not to give him Friends, which are,
after all, thought to be the greatest of external goods.

Again, if it is more characteristic of a friend to confer than to receive
kindnesses, and if to be beneficent belongs to the good man and to the
character of virtue, and if it is more noble to confer kindnesses on friends
than strangers, the good man will need objects for his benefactions. And
out of this last consideration springs a question whether the need of
Friends be greater in prosperity or adversity, since the unfortunate man
wants people to do him kindnesses and they who are fortunate want
objects for their kind acts.

Again, it is perhaps absurd to make our Happy man a solitary, because no man would choose the possession of all goods in the world on the
condition of solitariness, man being a social animal and formed by nature
for living with others: of course the Happy man has this qualification
since he has all those things which are good by nature: and it is obvious
that the society of friends and good men must be preferable to that of
strangers and ordinary people, and we conclude, therefore, that the
Happy man does need Friends.

But then, what do they mean whom we quoted first, and how are they
right? Is it not that the mass of mankind mean by Friends those who are
useful? and of course the Happy man will not need such because he has
all good things already; neither will he need such as are Friends with a
view to the pleasurable, or at least only to a slight extent; because his
life, being already pleasurable, does not want pleasure imported from
without; and so, since the Happy man does not need Friends of these
kinds, he is thought not to need any at all.

But it may be, this is not true: for it was stated originally, that Happiness is a kind of Working; now Working plainly is something that must
come into being, not be already there like a mere piece of property.

If then the being happy consists in living and working, and the good
man's working is in itself excellent and pleasurable, and if what is our
own reckons among things pleasurable, and if we can view our neighbours
better than ourselves and their actions better than we can our own, then
the actions of their Friends who are good men are pleasurable to the
good; inasmuch as they have both the requisites which are naturally pleasant. So the man in the highest state of happiness will need Friends of this

kind, since he desires to contemplate good actions, and actions of his own, which those of his friend, being a good man, are.

Are we then to make our Friends as numerous as possible? Or, as in respect of acquaintance it is thought to have been well said, "Have not thou many acquaintances yet be not without," so too in respect of Friendship may we adopt the precept and say that a man should not be without Friends, nor again have exceeding many Friends?

Now as for Friends who are intended for use, the maxim I have quoted will, it seems, fit in exceedingly well, because to requite the services of many is a matter of labour, and a whole life would not be long enough to do this for them. So that, if more numerous than what will suffice for one's own life, they become officious, and are hindrances in respect of living well: and so we do not want them. And again, of those who are to be for pleasure a few are quite enough, just like sweetening in our food.

But of the good are we to make as many as ever we can, or is there any measure of the number of Friends, as there is of the number to constitute a Political Community? I mean, you cannot make one out of ten men, and if you increase the number to one hundred thousand it is not any longer a Community. However, the number is not perhaps some one definite number but any between certain extreme limits.

Well, of Friends likewise there is a limited number, which perhaps may be laid down to be the greatest number with whom it would be possible to keep up intimacy; this being thought to be one of the greatest marks of Friendship, and it being quite obvious that it is not possible to be intimate with many, in other words, to part one's self among many. And besides it must be remembered that they also are to be Friends to one another if they are all to live together: but it is a matter of difficulty to find this in many men at once.

Book Ten

NEXT, it would seem, follows a discussion respecting Pleasure, for it is thought to be most closely bound up with our kind: and so men train the young, guiding them on their course by the rudders of Pleasure and Pain. And to like and dislike what one ought is judged to be most important for the formation of good moral character: because these feelings extend all one's life through, giving a bias towards and exerting an influence on the side of Virtue and Happiness, since men choose what is pleasant and avoid what is painful.

Now Eudoxus thought Pleasure to be the Chief Good because he saw all, rational and irrational alike, aiming at it: and he argued that, since in all what was the object of choice must be good and what most so the best, the fact of all being drawn to the same thing proved this thing to be the best for all: "For each," he said, "finds what is good for itself just as it does its proper nourishment, and so that which is good for all, and the object of the aim of all, is their Chief Good."

And he thought his position was not less proved by the argument from the contrary: that is, since Pain was in itself an object of avoidance to all, the contrary must be in like manner an object of choice.

Again he urged that that is most choiceworthy which we choose, not by reason of, or with a view to, anything further; and that Pleasure is confessedly of this kind because no one ever goes on to ask to what purpose he is pleased, feeling that Pleasure is in itself choiceworthy.

Again, that when added to any other good it makes it more choiceworthy; as, for instance, to actions of justice, or perfected self-mastery; and good can only be increased by itself.

However, this argument at least seems to prove only that it belongs to the class of goods, and not that it does so more than anything else: for every good is more choiceworthy in combination with some other than when taken quite alone. In fact, it is by just such an argument that Plato proves that Pleasure is not the Chief Good: "For," says he, "the life of Pleasure is more choiceworthy in combination with Practical Wisdom than apart from it; but, if the compound be better, then simple Pleasure cannot be the Chief Good; because the very Chief Good cannot by any addition become more choiceworthy than it is already": and it is obvious that nothing else can be the Chief Good, which by combination with any of the things in themselves good comes to be more choiceworthy.

Nor again is Pleasure therefore excluded from being a good because it does not belong to the class of qualities: the acts of virtue are not qualities, neither is Happiness, yet surely both are goods.

Again, they say the Chief Good is limited but Pleasure unlimited, in that it admits of degrees.

Now if they judge this from the act of feeling Pleasure, then the same thing will apply to justice and all the other virtues, in respect of which clearly it is said that men are more or less of such and such characters (according to the different virtues), they are more just or more brave, or one may practise justice and self-mastery more or less.

If, on the other hand, they judge in respect of the Pleasures themselves, then it may be they miss the true cause, namely, that some are unmixed and others mixed: for just as health, being in itself limited, admits of degrees, why should not Pleasure do so and yet be limited? In the former case we account for it by the fact that there is not the same adjustment of parts in all men, nor one and the same always in the same individual: but health, though relaxed, remains up to a certain point, and differs in degrees; and of course the same may be the case with Pleasure.

Again, assuming the Chief Good to be perfect and all Movements and Generations imperfect, they try to show that Pleasure is a Movement and a Generation.

Yet they do not seem warranted in saying even that it is a Movement: for to every Movement are thought to belong swiftness and slowness, and if not in itself, as to that of the universe, yet relatively: but to Pleasure. neither of these belongs: for though one may have got quickly into the state of Pleasure, as into that of anger, one cannot be in the state quickly, nor relatively to the state of any other person; but we can walk or grow, and so on, quickly or slowly.

An act of Sight is thought to be complete at any moment; that is to say, it lacks nothing the accession of which subsequently will complete its whole nature.

Well, Pleasure resembles this: because it is a whole, as one may say; and one could not at any moment of time take a Pleasure whose whole nature would be completed by its lasting for a longer time. And for this reason it is not a Movement: for all Movement takes place in time of certain duration and has a certain End to accomplish; for instance, the Movement of house-building is then only complete when the builder has produced what he intended, that is, either in the whole time [necessary to complete the whole design], or in a given portion. But all the subordinate Movements are incomplete in the parts of the time, and are different in kind from the whole Movement and from one another (I mean, for instance, that the fitting the stones together is a Movement different from that of fluting the column, and both again from the construction of the Temple as a whole: but this last is complete as lacking nothing to the result proposed; whereas that of the basement, or of the triglyph, is incomplete, because each is a Movement of a part merely).

As I said then, they differ in kind, and you cannot at any time you choose find a Movement complete in its whole nature, but, if at all, in the whole time requisite.

And so it is with the Movement of walking and all others: for, if motion be a Movement from one place to another place, then of it too there are different kinds, flying, walking, leaping, and suchlike. And not only so, but there are different kinds even in walking: the where-from and where-to are not the same in the whole Course as in a portion of it; nor in one portion as in another; nor is crossing this line the same as crossing that: because a man is not merely crossing a line but a line in a given place, and this is in a different place from that.

Of Movement I have discoursed exactly in another treatise. I will now therefore only say that it seems not to be complete at any given moment; and that most Movements are incomplete and specifically different, since the whence and whither constitute different species.

But of Pleasure the whole nature is complete at any given moment: it is plain then that Pleasure and Movement must be different from one another, and that Pleasure belongs to the class of things whole and complete. And this might appear also from the impossibility of moving except in a definite time, whereas there is none with respect to the sensation of Pleasure, for what exists at the very present moment is a kind of "whole."

From these considerations then it is plain that people are not warranted in saying that Pleasure is a Movement or a Generation: because these terms are not applicable to all things, only to such as are divisible and not "wholes": I mean that of an act of Sight there is no Generation, nor is there of a point, nor of a monad, nor is any one of these a Movement or a Generation: neither then of Pleasure is there Movement or Generation, because it is, as one may say, "a whole."

Now that we have spoken about the Excellences of both kinds, and Friendship in its varieties, and Pleasures, it remains to sketch out Happiness, since we assume that to be the one End of all human things: and we shall save time and trouble by recapitulating what was stated before.

Well then, we said that it is not a State merely; because, if it were, it might belong to one who slept all his life through and merely vegetated, or to one who fell into very great calamities: and so, if these possibilities displease us and we would rather put it into the rank of some kind of Working, and Workings are of different kinds, it is plain we must rank Happiness among those choiceworthy for their own sakes and not among those which are so with a view to something further: because Happiness has no lack of anything but is self-sufficient.

By choiceworthy in themselves are meant those from which nothing is sought beyond the act of Working: and of this kind are thought to be the actions according to Virtue, because doing what is noble and excellent is one of those things which are choiceworthy for their own sake alone.

Now if Happiness is a Working in the way of Excellence, of course that Excellence must be the highest, that is to say, the Excellence of the best Principle. Whether then this best Principle is Intellect or some other which is thought naturally to rule and to lead and to conceive of noble and divine things, whether being in its own nature divine or the most divine of all our internal Principles, the Working of this in accordance with its own proper Excellence must be the perfect Happiness.

It is Contemplative; and this would seem to be consistent with what we said before and with truth: for, in the first place, this Working is of

the highest kind, since the Intellect is the highest of our internal Principles and the subjects with which it is conversant the highest of all
which fall within the range of our knowledge.

Next, it is also most Continuous: for we are better able to contemplate
than to do anything else whatever, continuously.

Again, we think Pleasure must be in some way an ingredient in
Happiness, and of all Workings in accordance with Excellence that in the
way of Science is confessedly most pleasant: at least the pursuit of Science
is thought to contain Pleasures admirable for purity and permanence;
and it is reasonable to suppose that the employment is more pleasant to
those who have mastered, than to those who are yet seeking for, it.

And the Self-Sufficiency which people speak of will attach chiefly
to the Contemplative Working: of course the actual necessaries of life
are needed alike by the man of science, and the just man, and all the
other characters; but, supposing all sufficiently supplied with these, the
just man needs people towards whom, and in concert with whom, to
practise his justice; and in like manner the man of perfected self-mastery,
and the brave man, and so on of the rest; whereas the man of science
can contemplate and speculate even when quite alone, and the more
entirely he deserves the appellation the more able is he to do so: it may be
he can do better for having fellow-workers, but still he is certainly most
Self-Sufficient.

Again, this alone would seem to be rested in for its own sake, since
nothing results from it beyond the fact of having contemplated; whereas
from all things which are objects of moral action we do mean to get
something beside the doing them, be the same more or less.

Also, Happiness is thought to stand in perfect rest; for we toil that
we may rest, and war that we may be at peace. Now all the Practical
Virtues require either society or war for their Working, and the actions
regarding these are thought to exclude rest; those of war entirely, because
no one chooses war, nor prepares for war, for war's sake: he would indeed be thought a bloodthirsty villain who should make enemies of his
friends to secure the existence of fighting and bloodshed. The Working
also of the statesman excludes the idea of rest, and, beside the actual
work of government, seeks for power and dignities or at least Happiness
for the man himself and his fellow-citizens: a Happiness distinct from
the national Happiness which we evidently seek as being different
and distinct.

And second in degree of Happiness will be that Life which is in
accordance with the other kind of Excellence, for the Workings in accordance with this are proper to Man: I mean, we do actions of justice,
courage, and the other virtues, towards one another, in contracts, services
of different kinds, and in all kinds of actions and feelings too, by ob-

serving what is befitting for each: and all these plainly are proper to man. Further, the Excellence of the Moral character is thought to result in some points from physical circumstances, and to be, in many, very closely connected with the passions.

Again, Practical Wisdom and Excellence of the Moral character are very closely united; since the Principles of Practical Wisdom are in accordance with the Moral Virtues and these are right when they accord with Practical Wisdom.

These moreover, as bound up with the passions, must belong to the composite nature, and the Excellences or Virtues of the composite nature are proper to man: therefore so too will be the life and Happiness which is in accordance with them. But that of the Pure Intellect is separate and distinct: and let this suffice upon the subject, since great exactness is beyond our purpose.

It would seem, moreover, to require supply of external goods to a small degree, or certainly less than the Moral Happiness: for, as far as necessaries of life are concerned, we will suppose both characters to need them equally, but when we come to consider their Workings there will be found a great difference.

Now then that we have said enough in our sketchy kind of way on these subjects—I mean, on the Virtues, and also on Friendship and Pleasure—are we to suppose that our original purpose is completed? Must we not rather acknowledge, what is commonly said, that in matters of moral action mere Speculation and Knowledge is not the real End but rather Practice: and if so, then neither in respect of Virtue is Knowledge enough; we must further strive to have and exert it, and take whatever other means there are of becoming good.

Now if talking and writing were of themselves sufficient to make men good, they would justly, as Theognis observes, have reaped numerous and great rewards, and the thing to do would be to provide them: but in point of fact, while they plainly have the power to guide and stimulate the generous among the young and to base upon true virtuous principle any noble and truly high-minded disposition, they as plainly are powerless to guide the mass of men to Virtue and goodness; because it is not their nature to be amenable to a sense of shame but only to fear; nor to abstain from what is low and mean because it is disgraceful to do it but because of the punishment attached to it: in fact, as they live at the beck and call of passion, they pursue their own proper pleasures and the means of securing them, and they avoid the contrary pains; but as for what is noble and truly pleasurable they have not an idea of it, inasmuch as they have never tasted of it.

Men such as these then what mere words can transform? No, indeed! it is either actually impossible, or a task of no mean difficulty, to alter by words what has been of old taken into men's very dispositions: and, it may be, it is a ground for contentment if with all the means and appliances for goodness in our hands we can attain to Virtue.

The formation of a virtuous character some ascribe to Nature, some to Custom, and some to Teaching. Now Nature's part, be it what it may, obviously does not rest with us; but belongs to those who in the truest sense are fortunate, by reason of certain divine agency.

NOVUM ORGANUM

by

FRANCIS BACON

CONTENTS

Novum Organum

FRANCIS BACON

1561–1626

IN MANY WAYS Francis Bacon is one of the most tragic characters in the history of philosophy. His overmastering desire was to be of service to humanity, the state, the Church, and—it must be reluctantly admitted—himself. He rose to the highest legal office in the kingdom and, on the way up, composed philosophical works which have profoundly influenced the world down to the present day. But at the height of his career he was accused, tried, and sentenced for having taken bribes from men whose cases he had been appointed to decide in the courts. He was condemned and disgraced and died in retirement.

The son of Nicholas Bacon, Keeper of the Great Seal under Queen Elizabeth, and the nephew of the Queen's principal adviser, Lord Burghley, Bacon had every opportunity for rapid advancement. But his rise was slow. Because his health was always delicate, he received the greater part of his early education at home. At the age of twelve he entered Trinity College, Cambridge, where he became interested in the sciences and gradually reached the conclusion that the methods employed and the results attained were alike erroneous. This led him to begin a search for a "true and fruitful" method of science.

At fifteen Bacon decided to study law and entered Gray's Inn, one of the famous law schools of England. Here he began to show that hungry ambition which dominated his entire life. He applied for a minor post in court, and his application was successful.

Then, in 1588, he made the acquaintance of the Earl of Essex, the favorite of Queen Elizabeth. Shortly thereafter he became confidential adviser to the earl and worked closely with him for many years.

In 1593 Bacon won a seat in Parliament. Here he distinguished himself for his deep loyalty to the Crown. Indeed, he felt that the Crown was supreme in the realm and that everything else must be subordinated to its authority. Thus when Essex was arrested for treason—an arrest which to Bacon seemed wholly justified—Bacon turned from him and helped to send him to the block.

Upon the death of Elizabeth, Bacon transferred his loyalty to James and worked constantly for his sovereign's welfare. The King, nevertheless, was slow in promoting Bacon to high office—a tardiness due in some degree to the machinations of court favorites.

But a man like Bacon could not be kept down. On January 4, 1617, he was made Lord Chancellor, and in 1620 he was created Viscount St. Albans. In that same year (1620) Bacon published his most famous work, the *Novum Organum*. The philosopher-politician had now attained the heights.

But one so high may fall far, and Bacon toppled downward in a most tragic manner. He had received "gifts" from individuals who were to come before him as jurist. In several of the cases, to be sure, he decided against the givers of these gifts. But the fact that he had accepted their bounty was sufficient ground for the charge of bribery; and it was on this charge that Bacon was brought to trial. The evidence was unmistakable. Bacon made an eloquent plea in his behalf. But the judges were unimpressed. On May 3, 1621, they returned a verdict imposing a fine of £40,000, imprisoning him in the Tower during the King's pleasure, denying him forever any office in the state, debarring him from ever sitting in Parliament, and excluding him from the court.

This was indeed a harsh sentence. But actually it was never enforced. The fine was remitted by the King, and Bacon's imprisonment lasted only four days. In 1621 he received a general pardon from the King. But Bacon never again sat in Parliament. He was disgraced.

For the remaining five years of his life Bacon devoted himself to writings which have proved to be of far greater value to society than all his political and judicial activities in England.

Then, on the ninth of April, 1626, Bacon died of bronchitis brought on as he was attempting an experiment on the effect of snow in preserving flesh.

The *Novum Organum,* Bacon's greatest work, is the second part of a magnificent *Instauration* in which he planned to rethink the sciences and philosophy. This masterpiece was to contain six parts as follows:

1—The Divisions of the Sciences.
2—The New Organon; or, Directions concerning the Interpretation of Nature.
3—The Phenomena of the Universe; or a Natural and Experimental History of the Foundation of Philosophy.
4—The Ladder of the Intellect.
5—The Forerunners; or, Anticipations of the New Philosophy.
6—The New Philosophy; or, Active Science.

This great *Instauration* was to be "nothing less than a complete renovation of the sciences." Bacon was unable to complete this undertaking. The period in which he lived afforded him neither the technique nor the breadth of vision sufficient to do more than to suggest the general line of thinking in this direction.

Yet this general line of thinking, as outlined in the *Novum Organum,* has given the world a new method of scientific inquiry—"an easier approach to the truth."

Before we can investigate the truth, said Bacon, we must do away with a number of fallacies, or *Idols,* that have hampered us in our search.

Fallacy Number 1—the *Idols of the Tribe.* This class of idols assumes the foolish tribal doctrine that the universe has been created for any individual man or for any group of men. It impels us to seek for an order in a world which has not been made to our design. "The human understanding, from its peculiar nature, supposes a greater degree of regularity in things than it really finds . . . although most cogent and abundant instances may exist to the contrary. . . ."

Fallacy Number 2—the *Idols of the Cave.* "Every one of us," observes Bacon, "has a cave or den of his own, which refracts and discolors the light of nature." Every mind, in other words, sees the world through spectacles of a different color. Some minds are analytic—they see the world divided into diverse elements; other minds are synthetic—they visualize the world united into a coherent structure. To the first group belongs the scientist; to the second, the artist. But all of us, insists Bacon, must realize that the truth is independent both of analysis and of synthesis. There are more facets to the universe than are dreamt of either in our philosophies or in our sciences.

Fallacy Number 3—the *Idols of the Market Place.* These idols, or false images, arise "from the commerce and association of men with one another." There is too much loose talk about the world; too many erroneous definitions are taken for granted by laymen and scholars alike. "There arises, from a bad and inept formation of words, a wonderful obstruction of the mind." We must remove this obstruction through a clearer understanding of our terms. Let us learn to say what we mean, and to mean what we say.

Fallacy Number 4—the *Idols of the Theater.* These idols emanate from the dogmas of the philosophers, who dramatize all life into an artificial plot. Our various systems of philosophy "are but so many stage plays, representing worlds of their own creation after an unreal and scenic fashion." These fanciful worlds of the philosophers are "more as we should wish them to be than true stories . . . out of history."

These, then, are the old fallacies, the smoky lamps that have blurred our vision in the past. Let us replace them with the light of our new method. And what is this new method? It is the procedure of doubt, of trial and error, of classification and reclassification. It is, in short, the method of *simple experiment.* Bacon's *Novum Organum* is the philosopher's—and the scientist's—Declaration of Independence. It marks the birth of the "laboratory method" in man's experimental pursuit of the truth.

———————————

NOVUM ORGANUM

PREFACE

THOSE who have taken upon them to lay down the law of nature as a thing already searched out and understood, whether they have spoken in simple assurance or professional affectation, have therein done philosophy and the sciences great injury. For as they have been successful in inducing belief, so they have been effective in quenching and stopping inquiry; and have done more harm by spoiling and putting an end to other men's efforts than good by their own. Those on the other hand who have taken a contrary course, and asserted that absolutely nothing can be known—whether it were from hatred of the ancient sophists, or from uncertainty and fluctuation of mind, or even from a kind of fulness of learning, that they fell upon this opinion,—have certainly advanced reasons for it that are not to be despised; but yet they have neither started from true principles nor rested in the just conclusion, zeal and affectation having carried them much too far. The more ancient of the Greeks took up with better judgment a position between these two extremes,—between the presumption of pronouncing on everything, and the despair of comprehending anything; and though frequently and bitterly complaining of the difficulty of inquiry and the obscurity of things, and like impatient horses champing the bit, they did not the less follow up their object and engage with nature; thinking that this very question—viz., whether or no anything can be known—was to be settled not by arguing, but by trying. And yet they too, trusting entirely to the force of their understanding, applied no rule, but made everything turn upon hard thinking and perpetual working and exercise of the mind.

Now my method, though hard to practice, is easy to explain; and it is this. I propose to establish progressive stages of certainty. The evidence of the sense, helped and guarded by a certain process of correction, I retain. But the mental operation which follows the act of sense I for the most part reject; and instead of it, I open and lay out a new and certain path for the mind to proceed in, starting directly from the simple sensuous perception. The necessity of this was felt no doubt by those who attributed so much importance to logic; showing thereby that they were in search of helps for the understanding, and had no confidence in the native and spontaneous process of the mind. But this remedy comes too late to do any good, when the mind is already, through the daily intercourse and conversation of life, occupied with unsound doctrines and beset on all sides by vain imaginations. And therefore that art of logic, coming too late to the rescue, and no way able to set matters right again, has had the effect of fixing errors rather than disclosing truth. There remains but one course for the recovery of a sound and healthy condition,—namely, that the entire work of the understanding be commenced afresh, and the mind itself be from the very outset not left to take its own course, but guided at every step; and the business be done as if by machinery. Certainly if in things mechanical men had set to work with their naked hands, without help or force of instruments, just as in things intellectual they have set to work with little else than the naked forces of the understanding, very small would the matters have been which, even with their best efforts applied in conjunction, they could have attempted or accomplished.

Upon these premises two things occur to me of which, that they may not be overlooked, I would have men reminded. First it falls out, fortunately as I think for the allaying of contradictions and heart-burnings, that the honor and reverence due to the ancients remains untouched and undiminished; while I may carry out my designs and at the same time reap the fruit of my modesty. For if I should profess that I, going the same road as the ancients, have something better to produce, there must needs have been some comparison or rivalry between us in respect of excellency or ability of wit; and though in this there would be nothing unlawful or new, yet the contest, however just and allowable, would have been an unequal one perhaps, in respect of the measure of my own powers. As it is, however,—my object being to open a new way for the understanding, a way by them untried and unknown,—the case is altered; party zeal and emulation are at an end; and I appear merely as a guide to point out the road; an office of small authority, and depending more upon a kind of luck than upon any ability or excellency. And thus much relates to the persons only. The other point of which I would have men reminded relates to the matter itself.

Be it remembered then that I am far from wishing to interfere with the philosophy which now flourishes, or with any other philosophy more correct and complete than this which has been or may hereafter be propounded. For I do not object to the use of this received philosophy, or others like it, for supplying matter for disputations or ornaments for discourse,—for the professor's lecture and for the business of life. Nay more, I declare openly that for these uses the philosophy which I bring forward will not be much available. It does not lie in the way. It cannot be caught up in passage. It does not flatter the understanding by conformity with preconceived notions. Nor will it come down to the apprehension of the vulgar except by its utility and effects.

Let there be therefore two streams and two dispensations of knowledge; and in like manner two tribes or kindreds of students in philosophy —tribes not hostile or alien to each other, but bound together by mutual services;—let there in short be one method for the cultivation, another for the invention, of knowledge.

And for those who prefer the former, either from hurry or from considerations of business or for want of mental power to take in and embrace the other, I wish that they may succeed to their desire in what they are about, and obtain what they are pursuing. But if any man there be who, not content to rest in and use the knowledge which has already been discovered, aspires to penetrate further; to overcome, not an adversary in argument, but nature in action; to seek, not pretty and probable conjectures, but certain and demonstrable knowledge;—I invite all such to join themselves, as true sons of knowledge, with me, that passing by the outer courts of nature, which numbers have trodden, we may find a way at length into her inner chambers. And to make my meaning clearer and to familiarize the thing by giving it a name, I have chosen to call one of these methods or ways *Anticipation of the Mind,* the other *Interpretation of Nature.*

Aphorisms Concerning the Interpretation of Nature and the Kingdom of Man

APHORISM

i

MAN, being the servant and interpreter of nature, can do and understand so much and so much only as he has observed in fact or in thought of the course of nature: beyond this he neither knows anything nor can do anything.

ii

Neither the naked hand nor the understanding left to itself can effect much. It is by instruments and helps that the work is done, which are as much wanted for the understanding as for the hand. And as the instruments of the hand either give motion or guide it, so the instruments of the mind supply either suggestions for the understanding or cautions.

iii

Human knowledge and human power meet in one; for where the cause is not known the effect cannot be produced. Nature to be commanded must be obeyed; and that which in contemplation is as the cause is in operation as the rule

iv

Towards the effecting of works, all that man can do is to put together or put asunder natural bodies. The rest is done by nature working within.

v

The study of nature with a view to works is engaged in by the mechanic, the mathematician, the physician, the alchemist, and the magician; but by all with slight endeavor and scanty success.

vi

It would be an unsound fancy and self-contradictory to expect that things which have never yet been done can be done except by means which have never yet been tried.

vii

The productions of the mind and hand seem very numerous in books and manufactures. But all this variety lies in an exquisite subtlety and derivations from a few things already known; not in the number of axioms.

viii

Moreover the works already known are due to chance and experiment rather than to sciences; for the sciences we now possess are merely systems for the nice ordering and setting forth of things already invented; not methods of invention or directions for new works.

ix

The cause and root of nearly all evils in the sciences is this—that while we falsely admire and extol the powers of the human mind we neglect to seek for its true helps.

x

The subtlety of nature is greater many times over than the subtlety of the senses and understanding; so that all those specious meditations, speculations, and glosses in which men indulge are quite from the purpose, only there is no one by to observe it.

xi

As the sciences which we now have do not help us in finding out new works, so neither does the logic which we now have help us in finding out new sciences.

xii

The logic now in use serves rather to fix and give stability to the errors which have their foundation in commonly received notions, than to help the search after truth. So it does more harm than good.

xiii

The syllogism is not applied to the first principles of sciences, and is applied in vain to intermediate axioms; being no match for the subtlety of nature. It commands assent therefore to the proposition, but does not take hold of the thing.

xiv

The syllogism consists of propositions, propositions consist of words, words are symbols of notions. Therefore if the notions themselves are confused and overhastily abstracted from the facts, there can be no firmness in the superstructure. Our only hope therefore lies in a true induction.

xv

There is no soundness in our notions whether logical or physical. Substance, Quality, Action, Passion, Essence itself, are not sound notions: much less are Heavy, Light, Dense, Rare, Moist, Dry, Generation, Corruption, Attraction, Repulsion, Element, Matter, Form, and the like; but all are fantastical and ill defined.

xvi

Our notions of less general species as Man, Dog, Dove, and of the immediate perceptions of the sense, as Hot, Cold, Black, White, do not materially mislead us; yet even these are sometimes confused by the flux and alteration of matter and the mixing of one thing with another. All the others which men have hitherto adopted are but wanderings, not being abstracted and formed from things by proper methods.

xvii

Nor is there less of willfulness and wandering in the construction of axioms than in the formations of notions; not excepting even those very principles which are obtained by common induction; but much more in the axioms and lower propositions educed by the syllogism.

xviii

The discoveries which have hitherto been made in the sciences are such as lie close to vulgar notions, scarcely beneath the surface. In order to penetrate into the inner and further recesses of nature, it is necessary that both notions and axioms be derived from things by a more sure and guarded way; and that a method of intellectual operation be introduced altogether better and more certain.

xix

There are and can be only two ways of searching into and discovering truth. The one flies from the senses and particulars to the most general axioms, and from these principles, the truth of which it takes for settled and immovable, proceeds to judgment and to the discovery of middle axioms. And this way is now in fashion. The other derives axioms from the senses and particulars, rising by a gradual and unbroken ascent, so that it arrives at the most general axioms last of all. This is the true way, but as yet untried.

xx

The understanding left to itself takes the same course which it takes in accordance with logical order. For the mind longs to spring up to positions of higher generality, that it may find rest there; and so after a little while wearies of experiment. But this evil is increased by logic, because of the order and solemnity of its disputations.

xxi

The understanding left to itself, in a sober, patient, and grave mind, especially if it be not hindered by received doctrines, tries a little that other way, which is the right one, but with little progress; since the understanding, unless directed and assisted, is a thing unequal, and quite unfit to contend with the obscurity of things.

xxii

Both ways set out from the senses and particulars, and rest in the highest generalities; but the difference between them is infinite. For the one just glances at experiment and particulars in passing, the other dwells duly and orderly among them. The one, again, begins at once by establishing certain abstract and useless generalities, the other rises by gradual steps to that which is prior and better known in the order of nature.

xxiii

There is a great difference between the *Idols* of the human mind and the *Idéas* of the divine. That is to say, between certain empty dogmas, and the true signatures and marks set upon the works of creation as they are found in nature.

xxiv

It cannot be that axioms established by argumentation should avail for the discovery of new works; since the subtlety of nature is greater many times over than the subtlety of argument. But axioms duly and orderly formed from particulars easily discover the way to new particulars, and thus render sciences active.

xxv

The axioms now in use, having been suggested by a scanty and manipular experience and a few particulars of most general occurrence, are made for the most part just large enough to fit and take these in: and therefore it is no wonder if they do not lead to new particulars. And if some opposite instance. not observed or not known before, chance to come in the way, the axiom is rescued and preserved by some frivolous distinction; whereas the truer course would be to correct the axiom itself.

xxvi

The conclusions of human reason as ordinarily applied in matter of nature, I call for the sake of distinction *Anticipations of Nature*. That reason which is elicited from facts by a just and methodical process, I call *Interpretation of Nature*.

xxvii

Anticipations are a ground sufficiently firm for consent; for even if men went mad all after the same fashion, they might agree one with another well enough.

xxviii

For the winning of assent, indeed, anticipations are far more powerful than interpretations; because being collected from a few instances, and those for the most part of familiar occurrence, they straightway touch the understanding and fill the imagination; whereas interpretations on the other hand, being gathered here and there from very various and widely dispersed facts, cannot suddenly strike the understanding; and therefore they must needs, in respect of the opinions of the time, seem harsh and out of tune; much as the mysteries of faith do.

xxix

In sciences founded on opinions and dogmas, the use of anticipations and logic is good; for in them the object is to command assent to the proposition, not to master the thing.

xxx

Though all the wits of all the ages should meet together and combine and transmit their labors, yet will no great progress ever be made in science by means of anticipations; because radical errors in the first concoction of the mind are not to be cured by the excellence of functions and remedies subsequent.

xxxi

It is idle to expect any great advancement in science from the superinducing and engrafting of new things upon old. We must begin anew from the very foundations, unless we would revolve forever in a circle with mean and contemptible progress.

xxxii

The honor of the ancient authors, and indeed of all, remains untouched; since the comparison I challenge is not of wits or faculties, but of ways and methods, and the part I take upon myself is not that of a judge, but of a guide.

xxxiii

This must be plainly avowed: no judgment can be rightly formed either of my method or of the discoveries to which it leads, by means of anticipations; since I cannot be called on to abide by the sentence of a tribunal which is itself on its trial.

xxxiv

Even to deliver and explain what I bring forward is no easy matter; for things in themselves new will yet be apprehended with reference to what is old.

xxxv

It was said by Borgia of the expedition of the French into Italy, that they came with chalk in their hands to mark out their lodgings, not with arms to force their way in. I in like manner would have my doctrine enter quietly into the minds that are fit and capable of receiving it; for confutations cannot be employed, when the difference is upon first principles and very notions and even upon forms of demonstration.

xxxvi

One method of delivery alone remains to us; which is simply this: we must lead men to the particulars themselves, and their series and order; while men on their side must force themselves for a while to lay their notions by and begin to familiarize themselves with facts.

xxxvii

The doctrine of those who have denied that certainty could be attained at all, has some agreement with my way of proceeding at the first setting out; but they end in being infinitely separated and opposed. For the holders of that doctrine assert simply that nothing can be known; I also assert that not much can be known in nature by the way which is now in use. But then they go on to destroy the authority of the senses and understanding; whereas I proceed to devise and supply helps for the same.

xxxviii

The idols and false notions which are now in possession of the human understanding, and have taken deep root therein, not only so beset men's minds that truth can hardly find entrance, but even after entrance obtained, they will again in the very instauration of the sciences meet and trouble us, unless men being forewarned of the danger fortify themselves as far as may be against their assaults.

xxxix

There are four classes of idols which beset men's minds. To these for distinction's sake I have assigned names,—calling the first class *Idols of the Tribe;* the second, *Idols of the Cave;* the third, *Idols of the Market Place;* the fourth, *Idols of the Theater.*

xl

The formation of ideas and axioms by true induction is no doubt the proper remedy to be applied for the keeping off and clearing away of idols. To point them out, however, is of great use, for the doctrine of idols is to the interpretation of nature what the doctrine of the refutation of sophisms is to common logic.

xli

The *Idols of the Tribe* have their foundation in human nature itself, and in the tribe or race of men. For it is a false assertion that the sense of man is the measure of things. On the contrary, all perceptions, as well of the sense as of the mind, are according to the measure of the individual and not according to the measure of the universe. And the human understanding is like a false mirror, which, receiving rays irregularly, distorts and discolors the nature of things by mingling its own nature with it.

xlii

The *Idols of the Cave* are the idols of the individual man. For everyone has a cave or den of his own, which refracts and discolors the light of nature; owing either to his own proper and peculiar nature or to his education and conversation with others; or to the reading of books, and the authority of those whom he esteems and admires; or to the differences of impressions, accordingly as they take place in a mind preoccupied and predisposed or in a mind indifferent and settled; or the like. So that the spirit of man is in fact a thing variable and full of perturbation, and governed as it were by chance. Whence it was well observed by Heraclitus that men look for sciences in their own lesser worlds, and not in the greater or common world.

xliii

There are also idols formed by the intercourse and association of men with each other, which I call *Idols of the Market Place,* on account of the commerce and consort of men there. For it is by discourse that men associate; and words are imposed according to the apprehension of the vulgar. And therefore the ill and unfit choice of words wonderfully obstructs the understanding. Nor do the definitions or explanations wherewith in some things learned men are wont to guard and defend themselves, by any means set the matter right. But words plainly force and overrule the understanding, and throw all into confusion, and lead men away into numberless empty controversies and idle fancies.

xliv

Lastly, there are idols which have immigrated into men's minds from the various dogmas of philosophies, and also from wrong laws of demonstration. These I call *Idols of the Theater;* because in my judgment all the received systems are but so many stage-plays, representing worlds of their own creation after an unreal and scenic fashion. Nor is it only of the systems now in vogue, or only of the ancient sects and philosophies, that I speak: for many more plays of the same kind may yet be composed and in like artificial manner set forth; seeing that errors the most widely different have nevertheless causes for the most part alike. Neither again do I mean this only of entire systems, but also of many principles and axioms in science, which by tradition, credulity, and negligence have come to be received.

xlv

The human understanding is of its own nature prone to suppose the existence of more order and regularity in the world than it finds. And though there be many things in nature which are singular and unmatched, yet it devises for them parallels and conjugates and relatives which do not exist.

xlvi

The human understanding when it has once adopted an opinion (either as being the received opinion or as being agreeable to itself) draws all things else to support and agree with it. And though there be a greater number and weight of instances to be found on the other side, yet these it either neglects and despises, or else by some distinction sets aside and rejects; in order that by this great and pernicious predetermination the authority of its former conclusions may remain inviolate.

xlvii

The human understanding is moved by those things most which strike and enter the mind simultaneously and suddenly, and so fill the imagination; and then it feigns and supposes all other things to be somehow, though it cannot see how, similar to those few things by which it is surrounded. But for that going to and fro to remote and heterogeneous instances, by which axioms are tried as in the fire, the intellect is altogether slow and unfit, unless it be forced thereto by severe laws and overruling authority.

xlviii

The human understanding is unquiet; it cannot stop or rest, and still presses onward, but in vain. Therefore it is that we cannot conceive of any end or limit to the world; but always as of necessity it occurs to us that there is something beyond. Neither again can it be conceived how eternity has flowed down to the present day: for that distinction which is commonly received of infinity in time past and in time to come can by no means hold; for it would thence follow that one infinity is greater than another, and that infinity is wasting away and tending to become finite. The like subtlety arises touching the infinite divisibility of lines, from the same inability of thought to stop.

xlix

The human understanding is no dry light, but receives an infusion from the will and affections; whence proceed sciences which may be called "sciences as one would." For what a man had rather were true he more readily believes.

l

But by far the greatest hindrance and aberration of the human understanding proceeds from the dullness, incompetency, and deceptions of the senses; in that things which strike the sense outweigh things which do not immediately strike it, though they be more important. Hence it is that speculation commonly ceases where sight ceases, insomuch that of things invisible there is little or no observation. Hence all the working of the spirits inclosed in tangible bodies lies hid and unobserved of men. So also all the more subtle changes of form in the parts of coarser substances are in like manner unobserved. And yet unless these two things just mentioned be searched out and brought to light, nothing great can be achieved in nature, as far as the production of works is concerned.

li

The human understanding is of its own nature prone to abstractions and gives a substance and reality to things which are fleeting. But to resolve nature into abstractions is less to our purpose than to dissect her into parts; as did the school of Democritus, which went further into nature than the rest. Matter rather than forms should be the object of our attention, its configurations and changes of configuration, and simple action, and law of action or motion; for forms are figments of the human mind, unless you will call those laws of action forms.

lii

Such then are the idols which I call *Idols of the Tribe;* and which take their rise either from the homogeneity of the substance of the human spirit, or from its preoccupation, or from its narrowness, or from its restless motion, or from an infusion of the affections, or from the incompetency of the senses, or from the mode of impression.

liii

The *Idols of the Cave* take their rise in the peculiar constitution, mental or bodily, of each individual; and also in education, habit, and accident. Of this kind there is a great number and variety; but I will instance those the pointing out of which contains the most important caution, and which have most effect in disturbing the clearness of the understanding.

liv

Men become attached to certain particular sciences and speculations, either because they fancy themselves the authors and inventors thereof, or because they have bestowed the greatest pains upon them and become most habituated to them. But men of this kind, if they betake themselves to philosophy and contemplations of a general character, distort and color them in obedience to their former fancies; a thing especially to be noticed in Aristotle, who made his natural philosophy a mere bondservant to his logic, thereby rendering it contentious and well nigh useless.

lv

There is one principal and as it were radical distinction between different minds, in respect of philosophy and the sciences; which is this: that some minds are stronger and apter to mark the differences of things, others to mark their resemblances. The steady and acute mind can fix its contemplations and dwell and fasten on the subtlest distinctions; the lofty and discursive mind recognizes and puts together the finest and most general resemblances. Both kinds however easily err in excess, by catching the one at gradations the other at shadows.

lvi

There are found some minds given to an extreme admiration of antiquity, others to an extreme love and appetite for novelty; but few so duly tempered that they can hold the mean, neither carping at what has been well laid down by the ancients, nor despising what is well introduced by the moderns. This however turns to the great injury of the sciences and philosophy: since these affectations of antiquity and novelty are the humors of partisans rather than judgments; and truth is to be sought for not in the felicity of any age, which is an unstable thing, but in the light of nature and experience, which is eternal. These factions therefore must be abjured, and care must be taken that the intellect be not hurried by them into assent.

lvii

Contemplations of nature and of bodies in their simple form break up and distract the understanding, while contemplations of nature and bodies in their composition and configuration overpower and dissolve the understanding: a distinction well seen in the school of Leucippus and Democritus as compared with the other philosophies. For that school is so busied with the particles that it hardly attends to the structure; while the others are so lost in admiration of the structure that they do not penetrate to the simplicity of nature. These kinds of contemplation should therefore be alternated and taken by turns; that so the understanding may be rendered at once penetrating and comprehensive, and the inconveniences above mentioned, with the idols which proceed from them, may be avoided.

lviii

Let such then be our provision and contemplative prudence for keeping off and dislodging the *Idols of the Cave,* which grow for the most part either out of the predominance of a favorite subject, or out of an excessive tendency to compare or to distinguish, or out of partiality for particular ages, or out of the largeness or minuteness of the objects contemplated. And generally let every student of nature take this as a rule, —that whatever his mind seizes and dwells upon with peculiar satisfaction is to be held in suspicion, and that so much the more care is to be taken in dealing with such questions to keep the understanding even and clear.

lix

But the *Idols of the Market Place* are the most troublesome of all: idols which have crept into the understanding through the alliances of words and names. For men believe that their reason governs words; but it is also true that words react on the understanding; and this it is that has rendered philosophy and the sciences sophistical and inactive. Now words, being commonly framed and applied according to the capacity of the vulgar, follow those lines of division which are most obvious to the vulgar understanding. And whenever an understanding of greater acuteness or a more diligent observation would alter those lines to suit the true divisions of nature, words stand in the way and resist the change. Whence it comes to pass that the high and formal discussions of learned men end oftentimes in disputes about words and names; with which it would be more prudent to begin, and so by means of definitions reduce them to order. Yet even definitions cannot cure this evil in dealing with natural and material things; since the definitions themselves consist of words, and those words beget others: so that it is necessary to recur to individual instances, and those in due series and order; as I shall say presently when I come to the method and scheme for the formation of notions and axioms.

lx

The idols imposed by words on the understanding are of two kinds. They are either names of things which do not exist, or they are names of things which exist, but yet confused and ill-defined, and hastily and irregularly derived from realities. And this class of idols is more easily expelled, because to get rid of them it is only necessary that all theories should be steadily rejected and dismissed as obsolete.

But the other class, which springs out of a faulty and unskillful abstraction, is intricate and deeply rooted.

lxi

But the *Idols of the Theater* are not innate, nor do they steal into the understanding secretly, but are plainly impressed and received into the mind from the play-books of philosophical systems and the perverted rules of demonstration. To attempt refutations in this case would be merely inconsistent with what I have already said: for since we agree neither upon principles nor upon demonstrations there is no place for argument.

lxii

Idols of the Theater, or of Systems, are many, and there can be and perhaps will be yet many more. For were it not that now for many ages men's minds have been busied with religion and theology; and were it not that civil governments, especially monarchies, have been averse to such novelties, even in matters speculative; so that men labor therein to the peril and harming of their fortunes,—not only unrewarded, but exposed also to contempt and envy: doubtless there would have arisen many other philosophical sects like to those which in great variety flourished once among the Greeks. For as on the phenomena of the heavens many hypotheses may be constructed, so likewise many various dogmas may be set up and established on the phenomena of philosophy. And in the plays of this philosophical theater you may observe the same thing which is found in the theater of the poets, that stories invented for the stage are more compact and elegant, and more as one would wish them to be, than true stories out of history.

So that this parent stock of errors—this false philosophy—is of three kinds; the *sophistical,* the *empirical,* and the *superstitious.*

lxiii

The most conspicuous example of the first class was Aristotle, who corrupted natural philosophy by his logic: fashioning the world out of categories; assigning to the human soul, the noblest of substances, a genus from words of the second intention; doing the business of density and rarity by the frigid distinction of act and power; asserting that single bodies have each a single and proper motion, and that if they participate in any other, then this results from an external cause; and imposing countless other arbitrary restrictions on the nature of things: being always more solicitous to provide an answer to the question and affirm something positive in words, than about the inner truth of things; a failing best shown when his philosophy is compared with other systems of note among the Greeks.

lxiv

But the empirical school of philosophy gives birth to dogmas more deformed and monstrous than the sophistical or rational school. For it has its foundations not in the light of common notions but in the narrowness and darkness of a few experiments. To those therefore who are daily busied with these experiments, and have infected their imagination with them, such a philosophy seems probable and all but certain; to all men else incredible and vain.

lxv

But the corruption of philosophy by superstition and an admixture of theology is far more widely spread, and does the greatest harm, whether to entire systems or to their parts. For the human understanding is obnoxious to the influence of the imagination no less than to the influence of common notions. For the contentious and sophistical kind of philosophy ensnares the understanding; but this kind, being fanciful and tumid and half poetical, misleads it more by flattery. For there is in man an ambition of the understanding, no less than of the will, especially in high and lofty spirits.

lxvi

So much then for the mischievous authorities of systems, which are founded either on common notions, or on a few experiments, or on superstition. It remains to speak of the faulty subject-matter of contemplations, especially in natural philosophy. Now the human understanding is infected by the sight of what takes place in the mechanical arts, in which the alteration of bodies proceeds chiefly by composition or separation, and so imagines that something similar goes on in the universal nature of things. From this source has flowed the fiction of elements, and of their concourse for the formation of natural bodies. Again, when man contemplates nature working freely, he meets with different species of things, of animals, of plants, of minerals; whence he readily passes into the opinion that there are in nature certain primary forms which nature intends to educe, and that the remaining variety proceeds from hindrances and aberrations of nature in the fulfillment of her work, or from the collision of different species and the transplanting of one into another. To the first of these speculations we owe our primary qualities of the elements; to the other our occult properties and specific virtues; and both of them belong to those empty *compendia* of thought wherein the mind rests, and whereby it is diverted from more solid pursuits. It is to better purpose that the physicians bestow their labor on the secondary qualities of matter, and the operations of attraction, repulsion, attenuation, conspissation, dilatation, astriction, dissipation, maturation, and the like; and were it not that by those two compendia which I have mentioned they corrupted their correct observations in these other matters,—either reducing them to first qualities and their subtle and incommensurable mixtures, or not following them out with greater and more diligent observation to third and fourth qualities, but breaking off the scrutiny prematurely,—they had made much greater progress. Nor are powers of this kind to be sought for only in the medicines of the human body, but also in the changes of all other bodies.

lxvii

A caution must also be given to the understanding against the intemperance which systems of philosophy manifest in giving or withholding assent; because intemperance of this kind seems to establish idols and in some sort to perpetuate them, leaving no way open to reach and dislodge them.

This excess is of two kinds: the first being manifest in those who are ready in deciding; and render sciences dogmatic and magisterial; the other in those who deny that we can know anything, and so introduce a wandering kind of inquiry that leads to nothing; of which kinds the former subdues, the latter weakens the understanding.

lxviii

So much concerning the several classes of idols, and their equipage: all of which must be renounced and put away with a fixed and solemn determination, and the understanding thoroughly freed and cleansed; the entrance into the kingdom of man, founded on the sciences, being not much other than the entrance into the kingdom of heaven, whereinto none may enter except as a little child.

lxix

But vicious demonstrations are as the strongholds and defenses of idols; and those we have in logic do little else than make the world the bondslave of human thought, and human thought the bondslave of words. Demonstrations truly are in effect the philosophies themselves and the sciences. For such as *they* are, well or ill established, such are the systems of philosophy and the contemplations which follow. Now in the whole of the process which leads from the sense and objects to axioms and conclusions, the demonstrations which we use are deceptive and incompetent. This process consists of four parts, and has as many faults. In the first place, the impressions of the sense itself are faulty; for the sense both fails us and deceives us. But its shortcomings are to be supplied, and its deceptions to be corrected. Secondly, notions are ill drawn from the impressions of the senses, and are indefinite and confused, whereas they should be definite and distinctly bounded. Thirdly, the induction is amiss which infers the principles of sciences by simple enumeration, and does not, as it ought, employ exclusions and solutions (or separations) of nature. Lastly, that method of discovery and proof according to which the most general principles are first established, and then intermediate axioms are tried and proved by them, is the parent of error and the curse of all science.

lxx

But the best demonstration by far is experience, if it go not beyond the actual experiment. For if it be transferred to other cases which are deemed similar, unless such transfer be made by a just and orderly process, it is a fallacious thing. But the manner of making experiments which men now use is blind and stupid. And therefore, wandering and straying as they do with no settled course, and taking counsel only from things as they fall out, they fetch a wide circuit and meet with many matters, but make little progress; and sometimes are full of hope, sometimes are distracted; and always find that there is something beyond to be sought. For it generally happens that men make their trials carelessly, and as it were in play; slightly varying experiments already known, and, if the thing does not answer, growing weary and abandoning the attempt. And even if they apply themselves to experiments more seriously and earnestly and laboriously, still they spend their labor in working out some one experiment, as Gilbert with the magnet, and the chemists with gold,—a course of proceeding not less unskillful in the design than small in the attempt. For no one successfully investigates the nature of a thing in the thing itself; the inquiry must be enlarged, so as to become more general.

lxxi

The sciences which we possess come for the most part from the Greeks. For what has been added by Roman, Arabic, or later writers is not much nor of much importance; and whatever it is, it is built on the foundation of Greek discoveries. Now the wisdom of the Greeks was professorial and much given to disputations; a kind of wisdom most adverse to the inquisition of truth.

lxxii

Nor does the character of the time and age yield much better signs than the character of the country and nation. For at that period there was but a narrow and meager knowledge either of time or place; which is the worst thing that can be, especially for those who rest all on experience. For they had no history, worthy to be called history, that went back a thousand years; but only fables and rumors of antiquity. In our times on the other hand both many parts of the New World and the limits on every side of the Old World are known, and our stock of experience has increased to an infinite amount. Wherefore if we draw signs from the season of their nativity or birth, nothing great can be predicted of those systems of philosophy.

lxxiii

Of all signs there is none more certain or more noble than that taken from fruits. For fruits and works are as it were sponsors and sureties for the truth of philosophies. Now, from all these systems of the Greeks and their ramifications through particular sciences there can hardly after the lapse of so many years be adduced a single experiment which tends to relieve and benefit the condition of man, and which can with truth be referred to the speculations and theories of philosophy.

Some little has indeed been produced by the industry of chemists; but it has been produced accidentally and in passing, or else by a kind of variation of experiments, such as mechanics use; and not by any art or theory; for the theory which they have devised rather confuses the experiments than aids them. They too who have busied themselves with natural magic, as they call it, have but few discoveries to show, and those trifling and imposture-like. Wherefore, as in religion we are warned to show our faith by works, so in philosophy by the same rule the system should be judged of by its fruits, and pronounced frivolous if it be barren; more especially if, in place of fruits of grape and olive, it bear thorns and briars of dispute and contention.

lxxiv

Signs also are to be drawn from the increase and progress of systems and sciences. For what is founded on nature grows and increases; while what is founded on opinion varies but increases not. If therefore those doctrines had not plainly been like a plant torn up from its roots, but had remained attached to the womb of nature and continued to draw nourishment from her, that could never have come to pass which we have seen now for twice a thousand years; namely, that the sciences stand where they did and remain almost in the same condition; receiving no noticeable increase, but on the contrary, thriving most under their first founder, and then declining. Whereas in the mechanical arts, which are founded on nature and the light of experience, we see the contrary happen, for these are continually thriving and growing, as having in them a breath of life; at first rude, then convenient, afterwards adorned, and at all times advancing.

lxxv

There is still another sign remaining; I mean the confession of the very authorities whom men now follow. For even they who lay down the law on all things so confidently, do still in their more sober moods fall to complaints of the subtlety of nature, the obscurity of things, and the weakness of the human mind. Now if this were all they did, some perhaps of a timid disposition might be deterred from further search, while others of a more ardent and hopeful spirit might be whetted and incited to go on farther. But not content to speak for themselves, whatever is beyond their own or their master's knowledge or reach they set down as beyond the bounds of possibility, and pronounce, as if on the authority of their art, that it cannot be known or done; thus most presumptuously and invidiously turning the weakness of their own discoveries into a calumny on nature herself, and the despair of the rest of the world.

lxxvi

Neither is this other sign to be omitted;—that formerly there existed among philosophers such great disagreement, and such diversities in the schools themselves; a fact which sufficiently shows that the road from the senses to the understanding was not skillfully laid out, when the same groundwork of philosophy was torn and split up into such vague and multifarious errors. And although in these times disagreements and diversities of opinion on first principles and entire systems are for the most part extinguished, still on parts of philosophy there remain innumerable questions and disputes, so that it plainly appears that neither in the systems themselves nor in the modes of demonstration is there anything certain or sound.

lxxvii

And as for the general opinion that in the philosophy of Aristotle at any rate there is great agreement; since after its publication the systems of older philosophers died away, while in the times which followed nothing better was found; so that it seems to have been so well laid and established as to have drawn both ages in its train; I answer in the first place, that the common notion of the falling off of the old systems upon the publication of Aristotle's works is a false one; for long afterwards, down even to the times of Cicero and subsequent ages, the works of the old philosophers still remained. But in the times which followed, when on the inundation of barbarians into the Roman empire human learning had suffered shipwreck, then the systems of Aristotle and Plato, like planks of lighter and less solid material, floated on the waves of time, and were preserved. Upon the point of consent also men are deceived, if the matter be looked into more keenly. For true consent is that which consists in the coincidence of free judgments, after due examination. But far the greater number of those who have assented to the philosophy of Aristotle have addicted themselves thereto from prejudgment and upon the authority of others; so that it is a following and going along together, rather than consent. But even if it had been a real and widespread consent, still so little ought consent to be deemed a sure and solid confirmation, that it is in fact a strong presumption the other way.

lxxviii

I now come to the *causes* of these errors, and of so long a continuance in them through so many ages; which are very many and very potent; —that all wonder how these considerations which I bring forward should have escaped men's notice till now, may cease; and the only wonder be, how now at last they should have entered into any man's head and become the subject of his thoughts; which truly I myself esteem as the result of some happy accident, rather than of any excellence of faculty in me; a birth of time rather than a birth of wit. Now, in the first place, those so many ages, if you weigh the case truly, shrink into a very small compass. For out of the five and twenty centuries over which the memory and learning of men extends, you can hardly pick out six that were fertile in sciences or favorable to their development. In times no less than in regions there are wastes and deserts.

lxxix

In the second place there presents itself a cause of great weight in all ways; namely, that during those very ages in which the wits and learning of men have flourished most, or indeed flourished at all, the least part of their diligence was given to natural philosophy. Yet this very philosophy it is that ought to be esteemed the great mother of the sciences. For all arts and all sciences, if torn from this root, though they may be polished and shaped and made fit for use, yet they will hardly grow.

lxxx

To this it may be added that natural philosophy, even among those who have attended to it, has scarcely ever possessed, especially in these later times, a disengaged and whole man (unless it were some monk studying in his cell, or some gentleman in his country house), but that it has been made merely a passage and bridge to something else. And so this great mother of the sciences has with strange indignity been degraded to the offices of a servant; having to attend on the business of medicine or mathematics, and likewise to wash and imbue youthful and unripe wits with a sort of first dye, in order that they may be the fitter to receive another afterwards. Meanwhile let no man look for much progress in the sciences—especially in the practical part of them—unless natural philosophy be carried on and applied to particular sciences, and particular sciences be carried back again to natural philosophy.

lxxxi

Again there is another great and powerful cause why the sciences have made but little progress; which is this: it is not possible to run a course aright when the goal itself has not been rightly placed. Now the true and lawful goal of the sciences is none other than this: that human life be endowed with new discoveries and powers. But of this the great majority have no feeling, but are merely hireling and professorial; except when it occasionally happens that some workman of acuter wit and covetous of honor applies himself to a new invention; which he mostly does at the expense of his fortunes. But in general, so far are men from proposing to themselves to augment the mass of arts and sciences, that from the mass already at hand they neither take nor look for anything more than what they may turn to use in their lectures, or to gain, or to reputation, or to some similar advantage.

lxxxii

And as men have misplaced the end and goal of the sciences; so again, even if they had placed it right, yet they have chosen a way to it which is altogether erroneous and impassable. And an astonishing thing it is to one who rightly considers the matter, that no mortal should have seriously applied himself to the opening and laying out of a road for the human understanding direct from the sense, by a course of experiment orderly conducted and well built up; but that all has been left either to the mist of tradition, or the whirl and eddy of argument, or the fluctuations and mazes of chance and of vague and ill-digested experience.

lxxxiii

This evil however has been strangely increased by an opinion or conceit, which though of long standing is vain and hurtful; namely, that the dignity of the human mind is impaired by long and close intercourse with experiments and particulars, subject to sense and bound in matter; especially as they are laborious to search, ignoble to meditate, harsh to deliver, illiberal to practice, infinite in number, and minute in subtlety. So that it has come at length to this, that the true way is not merely deserted, but shut out and stopped up; experience being, I do not say abandoned or badly managed, but rejected with disdain.

lxxxiv

Again, men have been kept back as by a kind of enchantment from progress in the sciences by reverence for antiquity, by the authority of men accounted great in philosophy, and then by general consent.

lxxxv

Nor is it only the admiration of antiquity, authority, and consent that has forced the industry of man to rest satisfied with the discoveries already made; but also an admiration for the works themselves of which the human race has long been in possession. For when a man looks at the variety and the beauty of the provision which the mechanical arts have brought together for men's use, he will certainly be more inclined to admire the wealth of man than to feel his wants: not considering that the original observations and operations of nature are not many nor deeply fetched, and that the rest is but patience, and the subtle and ruled motion of the hand and instruments;—as the making of clocks is certainly a subtle and exact work: their wheels seem to imitate the celestial orbs, and their alternating and orderly motion, the pulse of animals: and yet all this depends on one or two axioms of nature.

lxxxvi

Further, this admiration of men for knowledges and arts,—an admiration in itself weak enough, and well-nigh childish,—has been increased by the craft and artifices of those who have handled and transmitted sciences. For they set them forth with such ambition and parade, and bring them into the view of the world so fashioned and masked, as if they were complete in all parts and finished. For if you look at the method of them and the divisions, they seem to embrace and comprise everything which can belong to the subject. And although these divisions are ill filled out and are but as empty cases, still to the common mind they present the form and plan of a perfect science. But the first and most ancient seekers after truth were wont, with better faith and better fortune too, to throw the knowledge which they gathered from the contemplation of things, and which they meant to store up for use, into aphorisms; that is, into short and scattered sentences, not linked together by an artificial method; and did not pretend or profess to embrace the entire art. But as the matter now is, it is nothing strange if men do not seek to advance in things delivered to them as long since perfect and complete.

lxxxvii

Moreover the ancient systems have received no slight accession of reputation and credit from the vanity and levity of those who have propounded new ones; especially in the active and practical department of natural philosophy.

lxxxviii

Far more however has knowledge suffered from littleness of spirit and the smallness and slightness of the tasks which human industry has proposed to itself. And what is worst of all, this very littleness of spirit comes with a certain air of arrogance and superiority.

Thus then it is no wonder if noble inventions and worthy of mankind have not been brought to light, when men have been contented and delighted with such trifling and puerile tasks, and have even fancied that in them they have been endeavoring after, if not accomplishing, some great matter.

lxxxix

Neither is it to be forgotten that in every age natural philosophy has had a troublesome adversary and hard to deal with; namely, superstition, and the blind and immoderate zeal of religion.

xc

Again, in the customs and institutions of schools, academies, colleges, and similar bodies destined for the abode of learned men and the cultivation of learning, everything is found adverse to the progress of science.

For the lectures and exercises there are so ordered, that to think or speculate on anything out of the common way can hardly occur to any man. And if one or two have the boldness to use any liberty of judgment, they must undertake the task all by themselves; they can have no advantage from the company of others. And if they can endure this also, they will find their industry and largeness of mind no slight hindrance to their fortune.

xci

Nay, even if that jealousy were to cease, still it is enough to check the growth of science, that efforts and labors in this field go unrewarded. For it does not rest with the same persons to cultivate sciences and to reward them. The growth of them comes from great wits; the prizes and rewards of them are in the hands of the people, or of great persons, who are but in very few cases even moderately learned. Moreover this kind of progress is not only unrewarded with prizes and substantial benefits; it has not even the advantage of popular applause. For it is a greater matter than the generality of men can take in, and is apt to be overwhelmed and extinguished by the gales of popular opinions. And it is nothing strange if a thing not held in honor does not prosper.

xcii

But by far the greatest obstacle to the progress of science and to the undertaking of new tasks and provinces therein, is found in this—that men despair and think things impossible. For wise and serious men are wont in these matters to be altogether distrustful; considering with themselves the obscurity of nature, the shortness of life, the deceitfulness of the senses, the weakness of the judgment, the difficulty of experiment and the like; and so supposing that in the revolution of time and of the ages of the world the sciences have their ebbs and flows; that at one season they grow and flourish, at another wither and decay, yet in such sort that when they have reached a certain point and condition they can advance no further. If therefore anyone believes or promises more, they think this comes of an ungoverned and unripened mind, and that such attempts have prosperous beginnings, become difficult as they go on, and end in confusion. Now since these are thoughts which naturally present themselves to grave men and of great judgment, we must take good heed that we be not led away by our love for a most fair and excellent object to relax or diminish the severity of our judgment; we must observe diligently what encouragement dawns upon us and from what quarter; and, putting aside the lighter breeze of hope, we must thoroughly sift and examine those which promise greater steadiness and constancy. Nay, and we must take state-prudence too into our counsels, whose rule is to distrust, and to take the less favorable view of human affairs. I am now therefore to speak touching *hope*.

xciii

The beginning is from God: for the business which is in hand, having the character of good so strongly impressed upon it, appears manifestly to proceed from God, who is the Author of Good, and the Father of Lights. Now in divine operations even the smallest beginnings lead of a certainty to their end.

xciv

Next comes a consideration of the greatest importance as an argument of hope; I mean that drawn from the errors of past time, and of the ways hitherto trodden. For most excellent was the censure once passed upon a government that had been unwisely administered. "That which is the worst thing in reference to the past, ought to be regarded as best for the future. For if you had done all that your duty demanded, and yet your affairs were no better, you would not have even a hope left you that further improvement is possible. But now, when your misfortunes are owing, not to the force of circumstances, but to your own errors, you may hope that by dismissing or correcting these errors, a great change may be made for the better."

xcv

Those who have handled sciences have been either men of experiment or men of dogmas. The men of experiment are like the ant; they only collect and use: the reasoners resemble spiders, who make cobwebs out of their own substance. But the bee takes a middle course, it gathers its material from the flowers of the garden and of the field, but transforms and digests it by a power of its own. Not unlike this is the true business of philosophy: for it neither relies solely or chiefly on the powers of the mind, nor does it take the matter which it gathers from natural history and mechanical experiments and lay it up in the memory whole, as it finds it; but lays it up in the understanding altered and digested.

xcvi

We have as yet no natural philosophy that is pure; all is tainted and corrupted: in Aristotle's school by logic; in Plato's by natural theology;

in the second school of Platonists, such as Proclus and others, by mathematics, which ought only to give definiteness to natural philosophy, not to generate or give it birth. From a natural philosophy pure and unmixed, better things are to be expected.

xcvii

No one has yet been found so firm of mind and purpose as resolutely to compel himself to sweep away all theories and common notions, and to apply the understanding, thus made fair and even, to a fresh examination of particulars. Thus it happens that human knowledge, as we have it, is a mere medley and ill-digested mass, made up of much credulity and much accident, and also of the childish notions which we at first imbibed.

Now if anyone of ripe age, unimpaired senses, and well-purged mind apply himself anew to experience and particulars, better hopes may be entertained of that man.

xcviii

Now for grounds of experience—since to experience we must come— we have as yet had either none or very weak ones; no search has been made to collect a store of particular observations sufficient either in number, or in kind, or in certainty, to inform the understanding, or in any way adequate. On the contrary, men of learning, but easy withal and idle, have taken for the construction or for the confirmation of their philosophy certain rumors and vague fames or airs of experience, and allowed to these the weight of lawful evidence. And just as if some kingdom or state were to direct its counsels and affairs, not by letters and reports from ambassadors and trustworthy messengers, but by the gossip of the streets; such exactly is the system of management introduced into philosophy with relation to experience.

xcix

Again, even in the great plenty of mechanical experiments, there is yet a great scarcity of those which are of most use for the information of the understanding. For the mechanic, not troubling himself with the investigation of truth, confines his attention to those things which bear upon his particular work, and will not either raise his mind or stretch out his hand for anything else. But then only will there be good ground of hope for the further advance of knowledge, when there shall be received and gathered together into natural history a variety of experiments, which are of no use in themselves, but simply serve to discover causes and axioms; which I call *experimenta lucifera,* experiments of *light,* to distinguish them from those which I call *fructifera,* experiments of *fruit.*

c

But not only is a greater abundance of experiments to be sought for and procured, and that too of a different kind from those hitherto tried; an entirely different method, order, and process for carrying on and advancing experience must also be introduced. For experience, when it wanders in its own track, is, as I have already remarked, mere groping in the dark, and confounds men rather than instructs them. But when it shall proceed in accordance with a fixed law, in regular order, and without interruption, then may better things be hoped of knowledge.

ci

But even after such a store of natural history and experience as is required for the work of the understanding, or of philosophy, shall be ready at hand, still the understanding is by no means competent to deal with it offhand and by memory alone; no more than if a man should hope by force of memory to retain and make himself master of the computation of an ephemeris. And yet hitherto more has been done in matter of invention by thinking than by writing; and experience has not yet learned her letters. Now no course of invention can be satisfactory unless it be carried on in writing. But when this is brought into use, and experience has been taught to read and write, better things may be hoped.

cii

Moreover, since there is so great a number and army of particulars, and that army so scattered and dispersed as to distract and confound the understanding, little is to be hoped for from the skirmishings and slight attacks and desultory movements of the intellect, unless all the particulars which pertain to the subject of inquiry shall, by means of Tables of Discovery, apt, well arranged, and as it were animate, be drawn up and marshaled; and the mind be set to work upon the helps duly prepared and digested which these tables supply.

ciii

But after this store of particulars has been set out duly and in order before our eyes, we are not to pass at once to the investigation and discovery of new particulars or works; or at any rate if we do so we must not stop there. For although I do not deny that when all the experiments of all the arts shall have been collected and digested, and brought within one man's knowledge and judgment, the mere transferring of the experiments of one art to others may lead, by means of that experience which I term *literate,* to the discovery of many new things of service to the life and state of man; yet it is no great matter that can be hoped from that: but from the new light of axioms, which having been educed from those particulars by a certain method and rule, shall in their turn point out the way again to new particulars, greater things may be looked for. For our road does not lie on a level, but ascends and descends; first ascending to axioms, then descending to works.

civ

The understanding must not however be allowed to jump and fly from particulars to remote axioms and of almost the highest generality (such as the first principles, as they are called, of arts and things), and taking stand upon them as truths that cannot be shaken, proceed to prove and frame the middle axioms by reference to them: which has been the practice hitherto; the understanding being not only carried that way by a natural impulse, but also by the use of syllogistic demonstration trained and inured to it. But then, and then only, may we hope well of the sciences, when in a just scale of ascent, and by successive steps not interrupted or broken, we rise from particulars to lesser axioms; and then to middle axioms, one above the other; and last of all to the most general.

cv

In establishing axioms, another form of induction must be devised than has hitherto been employed; and it must be used for proving and discovering not first principles only, but also the lesser axioms, and the middle, and indeed all. For the induction which proceeds by simple enumeration is childish; its conclusions are precarious, and exposed to peril from a contradictory instance; and it generally decides on too small a number of facts, and on those only which are at hand. But the induction which is to be available for the discovery and demonstration of sciences and arts, must analyze nature by proper rejections and exclusions; and then, after a sufficient number of negatives, come to a conclusion on the affirmative instances: which has not yet been done or even attempted, save only by Plato, who does indeed employ this form of induction to a certain extent for the purpose of discussing definitions and ideas. But in order to furnish this induction or demonstration well and duly for its work, very many things are to be provided which no mortal has yet thought of; insomuch that greater labor will have to be spent in it than has hitherto been spent on the syllogism. And this induction must be used not only to discover axioms, but also in the formation of notions. And it is in this induction that our chief hope lies.

cvi

But in establishing axioms by this kind of induction, we must also examine and try whether the axiom so established be framed to the measure of those particulars only from which it is derived, or whether it be larger and wider. And if it be larger and wider, we must observe whether by indicating to us new particulars it confirm that wideness and largeness as by a collateral security: that we may not either stick fast in things already known, or loosely grasp at shadows and abstract forms; not at things solid and realized in matter. And when this process shall have come into use, then at last shall we see the dawn of a solid hope.

cvii

And here also should be remembered what was said above concerning the extending of the range of natural philosophy to take in the particular sciences, and the referring or bringing back of the particular sciences to natural philosophy; that the branches of knowledge may not be severed and cut off from the stem. For without this the hope of progress will not be so good.

cviii

So much then for the removing of despair and the raising of hope through the dismissal or rectification of the errors of past time. We must now see what else there is to ground hope upon. And this consideration occurs at once—that if many useful discoveries have been made by accident or upon occasion, when men were not seeking for them but were busy about other things; no one can doubt but that when they apply themselves to seek and make this their business, and that too by method and in order and not by desultory impulses, they will discover far more.

cix

Another argument of hope may be drawn from this—that some of the inventions already known are such as before they were discovered it could hardly have entered any man's head to think of; they would have been simply set aside as impossible. For in conjecturing what may be men set before them the example of what has been, and divine of the new with an imagination preoccupied and colored by the old; which way of forming opinions is very fallacious; for streams that are drawn from the springheads of nature do not always run in the old channels.

There is therefore much ground for hoping that there are still laid up in the womb of nature many secrets of excellent use, having no affinity or parallelism with anything that is now known, but lying entirely out of the beat of the imagination, which have not yet been found out. They too no doubt will some time or other, in the course and revolution of many ages, come to light of themselves, just as the others did; only by the method of which we are now treating they can be speedily and suddenly and simultaneously presented and anticipated.

cx

But we have also discoveries to show of another kind, which prove that noble inventions may be lying at our very feet, and yet mankind may step over without seeing them.

But such is the infelicity and unhappy disposition of the human mind· in this course of invention, that it first distrusts and then despises itself: first will not believe that any such thing can be found out; and when it is found out, cannot understand how the world should have missed it so long. And this very thing may be justly taken as an argument of hope; namely, that there is a great mass of inventions still remaining, which not only by means of operations that are yet to be discovered, but also through the transferring, comparing, and applying of those already known, by the help of that learned experience of which I spoke, may be deduced and brought to light.

cxi

There is another ground of hope that must not be omitted. Let men but think over their infinite expenditure of understanding, time, and means on matters and pursuits of far less use and value; whereof if but a small part were directed to sound and solid studies, there is no difficulty that might not be overcome. This I thought good to add, because I plainly confess that a collection of history natural and experimental, such as I conceive it and as it ought to be, is a great, I may say a royal work, and of much labor and expense.

cxii

Meantime, let no man be alarmed at the multitude of particulars, but let this rather encourage him to hope. For the particular phenomena of

art and nature are but a handful to the inventions of the wit, when dis-
joined and separated from the evidence of things. Moreover this road
has an issue in the open ground and not far off; the other has no issue
at all, but endless entanglement. For men hitherto have made but short
stay with experience, but passing her lightly by, have wasted an infinity
of time on meditations and glosses of the wit. But if someone were by
that could answer our questions and tell us in each case what the fact
in nature is, the discovery of all causes and sciences would be but the
work of a few years.

cxiii

Moreover I think that men may take some hope from my own example. And this I say not by way of boasting, but because it is useful
to say it. If there be any that despond, let them look at me, that being
of all men of my time the most busied in affairs of state, and a man of
health not very strong, and in this course altogether a pioneer, following
in no man's track, nor sharing these counsels with anyone, have nevertheless by resolutely entering on the true road, and submitting my mind to
things, advanced these matters, as I suppose, some little way. And then
let them consider what may be expected from men abounding in leisure,
and from association of labors, and from successions of ages: the rather
because it is not a way over which only one man can pass at a time, but
one in which the labors and industries of men may with the best effect
be first distributed and then combined. For then only will men begin to
know their strength, when instead of great numbers doing all the same
things, one shall take charge of one thing and another of another.

cxiv

Lastly, even if the breath of hope which blows on us from that new
continent were fainter than it is and harder to perceive; yet the trial
must by all means be made. For there is no comparison between that
which we may lose by not trying and by not succeeding; since by not
trying we throw away the chance of an immense good; by not succeeding
we only incur the loss of a little human labor. But as it is, it appears to
me from what has been said, and also from what has been left unsaid,
that there is hope enough and to spare, not only to make a bold man
try, but also to make a sober-minded and wise man believe.

cxv

Concerning the grounds then for putting away despair, which has
been one of the most powerful causes of delay and hindrance to the

progress of knowledge, I have now spoken. And this also concludes what I had to say touching the *signs* and *causes* of the errors, sluggishness, and ignorance which have prevailed; especially since the more subtle causes, which do not fall under popular judgment and observation, must be referred to what has been said on the idols of the human mind.

It is time therefore to proceed to the art itself and rule of interpreting nature; still however there remains something to be premised. For whereas in this first book of aphorisms I proposed to prepare men's minds as well for understanding as for receiving what is to follow; now that I have purged and swept and leveled the floor of the mind, it remains that I place the mind in a good position and as it were in a favorable aspect towards what I have to lay before it. For in a new matter, it is not only the strong preoccupation of some old opinion that tends to create a prejudice, but also a false preconception or prefiguration of the new thing which is presented. I will endeavor therefore to impart sound and true opinions as to the things I propose, although they are to serve only for the time and by way of interest (so to speak), till the thing itself, which is the principal, be fully known.

cxvi

First, then, I must request men not to suppose that after the fashion of ancient Greeks, and of certain moderns, as Telesius, Patricius, Severinus, I wish to found a new sect in philosophy. For this is not what I am about; nor do I think that it matters much to the fortunes of men what abstract notions one may entertain concerning nature and the principles of things; and no doubt many old theories of this kind can be revived and many new ones introduced; just as many theories of the heavens may be supposed, which agree well enough with the phenomena and yet differ with each other.

cxvii

And as I do not seek to found a school, so neither do I hold out offers or promises of particular works. It may be thought indeed, that I who make such frequent mention of works and refer everything to that end, should produce some myself by way of earnest. But my course and method, as I have often clearly stated and would wish to state again, is this—not to extract works from works or experiments from experiments, but from works and experiments to extract causes and axioms, and again from those causes and axioms new works and experiments, as a legitimate interpreter of nature. And although in my tables of discovery, and also in the examples of particulars (which I shall adduce in the second part), and moreover in my observations on the history, any reader of even moderate sagacity and intelligence will everywhere observe indications and outlines of many noble works; still I candidly confess that the natural history which I now have, whether collected from books or from my own investigations, is neither sufficiently copious nor verified with sufficient accuracy to serve the purposes of legitimate interpretation.

cxviii

It remains for me to say a few words touching the excellency of the end in view. Had they been uttered earlier, they might have seemed like idle wishes; but now that hopes have been raised and unfair prejudices removed, they may perhaps have greater weight. Also, if I had finished all myself, and had no occasion to call in others to help and take part in the work, I should even now have abstained from such language, lest it might be taken as a proclamation of my own deserts. But since I want to quicken the industry and rouse and kindle the zeal of others, it is fitting that I put men in mind of some things.

In the first place then, the introduction of famous discoveries appears to hold by far the first place among human actions; and this was the judgment of the former ages.

Again, discoveries are as it were new creations, and imitations of God's works.

Again, let a man only consider what a difference there is between the life of men in the most civilized province of Europe, and in the wildest and most barbarous districts of New India; he will feel it be great. enough to justify the saying that "man is a god to man," not only in regard of aid and benefit, but also by a comparison of condition. And this difference comes not from soil, not from climate, not from race, but from the arts.

Again, it is well to observe the force and virtue and consequences of discoveries; and these are to be seen nowhere more conspicuously than in those three which were unknown to the ancients, and of which the origin, though recent, is obscure and inglorious; namely, printing, gunpowder, and the magnet. For these three have changed the whole face and state of things throughout the world; the first in literature, the second in warfare, the third in navigation; whence have followed innumerable changes; insomuch that no empire, no sect, no star seems to have exerted greater power and influence in human affairs than these mechanical discoveries.

Lastly, if the debasement of arts and sciences to purposes of wickedness, luxury, and the like, be made a ground of objection, let no one be moved thereby. For the same may be said of all earthly goods; of wit, courage, strength, beauty, wealth, light itself, and the rest. Only let the human race recover the right over nature which belongs to it by divine bequest, and let power be given it; the exercise thereof will be governed by sound reason and true religion.

cxix

And now it is time for me to propound the art itself of interpreting nature; in which, although I conceive that I have given true and most useful precepts, yet I do not say either that it is absolutely necessary or that it is perfect. For I am of opinion that if men had ready at hand a just history of nature and experience, and labored diligently thereon; and if they could bind themselves to two rules,—the first, to lay aside received opinions and notions; and the second, to refrain the mind for a time from the highest generalizations, and those next to them,—they would be able by the native and genuine force of the mind, without any other art, to fall into my form of interpretation. For interpretation is the true and natural work of the mind when freed from impediments. It is true however that by my precepts everything will be in more readiness, and much more sure.

Nor again do I mean to say that no improvement can be made upon these. On the contrary, I that regard the mind not only in its own faculties but in its connection with things, must needs hold that the art of discovery may advance as discoveries advance.

The Second Book of Aphorisms Concerning the Interpretation of Nature and the Kingdom of Man

APHORISM

i

On a given body to generate and superinduce a new nature or new natures, is the work and aim of *human power*. Of a given nature to discover the form, or true specific difference, or nature-engendering nature, or source of emanation, is the work and aim of *human knowledge*. Subordinate to these primary works are two others that are secondary and of inferior mark: to the former, the transformation of concrete bodies, so far as this is possible; to the latter, the discovery, in every case of generation and motion, of the latent process carried on from the manifest efficient and the manifest material to the form which is engendered; and in like manner the discovery of the latent configuration of bodies at rest and not in motion.

ii

In what an ill condition human knowledge is at the present time, is apparent even from the commonly received maxims. It is a correct position that "true knowledge is knowledge by causes." And causes again are not improperly distributed into four kinds: the material, the formal, the efficient, and the final. But of these the final cause rather corrupts than advances the sciences, except such as have to do with human action. The discovery of the formal is despaired of. The efficient and the material are but slight and superficial, and contribute little, if anything, to true and active science.

iii

If a man be acquainted with the cause of any nature (as whiteness or heat) in certain subjects only, his knowledge is imperfect; and if he be able to superinduce an effect on certain substances only (of those susceptible of such effect), his power is in like manner imperfect. Now if a man's knowledge be confined to the efficient and material causes, he may arrive at new discoveries in reference to substances in some degree similar to one another, and selected beforehand; but he does not touch the deeper boundaries of things. But whosoever is acquainted with forms, embraces the unity of nature in substances the most unlike; and is able therefore to detect and bring to light things never yet done, and such as neither the vicissitudes of nature, nor industry in experimenting, nor accident itself, would ever have brought into act, and which would never have occurred to the thought of man. From the discovery of forms therefore results truth in speculation and freedom in operation.

iv

Although the roads to human power and to human knowledge lie close together, and are nearly the same, nevertheless on account of the pernicious and inveterate habit of dwelling on abstractions, it is safer to begin and raise the sciences from those foundations which have relation to practice, and to let the active part itself be as the seal which prints and determines the contemplative counterpart. We must therefore consider, if a man wanted to generate and superinduce any nature upon a given body, what kind of rule or direction or guidance he would most wish for, and express the same in the simplest and least abstruse language.

For a true and perfect rule of operation then the direction will be *that it be certain, free, and disposing or leading to action*. And this is the same thing with the discovery of the true form. For the form of a nature is such that, given the form, the nature infallibly follows. Therefore it is always present when the nature is present, and universally implies it, and is constantly inherent in it. Again, the form is such that if it be taken away, the nature infallibly vanishes. Therefore it is always absent when the nature is absent, and implies its absence, and inheres in nothing else. Lastly, the true form is such that it deduces the given nature from some source of being which is inherent in more natures, and which is better known in the natural order of things than the form itself. For a true and perfect axiom of knowledge then the direction and precept will be, *that another nature be discovered which is convertible with the given nature, and yet is a limitation of a more general nature, as of a true and real genus.* Now these two directions, the one active, the other contemplative, are one and the same thing; and what in operation is most useful, that in knowledge is most true.

v

The rule or axiom for the transformation of bodies is of two kinds. The first regards a body as a troop or collection of simple natures. For the principle of generating some one simple nature is the same as that of generating many; only that a man is more fettered and tied down in operation if more are required, by reason of the difficulty of combining into one so many natures, which do not readily meet except in the beaten and ordinary paths of nature. It must be said however that this mode of operation proceeds from what in nature is constant and eternal and universal, and opens broad roads to human power, such as human thought can scarcely comprehend or anticipate.

The second kind of axiom, which is concerned with the discovery of the Latent Process, proceeds not by simple natures, but by compound bodies, as they are found in nature in its ordinary course.

vi

But this Latent Process, of which I speak, is quite another thing than men, preoccupied as their minds now are, will easily conceive. For what I understand by it is not certain measures or signs or successive steps of process in bodies, which can be seen; but a process perfectly continuous, which for the most part escapes the sense.

vii

In like manner the investigation and discovery of the Latent Configuration in bodies is a new thing, no less than the discovery of the Latent Process and of the Form. For as yet we are but lingering in the outer courts of nature, nor are we preparing ourselves a way into her inner chambers. Yet no one can endow a given body with a new nature, or successfully and aptly transmute it into a new body, unless he has attained a competent knowledge of the body so to be altered or transformed. Otherwise he will run into methods which, if not useless, are at any rate difficult and perverse and unsuitable to the nature of the body on which he is operating. It is clear therefore that to this also a way must be opened and laid out.

viii

Nor shall we thus be led to the doctrine of atoms, which implies the hypothesis of a vacuum and that of the unchangeableness of matter (both false assumptions); we shall be led only to real particles, such as really exist. Nor again is there any reason to be alarmed at the subtlety of the investigation, as if it could not be disentangled: on the contrary, the nearer it approaches to simple natures, the easier and plainer will everything become; the business being transferred from the complicated to the simple, from the incommensurable to the commensurable, from surds to rational quantities, from the infinite and vague to the finite and certain,— as in the case of the letters of the alphabet and the notes of music. And inquiries into nature have the best result when they begin with physics and end in mathematics. Again, let no one be afraid of high numbers or minute fractions. For in dealing with numbers it is as easy to set down or conceive a thousand as one, or the thousandth part of an integer as an integer itself.

ix

From the two kinds of axioms which have been spoken of, arises a just division of philosophy and the sciences; taking the received terms in a sense agreeable to my own views. Thus, let the investigation of forms, which are (in the eye of reason at least, and in their essential law) eternal and immutable, constitute *metaphysics;* and let the investigation of the Efficient Cause, and of Matter, and of the Latent Process, and the Latent Configuration (all of which have reference to the common and ordinary course of nature, not to her eternal and fundamental laws) constitute *physics.* And to these let there be subordinate two practical divisions: to physics, *mechanics;* to metaphysics, what I call *magic,* on account of the broadness of the ways it moves in, and its greater command over nature.

x

Having thus set up the mark of knowledge, we must go on to precepts, and that in the most direct and obvious order. Now my directions for the interpretation of nature embrace two generic divisions: the one how to educe and form axioms from experience; the other how to deduce and derive new experiments from axioms. The former again is divided into three ministrations: a ministration to the sense, a ministration to the memory, and a ministration to the mind or reason.

For first of all we must prepare a *Natural and Experimental History,* sufficient and good; and this is the foundation of all; for we are not to imagine or suppose, but to discover, what nature does or may be made to do.

But natural and experimental history is so various and diffuse, that it confounds and distracts the understanding, unless it be ranged and presented to view in a suitable order. We must therefore form *Tables and Arrangements of Instances,* in such a method and order that the understanding may be able to deal with them.

And even when this is done, still the understanding, if left to itself and its own spontaneous movements, is incompetent and unfit to form axioms, unless it be directed and guarded. Therefore in the third place we must use *Induction,* true and legitimate induction, which is the very key of interpretation. But of this, which is the last, I must speak first, and then go back to the other ministrations.

xi

The investigation of Forms proceeds thus: a nature being given, we must first of all have a muster or presentation before the understanding of all known instances which agree in the same nature, though in substances the most unlike. And such collection must be made in the manner of a history, without premature speculation, or any great amount of subtlety. For example, let the investigation be into the Form of heat:

Instances Agreeing in the Nature of Heat

1. The rays of the sun, especially in summer and at noon.
2. The rays of the sun reflected and condensed, as between mountains, or on walls, and most of all in burning-glasses and mirrors.
3. Fiery meteors.
4. Burning thunderbolts.
5. Eruptions of flames from the cavities of mountains.
6. All flame.
7. Ignited solids.
8. Natural warm-baths.
9. Liquids boiling or heated.
10. Hot vapors and fumes, and the air itself, which conceives the most powerful and glowing heat, if confined, as in reverberatory furnaces.

This table I call the *Table of Essence and Presence.*

xii

Secondly, we must make a presentation to the understanding of instances in which the given nature is wanting; because the Form, as stated above, ought no less to be absent when the given nature is absent, than present when it is present. But to note all these would be endless.

The negatives should therefore be subjoined to the affirmatives, and the absence of the given nature inquired of in those subjects only that are most akin to the others in which it is present and forthcoming. This I call the *Table of Deviation, or of Absence in Proximity.*

Instances in Proximity where the Nature of Heat is Absent

1. The rays of the moon and of stars and comets are not found to be hot to the touch; indeed the severest colds are observed to be at the full moons.

The larger fixed stars however, when passed or approached by the sun, are supposed to increase and give intensity to the heat of the sun; as is the case when the sun is in the sign Leo, and in the Dog-days.

2. The rays of the sun in what is called the middle region of the air do not give heat; for which there is commonly assigned not a bad reason, viz., that that region is neither near enough to the body of the sun from which the rays emanate, nor to the earth from which they are reflected.

3. The reflection of the rays of the sun in regions near the polar circles is found to be very weak and ineffective in producing heat; insomuch that the Dutch who wintered in Nova Zembla, and expected their ship to be freed from the obstructions of the mass of ice which hemmed her in by the beginning of July, were disappointed of their expectation, and obliged to take to their boat.

4. Try the following experiment. Take a glass fashioned in a contrary manner to a common burning-glass, and placing it between your hand and the rays of the sun, observe whether it diminishes the heat of the sun, as a burning-glass increases and strengthens it. For it is evident in the case of optical rays that according as the glass is made thicker or thinner in the middle as compared with the sides, so do the objects seen through it appear more spread or more contracted. Observe therefore whether the same is the case with heat.

5. Let the experiment be carefully tried, whether by means of the most powerful and best constructed burning-glasses, the rays of the moon can be so caught and collected as to produce even the least degree of warmth. But should this degree of warmth prove too subtle and weak to be perceived and apprehended by the touch, recourse must be had to those glasses which indicate the state of the atmosphere in respect of heat and cold. Thus, let the rays of the moon fall through a burning-

glass on the top of a glass of this kind, and then observe whether there ensues a sinking of the water through warmth.

6. Let a burning-glass also be tried with a heat that does not emit rays or light, as that of iron or stone heated but not ignited, boiling water, and the like; and observe whether there ensues an increase of the heat, as in the case of the sun's rays.

7. Let a burning-glass also be tried with common flame.

8. Comets (if we are to reckon these too among meteors) are not found to exert a constant or manifest effect in increasing the heat of the season, though it is observed that they are often followed by droughts. Moreover bright beams and pillars and openings in the heavens appear more frequently in winter than in summer time, and chiefly during the intensest cold, but always accompanied by dry weather. Lightning, however, and coruscations and thunder, seldom occur in the winter, but about the time of great heat. Falling stars, as they are called, are commonly supposed to consist rather of some bright and lighted viscous substance, than to be of any strong fiery nature. But on this point let further inquiry be made.

9. There are certain coruscations which give light but do not burn. And these always come without thunder.

10. Eructations and eruptions of flame are found no less in cold than in warm countries, as in Iceland and Greenland. In cold countries too the trees are in many cases more inflammable and more pitchy and resinous than in warm; as the fir, pine, and others. The situations however and the nature of the soil in which eruptions of this kind usually occur have not been carefully enough ascertained to enable us to subjoin a Negative to this Affirmative Instance.

xiii

Thirdly, we must make a presentation to the understanding of instances in which the nature under inquiry is found in different degrees, more or less; which must be done by making a comparison either of its increase and decrease in the same subject, or of its amount in different subjects, as compared one with another. For since the Form of a thing is the very thing itself, and the thing differs from the form no otherwise than as the apparent differs from the real, or the external from the internal, or the thing in reference to man from the thing in reference to the universe; it necessarily follows that no nature can be taken as the true form, unless it always decrease when the nature in question decreases, and in like manner always increase when the nature in question increases. This Table therefore I call the *Table of Degrees* or the *Table of Comparison*.

Table of Degrees or Comparison in Heat

I will therefore first speak of those substances which contain no degree at all of heat perceptible to the touch, but seem to have a certain potential heat only, or disposition and preparation for hotness. After that I shall proceed to substances which are hot actually, and to the touch, and to their intensities and degrees.

1. In solid and tangible bodies we find nothing which is in its nature originally hot. For no stone, metal, sulphur, fossil, wood, water, or carcass of animal is found to be hot. And the hot water in baths seems to be heated by external causes; whether it be by flame or subterraneous fire, such as is thrown up from Aetna and many other mountains, or by the conflict of bodies, as heat is caused in the dissolutions of iron and tin. There is therefore no degree of heat palpable to the touch in animate substances; but they differ in degree of cold, wood not being equally cold with metal.

2. As far however as potential heat and aptitude for flame is concerned, there are many inanimate substances found strongly disposed thereto, as sulphur, naphtha, rock oil.

3. Substances once hot, as horse-dung from animal heat, and lime or perhaps ashes and soot from fire, retain some latent remains of their former heat. Hence certain distillations and resolutions of bodies are made by burying them in horse-dung, and heat is excited in lime by sprinkling it with water.

4. In the vegetable creation we find no plant or part of plant (as gum or pitch) which is warm to the human touch. But yet, as stated above, green herbs gain warmth by being shut up; and to the internal touch, as the palate or stomach, and even to external parts, after a little time, as in plasters and ointments, some vegetables are perceptibly warm and others cold.

5. In the parts of animals after death or separation from the body, we find nothing warm to the human touch. Not even horse-dung, unless enclosed and buried, retains its heat. But yet all dung seems to have a potential heat, as is seen in the fattening of the land. In like manner carcasses of animals have some such latent and potential heat; insomuch that in burying grounds, where burials take place daily, the earth collects a certain hidden heat, which consumes a body newly laid in it much more speedily than pure earth. We are told too that in the East there is discovered a fine soft texture, made of the down of birds, which by an innate force dissolves and melts butter when lightly wrapped in it.

6. Substances which fatten the soil, as dung of all kinds, chalk, sea-sand, salt, and the like, have some disposition to heat.

7. All putrefaction contains in itself certain elements of a slight heat,

though not so much as to be perceived by the touch. For not even those substances which on putrefaction turn to animalculae, as flesh, cheese, &c., feel warm to the touch; no more does rotten wood, which shines in the dark. Heat however in putrid substances sometimes betrays itself by foul and powerful odors.

8. The first degree of heat therefore among those substances which feel hot to the touch, seems to be the heat of animals, which has a pretty great extent in its degrees. For the lowest, as in insects, is hardly perceptible to the touch; but the highest scarce equals the sun's heat in the hottest countries and seasons, nor is it too great to be borne by the hand. It is said however of Constantius, and some others of a very dry constitution and habit of body, that in violent fevers they became so hot as somewhat to burn the hand that touched them.

9. Animals increase in heat by motion and exercise, wine, feasting, venus, burning fevers, and pain.

10. When attacked by intermittent fevers, animals are at first seized with cold and shivering, but soon after they become exceedingly hot, which is their condition from the first in burning and pestilential fevers.

xiv

How poor we are in history anyone may see from the foregoing tables; where I not only insert sometimes mere traditions and reports in place of history proved and instances certain, but am also forced to use the words "Let trial be made," or "Let it be further inquired."

xv

The work and office of these three tables I call the Presentation of Instances to the Understanding. Which presentation having been made, Induction itself must be set at work; for the problem is, upon a review of the instances, all and each, to find such a nature as is always present or absent with the given nature, and always increases and decreases with it; and which is, as I have said, a particular case of a more general nature. Now if the mind attempt this affirmatively from the first, as when left to itself it is always wont to do, the result will be fancies and guesses and notions ill defined and axioms that must be mended every day; unless like the schoolmen we have a mind to fight for what is false; though doubtless these will be better or worse according to the faculties and strength of the understanding which is at work. To God, truly, the Giver and Architect of Forms, and it may be to the angels and higher intelligences, it belongs to have an affirmative knowledge of Forms immediately, and from the first contemplation. But this assuredly is more than man can do, to whom it is granted only to proceed at first by negatives, and at last to end in affirmatives, after exclusion has been exhausted.

xvi

We must make therefore a complete solution and separation of nature, not indeed by fire, but by the mind, which is a kind of divine fire. The first work therefore of true induction is the rejection or exclusion of the several natures which are not found in some instance where the given nature is present, or are found in some instance where the given nature is absent, or are found to increase in some instance when the given nature decreases, or to decrease when the given nature increases. Then indeed after the rejection and exclusion has been duly made, there will remain at the bottom, all light opinions vanishing into smoke, a Form affirmative, solid and true and well defined. This is quickly said; but the way to come at it is winding and intricate. I will endeavor however not to overlook any of the points which may help us towards it.

xvii

But when I assign so prominent a part to Forms, I cannot too often warn and admonish men against applying what I say to those forms to which their thoughts and contemplations have hitherto been accustomed.

For in the first place I do not at present speak of Compound Forms, which are, as I have remarked, combinations of simple natures according to the common course of the universe; as of the lion, eagle, rose, gold, and the like. It will be time to treat of these when we come to the Latent Processes and Latent Configurations, and the discovery of them, as they are found in what are called substances or natures concrete.

And even in the case of simple natures I would not be understood to speak of abstract Forms and Ideas, either not defined in matter at all, or ill defined. For when I speak of Forms, I mean nothing more than those laws and determinations of absolute actuality, which govern and constitute any simple nature, as heat, light, weight, in every kind of matter and subject that is susceptible of them. Thus the Form of heat or the Form of light is the same thing as the Law of heat or the Law of light. Nor indeed do I ever allow myself to be drawn away from things themselves and the operative part. And therefore when I say in the investigation of the Form of heat, "Reject rarity," or "Rarity does not belong to the form of heat," it is the same as if I said, "It is possible to superinduce heat on a dense body," or "It is possible to take away or keep out heat from a rare body."

But if anyone conceive that my Forms too are of a somewhat abstract nature, because they mix and combine things heterogeneous (for the heat of heavenly bodies and the heat of fire seem to be very heterogeneous; so do the fixed red of the rose or the like, and the apparent red in the rainbow, the opal, or the diamond; so again do the different kinds of death, death by drowning, by hanging, by stabbing, by apoplexy, by atrophy; and yet they agree severally in the nature of heat, redness, death); if anyone, I say, be of this opinion, he may be assured that his mind is held in captivity by custom, by the gross appearance of things, and by men's opinions. For it is most certain that these things, however heterogeneous and alien from each other, agree in the Form or Law which governs heat, redness, and death; and that the power of man cannot possibly be emancipated and freed from the common course of nature, and expanded and exalted to new efficients and new modes of operation, except by the revelation and discovery of Forms of this kind. And yet, when I have spoken of this union of nature, which is the point of most importance, I shall proceed to the divisions and veins of nature, as well the ordinary as those that are more inward and exact, and speak of them in their place.

xviii

I must now give an example of the Exclusion or Rejection of natures which by the Tables of Presentation are found not to belong to the Form of heat; observing in the meantime that not only each table suffices for the rejection of any nature, but even any one of the particular instances contained in any of the tables. For it is manifest from what has been said that any one contradictory instance overthrows a conjecture as to the Form. But nevertheless for clearness' sake and that the use of the tables may be more plainly shown, I sometimes double or multiply an exclusion.

An Example of Exclusion, or Rejection of Natures from
the Form of Heat

1. On account of the rays of the sun, reject the nature of the elements.
2. On account of common fire, and chiefly subterraneous fires (which are the most remote and most completely separate from the rays of heavenly bodies), reject the nature of heavenly bodies.
3. On account of the warmth acquired by all kinds of bodies (minerals, vegetables, skin of animals, water, oil, air, and the rest) by mere approach to a fire, or other hot body, reject the distinctive or more subtle texture of bodies.
4. On account of ignited iron and other metals, which communicate heat to other bodies and yet lose none of their weight or substance, reject the communication or admixture of the substance of another hot body.

5. On account of boiling water and air, and also on account of metals and other solids that receive heat but not to ignition or red heat, reject light or brightness.

6. On account of the rays of the moon and other heavenly bodies, with the exception of the sun, also reject light and brightness.

7. By a comparison of ignited iron and the flame of spirit of wine (of which ignited iron has more heat and less brightness, while the flame of spirit of wine has more brightness and less heat), also reject light and brightness.

8. On account of ignited gold and other metals, which are of the greatest density as a whole, reject rarity.

9. On account of air, which is formed for the most part cold and yet remains rare, also reject rarity.

10. On account of ignited iron, which does not swell in bulk, but keeps within the same visible dimensions, reject local or expansive motion of the body as a whole.

There are other natures beside these; for these tables are not perfect, but meant only for examples.

All and each of the above-mentioned natures do *not* belong to the Form of heat. And from all of them man is freed in his operations on heat.

xix

In the process of Exclusion are laid the foundations of true Induction, which however is not completed till it arrives at an Affirmative. Nor is the Exclusive part itself at all complete, nor indeed can it possibly be so at first. For Exclusion is evidently the rejection of simple natures; and if we do not yet possess sound and true notions of simple natures, how can the process of Exclusion be made accurate? Now some of the above-mentioned notions (as that of the nature of the elements, of the nature of heavenly bodies, of rarity) are vague and ill-defined. I therefore, well knowing and nowise forgetting how great a work I am about, do not rest satisfied with the precepts I have laid down; but proceed further to devise and supply more powerful aids for the use of the understanding; which I shall now subjoin. And assuredly in the Interpretation of Nature the mind should by all means be so prepared and disposed, that while it rests and finds footing in due stages and degrees of certainty, it may remember withal that what it has before it depends in great measure upon what remains behind.

xx

And yet since truth will sooner come out from error than from confusion, I think it expedient that the understanding should have permission, after the three Tables of First Presentation (such as I have exhibited) have been made and weighed, to make an essay of the Interpretation of Nature in the affirmative way; on the strength both of the instances given in the tables, and of any others it may meet with elsewhere. Which kind of essay I call the *indulgence of the understanding,* or the *commencement of interpretation,* or the *First Vintage.*

First Vintage concerning the Form of Heat

Let this then be the First Vintage or Commencement of Interpretation concerning the Form of Heat, made by way of indulgence to the understanding.

Now from this our First Vintage it follows that the Form or true definition of heat (heat, that is, in relation to the universe, not simply in relation to man) is in few words as follows: *Heat is a motion, expansive, restrained, and acting in its strife upon the smaller particles of bodies.* But the expansion is thus modified: *while it expands all ways, it has at the same time an inclination upwards.* And the struggle in the particles is modified also: *it is not sluggish, but hurried and with violence.*

Viewed with reference to operation it is the same thing. For the direction is this: *If in any natural body you can excite a dilating or expanding motion, and can so repress this motion and turn it back upon itself that the dilation shall not proceed equably, but have its way in one part and be counteracted in another, you will undoubtedly generate heat;*—without taking into account whether the body be elementary (as it is called) or subject to celestial influence; whether it be luminous or opaque; rare or dense; locally expanded or confined within the bounds of its first dimension; verging to dissolution or remaining in its original state; animal, vegetable, or mineral, water, oil or air, or any other substance whatever susceptible of the above-mentioned motion. Sensible heat is the same thing; only it must be considered with reference to the sense. Let us now proceed to further aids.

xxi

The Tables of First Presentation and the Rejection or process of Exclusion being completed, and also the First Vintage being made thereupon, we are to proceed to the other helps of the understanding in the Interpretation of Nature and true and perfect Induction. In propounding which, I mean, when Tables are necessary, to proceed upon the Instances of Heat and Cold; but when a small number of examples will suffice, I shall proceed at large; so that the inquiry may be kept clear, and yet more room be left for the exposition of the system.

xxii

Among Prerogative Instances I will place first *Solitary Instances.* Those are Solitary Instances which exhibit the nature under investigation in subjects which have nothing in common with other subjects except that nature; or, again, which do not exhibit the nature under investigation in subjects which resemble other subjects in every respect except in not having that nature. For it is clear that such instances make the way short, and accelerate and strengthen the process of exclusion; so that a few of them are as good as many.

For instance, if we are inquiring into the nature of Color, prisms, crystals, which show colors not only in themselves but externally on a wall, dews, &c., are Solitary Instances. For they have nothing in common with the colors fixed in flowers, colored stones, metals, woods, &c., except the color. From which we easily gather that color is nothing more than a modification of the image of light received upon the object, resulting in the former case from the different degrees of incidence, in the latter from the various textures and configurations of the body. These instances are Solitary in respect of resemblance.

Again, in the same investigation, the distinct veins of white and black in marble, and the variegation of color in flowers of the same species, are Solitary Instances. For the black and white streaks in marble, or the spots of pink and white in a pink, agree in everything almost except the color. From which we easily gather that color has little to do with the intrinsic nature of a body, but simply depends on the coarser and as it were mechanical arrangement of the parts. These instances are Solitary in respect of difference. Both kinds I call *Solitary Instances,* or *Ferine,* to borrow a term from astronomers.

xxiii

Among Prerogative Instances I will next place *Migratory Instances.* They are those in which the nature in question is in the process of being produced when it did not previously exist, or on the other hand of disappearing when it existed before. And therefore, in either transition, such instances are always twofold, or rather it is one instance in motion or passage, continued till it reaches the opposite state. Such instances not only accelerate and strengthen the exclusive process, but also drive the affirmative or Form itself into a narrow compass. For the Form of a thing must necessarily be something which in the course of this migration is communicated, or on the other hand which in the course of this migration is removed and destroyed. And though every exclusion promotes the affirmative, yet this is done more decidedly when it occurs in the same than in different subjects. And the betrayal of the form in a single instance leads the way (as is evident from all that has been said) to the discovery of it in all. And the simpler the Migration, the more must the instance be valued. Besides Migratory Instances are of great use with a view to operation; because in exhibiting the form in connection with that which causes it to be or not to be; they supply a clear direction for practice in some cases; whence the passage is easy to the cases that lie next. There is however in these instances a danger which requires caution; viz., lest they lead us to connect the Form too much with the efficient, and so possess the understanding, or at least touch it, with a false opinion concerning the Form, drawn from a view of the efficient. But the efficient is always understood to be merely the vehicle that carries the Form. This is a danger however easily remedied by the process of exclusion legitimately conducted.

I must now give an example of a Migratory Instance. Let the nature to be investigated be Whiteness; an instance migrating to production or existence is glass whole and pounded. Again, simple water and water agitated into froth. For glass and water in their simple state are transparent, not white; whereas pounded glass and water in froth are white, not transparent. We must therefore inquire what has happened to the glass of water from this Migration. For it is obvious that the Form of Whiteness is communicated and conveyed by that pounding of the glass and that agitation of the water. We find, however, that nothing has been added except the breaking up of the glass and water into small parts, and the introduction of air. But we have made no slight advance to the discovery of the Form of Whiteness when we know that two bodies, both transparent but in a greater or less degree (viz., air and water, or air and glass), do when mingled in small portions together exhibit whiteness, through the unequal refraction of the rays of light.

But an example must at the same time be given of the danger and caution to which I alluded. For at this point it might readily suggest itself to an understanding led astray by efficient causes of this kind, that air is always required for the Form of Whiteness, or that Whiteness is generated by transparent bodies only; notions entirely false, and refuted by numerous exclusions. Whereas it will be found that (setting air and the like aside) bodies entirely even in the particles which affect vision are transparent, bodies simply uneven are white; bodies uneven and in a compound yet regular texture are all colors except black; while bodies uneven and in a compound, irregular, and confused texture are black. Here then I have given an example of an Instance Migrating to production or existence in the proposed nature of Whiteness. An Instance Migrating to destruction in the same nature of Whiteness, is froth or snow in dissolution. For the water puts off Whiteness and puts on transparency, on returning to its integral state without air.

Nor must I by any means omit to mention that under Migratory Instances are to be included not only those which are passing towards production and destruction, but also those which are passing towards increase and decrease. Thus paper, which is white when dry, but when wetted (that is, when air is excluded and water introduced) is less white and approaches nearer to the transparent, is analogous to the above-given Instances.

xxiv

After Prerogative Instances I will put in the third place *Striking Instances,* which I also call *Shining Instances,* or *Instances Freed and Predominant.* They are those which exhibit the nature in question naked and standing by itself, and also in its exaltation or highest degree of power; as being disenthralled and freed from all impediments, or at any rate by virtue of its strength dominant over, suppressing and coercing them. For since every body contains in itself many forms of natures united together in a concrete state, the result is that they severally crush, depress, break, and enthrall one another, and thus the individual forms are obscured. But certain subjects are found wherein the required nature appears more in its vigor than in others, either through the absence of impediments or the predominance of its own virtue. And instances of this kind strikingly display the Form. At the same time in these instances also we must use caution, and check the hurry of the understanding. For whatever displays the Form too conspicuously, and seems to force it on the notice of the understanding, should be held suspect, and recourse be had to a rigid and careful exclusion.

PRINCIPLES OF PHILOSOPHY

by

RENÉ DESCARTES

CONTENTS

Principles of Philosophy

RENÉ DESCARTES

1596–1650

When René Descartes was born, March 31, 1596, the thinking world was in great confusion. Medievalism with its assurances and its simple theological and cosmological systems had been challenged and shaken to its depths by Renaissance scientists. Religious men were fearful that the foundations of the religious life would be swept away and morality would have no certain moorings. Keen minds everywhere were seeking certainty, and the scientists assured them that only in their sciences could this certainty be found.

Thus the scene was set for the entrance of the man who could discover certainty in the midst of complete doubt, who could assert with perfect confidence, "I think, therefore I am," and who from this assertion could build an entire philosophy which would serve as a foundation for religion and morality.

A child of delicate physique but of strenuous mind—his father called him "my little philosopher"—Descartes did not spend his time in the sports of other boys, but devoted himself to study and meditation. At eight he entered the Jesuit college of La Flèche, where he remained until he was sixteen. During this time he developed the habit of meditating in bed, a practice which he continued throughout his life. He began early to show great promise and openly criticized the authority of tradition and of his teachers. He studied physics and philosophy according to the scholastic system, but devoted much time to mathematics, which soon became his foremost love.

After his graduation from college he went to Paris and entered the brilliant social circles of that city. Here he met several famous personalities of the time. Among these were the mathematician Claude Mydorge and Father Mersenne of the order of Minim friars. These men became fast friends of Descartes and exerted considerable influence upon his thinking.

Dissatisfied with Parisian life, Descartes abandoned his social activities for a while and took up a military career. This he did, he tells us, so that he might "study the great book of the world." He served under Maurice of Orange in Holland, and under the Elector of Bavaria in Germany. But, despite his preoccupation with military affairs, he devoted a part of each day to the study of mathematics.

While in winter quarters at Newburg, November 10, 1619, Descartes experienced a mental crisis which "revealed" to him the general method of his philosophy. It was on the eve of St. Martin's day, he tells us, that he "was filled with enthusiasm, and discovered the foundations of a marvelous science." He secluded himself in his room for several days and devoted himself to thinking out the ideas which had come to him on this eventful day.

The next ten years he spent in military service, travel, and study; and then, in the spring of 1629, he moved to Holland, where he lived until 1649, devoting himself to the examination of truth, to writing, and to carrying on a voluminous correspondence with friends throughout Europe. Many of his letters during this period were written to Mersenne and to Princess Elizabeth, eldest daughter of the deposed Elector Palatine, who lived at The Hague. It was to her that he dedicated his *Principles of Philosophy*.

Holland at this time was the home of a brilliant group of men devoted to creative work in many fields. Dutch navigators were dominating world trade, Rembrandt was painting at his best, and Grotius, Vossius, and the elder Heinsius were leading the philosophic thought of the times. Many of these individuals were frequent visitors to Descartes's reception room and took a keen interest in the researches of this scientist-philosopher.

Early in this period Descartes wrote *Le Monde* (The World)—a book in which he advanced the then revolutionary theory that the earth was in motion. But he hesitated to publish this book because he saw how Galileo had been persecuted for a similar idea, and therefore abandoned the idea of giving the work to the public. He had the manuscript hidden away and told only a few close friends of its existence. The public did not see *Le Monde* until after Descartes's death.

Nevertheless, other writings published by Descartes resulted in his condemnation by the Church on the charge of infidelity and atheism. His attempt to prove the existence of God seemed to many churchmen to be meddling with matters which should be left to faith. Many biblical scholars attacked him, and some of his best ideas are to be found in the replies which he gave to their criticisms.

In 1644 the *Principles of Philosophy* appeared in Amsterdam. In this book Descartes was careful not to offend the Church. He rejected the Copernican theory in name but clung to it in principle; and he concluded the book with a statement: "I submit all my opinions to the authority of the Church." But this did not help him. His philosophy had offended the traditions of many a conservative group. In some circles the mere mention of his name was a high offense.

In Sweden, however, thanks to the interest of Queen Christina, who corresponded with the philosopher and to whom his *Passions of the Mind* was dedicated, Descartes was popular. In 1649 he accepted an invitation to the Swedish court. A vessel of the royal navy carried him to his destination, and a royal reception awaited him on his arrival.

But the climate of Sweden was too severe for a man of Descartes's frail constitution. His friend Pierre Chanut, the French ambassador to the court of Sweden, had fallen ill. Descartes attended him constantly, with the result that Chanut recovered but Descartes contracted the same disease—inflammation of the lungs—and died on February 1, 1650.

Only after his death did Descartes receive the honors rightfully due him. His philosophy spread throughout Europe. He was buried in a Catholic cemetery in Sweden, where his ashes remained for sixteen years. They were then taken to France and laid in the Church of Saint Geneviève du Mont, the modern Pantheon. In 1819 the ashes were again removed and interred at Saint Germain-des-Prés, where they still repose.

Descartes has been called "the father of modern philosophy." This philosophy, as developed in his *Discourse on Method* and his *Meditations,* is based upon "the method of mathematics," to quote his own words, "as applied to philosophy." To begin with, declares Descartes, we must take nothing for granted—we must accept nothing as true. We must look into the secret of the universe with an open mind.

And what do we discover? One certain, solid fact. "The fact of my thinking reveals to me something that thinks." *Cogito, ergo sum. I think, therefore I am.* This is the one fact I know—*I exist.*

But who is this *I* that exists? The answer to this is, a *Thinking Thing,* or a *Mind.* "I know that I am a substance whose entire nature it is to think and for whose existence there is no need of any place, nor does it depend on any material thing. . . . The soul (or mind) by which I am what I am, is entirely distinct from my body . . . and even if the body were not, the soul would not cease to be what it is."

And thus Descartes establishes, as he believes, the one certain fact of existence—the existence of the soul.

Does this lead, inquires Descartes, to any other facts? Yes, he replies—two other facts: the presence of my body and the existence of God.

PRINCIPLES OF PHILOSOPHY

PART ONE: OF THE PRINCIPLES OF HUMAN KNOWLEDGE

I. THAT in order to seek truth, it is necessary once in the course of our life to doubt, as far as possible, of all things.

As we were at one time children, and as we formed various judgments regarding the objects presented to our senses, when as yet we had not the entire use of our reason, numerous prejudices stand in the way of our arriving at the knowledge of truth; and of these it seems impossible for us to rid ourselves, unless we undertake, once in our lifetime, to doubt of all those things in which we may discover even the smallest suspicion of uncertainty.

II. That we ought also to consider as false all that is doubtful.

Moreover, it will be useful likewise to esteem as false the things of which we shall be able to doubt, that we may with greater clearness discover what possesses most certainty and is the easiest to know.

III. That we ought not meanwhile to make use of doubt in the conduct of life.

In the meantime, it is to be observed that we are to avail ourselves of this general doubt only while engaged in the contemplation of truth. For, as far as concerns the conduct of life, we are very frequently obliged to follow opinions merely probable, or even sometimes, though of two courses of action we may not perceive more probability in the one than in the other, to choose one or other, seeing the opportunity of acting would not unfrequently pass away before we could free ourselves from our doubts.

IV. Why we may doubt of sensible things.

Accordingly, since we now only design to apply ourselves to the investigation of truth, we will doubt, first, whether of all the things that have ever fallen under our senses, or which we have ever imagined, any one really exists; in the first place, because we know by experience that the senses sometimes err, and it would be imprudent to trust too much to what has even once deceived us; secondly, because in dreams we perpetually seem to perceive or imagine innumerable objects which have no existence. And to one who has thus resolved upon a general doubt, there appear no marks by which he can with certainty distinguish sleep from the waking state.

V. Why we may also doubt of mathematical demonstrations.

We will also doubt of the other things we have before held as most certain, even of the demonstrations of mathematics, and of their principles which we have hitherto deemed self-evident; in the first place, because we have sometimes seen men fall into error in such matters, and admit as absolutely certain and self-evident what to us appeared false, but chiefly because we have learnt that God who created us is all-powerful; for we do not yet know whether perhaps it was his will to create us so that we are always deceived, even in the things we think we know best: since this does not appear more impossible than our being occasionally deceived, which, however, as observation teaches us, is the case. And if we suppose that an all-powerful God is not the author of our being, and that we exist of ourselves or by some other means, still, the less powerful we suppose our author to be, the greater reason will we have for believing that we are not so perfect as that we may not be continually deceived.

VI. That we possess a free will, by which we can withhold our assent from what is doubtful, and thus avoid error.

But meanwhile, whoever in the end may be the author of our being, and however powerful and deceitful he may be, we are nevertheless conscious of a freedom, by which we can refrain from admitting to a place in our belief aught that is not manifestly certain and undoubted, and thus guard against ever being deceived.

VII. That we cannot doubt of our existence while we doubt, and that this is the first knowledge we acquire when we philosophise in order.

While we thus reject all of which we can entertain the smallest doubt, and even imagine that it is false, we easily indeed suppose that there is neither God, nor sky, nor bodies, and that we ourselves even have neither hands nor feet, nor, finally, a body; but we cannot in the same way suppose that we are not while we doubt of the truth of these things; for there is a repugnance in conceiving that what thinks does not exist at the very time when it thinks. Accordingly, the knowledge, *I think, therefore I am,* is the first and most certain that occurs to one who philosophises orderly.

VIII. That we hence discover the distinction between the mind and the body, or between a thinking and corporeal thing.

And this is the best mode of discovering the nature of the mind, and its distinctness from the body: for examining what we are, while supposing, as we now do, that there is nothing really existing apart from our thought, we clearly perceive that neither extension, nor figure, nor local motion, nor anything similar that can be attributed to body, pertains to our nature, and nothing save thought alone; and, consequently, that the notion we have of our mind precedes that of any corporeal thing, and is more certain, seeing we still doubt whether there is any body in existence, while we already perceive that we think.

IX. What thought is.

By the word thought, I understand all that which so takes place in us that we of ourselves are immediately conscious of it; and, accordingly, not only to understand, to will, to imagine, but even to perceive, are here the same as to think. For if I say, I see, or, I walk, therefore I am; and if I understand by vision or walking the act of my eyes or of my limbs, which is the work of the body, the conclusion is not absolutely certain, because, as is often the case in dreams, I may think that I see or walk, although I do not open my eyes or move from my place, and even, perhaps, although I have no body: but, if I mean the sensation itself, or consciousness of seeing or walking, the knowledge is manifestly certain, because it is then referred to the mind, which alone perceives or is conscious that it sees or walks.

X. That the notions which are simplest and self-evident are obscured by logical definitions; and that such are not to be reckoned among the cognitions acquired by study [but as born with us].

I do not here explain several other terms which I have used, or design to use in the sequel, because their meaning seems to me sufficiently self-evident. And I frequently remarked that philosophers erred in attempting to explain, by logical definitions, such truths as are most simple and self-evident; for they thus only rendered them more obscure. And when I said that the proposition, *I think, therefore I am,* is of all others the first and most certain which occurs to one philosophising orderly, I did not therefore deny that it was necessary to know what thought, existence, and certitude are, and the truth that, in order to think it is necessary to be, and the like; but, because these are the most simple notions, and such as of themselves afford the knowledge of nothing existing, I did not judge it proper there to enumerate them.

XI. How we can know our mind more clearly than our body.

But now that it may be discerned how the knowledge we have of the mind not only precedes, and has greater certainty, but is even clearer, than that we have of the body, it must be remarked, as a matter that is highly manifest by the natural light, that to nothing no affections or qualities belong; and, accordingly, that where we observe certain affections, there a thing or substance to which these pertain is necessarily found. The same light also shows us that we know a thing or substance more clearly in proportion as we discover in it a greater number of qualities. Now, it is manifest that we remark a greater number of qualities in our mind than in any other thing; for there is no occasion on which we know anything whatever when we are not at the same time led with much greater certainty to the knowledge of our own mind. For example, if I judge that there is an earth because I touch or see it, on the same ground, and with still greater reason, I must be persuaded that my mind exists; for it may be, perhaps, that I think I touch the earth while there is none in existence; but it is not possible that I should so judge, and my mind which thus judges not exist; and the same holds good of whatever object is presented to our mind.

XII. How it happens that every one does not come equally to know this.

Those who have not philosophised in order have had other opinions on this subject, because they never distinguished with sufficient care the mind from the body. For, although they had no difficulty in believing that they themselves existed, and that they had a higher assurance of this than of any other thing, nevertheless, as they did not observe that by *themselves,* they ought here to understand their *minds* alone; and since, on the contrary, they rather meant their bodies which they saw with their eyes, touched with their hands, and to which they erroneously attributed the faculty of perception, they were prevented from distinctly apprehending the nature of the mind.

XIII. In what sense the knowledge of other things depends upon the knowledge of God.

But when the mind, which thus knows itself but is still in doubt as to all other things, looks around on all sides, with a view to the farther extension of its knowledge, it first of all discovers within itself the ideas of many things; and while it simply contemplates them, and neither affirms nor denies that there is anything beyond itself corresponding to them, it is in no danger of erring. The mind also discovers certain common notions out of which it frames various demonstrations that carry conviction to such a degree as to render doubt of their truth impossible, so long as we give attention to them. For example, the mind has within itself ideas of numbers and figures, and it has likewise among its common notions the principle *that if equals be added to equals the wholes will be equal,* and the like; from which it is easy to demonstrate that the three angles of a triangle are equal to two right angles, etc. Now, so long as we attend to the premises from which this conclusion and others similar to it were deduced, we feel assured of their truth; but, as the mind cannot always think of these with attention, when it has the remembrance of a conclusion without recollecting the order of its deduction, and is uncertain whether the author of its being has created it of a nature that is liable to be deceived, even in what appears most evident, it perceives that there is just ground to distrust the truth of such conclusions, and that it cannot possess any certain knowledge until it has discovered its author.

XIV. That we may validly infer the existence of God from necessary existence being comprised in the concept we have of him.

When the mind afterwards reviews the different ideas that are in it, it discovers what is by far the chief among them—that of a Being omniscient, all-powerful, and absolutely perfect; and it observes that in this idea there is contained not only possible and contingent existence, as in the ideas of all other things which it clearly perceives, but existence absolutely necessary and eternal. And just as because, for example, the equality of its three angles to two right angles is necessarily comprised in the idea of a triangle, the mind is firmly persuaded that the three angles of a triangle are equal to two right angles; so, from its perceiving necessary and eternal existence to be comprised in the idea which it has of an all-perfect Being, it ought manifestly to conclude that this all-perfect Being exists.

XV. That necessary existence is not in the same way comprised in the notions which we have of other things, but merely contingent existence.

The mind will be still more certain of the truth of this conclusion, if it consider that it has no idea of any other thing in which it can discover that necessary existence is contained; for, from this circumstance alone, it will discern that the idea of an all-perfect Being has not been framed by itself, and that it does not represent a chimera, but a true and immutable nature, which must exist since it can only be conceived as necessarily existing.

XVI. That prejudices hinder many from clearly knowing the necessity of the existence of God.

Our mind would have no difficulty in assenting to this truth, if it were, first of all, wholly free from prejudices; but as we have been accustomed to distinguish, in all other things, essence from existence, and to imagine at will many ideas of things which neither are nor have been, it easily happens, when we do not steadily fix our thoughts on the contemplation of the all-perfect Being, that a doubt arises as to whether the idea we have of him is not one of those which we frame at pleasure, or at least of that class to whose essence existence does not pertain.

XVII. That the greater objective perfection there is in our idea of a thing, the greater also must be the perfection of its cause.

When we further reflect on the various ideas that are in us, it is easy to perceive that there is not much difference among them, when we consider them simply as certain modes of thinking, but that they are widely different, considered in reference to the objects they represent; and that their causes must be so much the more perfect according to the degree of objective perfection contained in them. For there is no difference between this and the case of a person who has the idea of a machine, in the construction of which great skill is displayed, in which circumstances we have a right to inquire how he came by this idea, whether, for example, he somewhere saw such a machine constructed by another, or whether he was so accurately taught the mechanical sciences, or is endowed with such force of genius, that he was able of himself to invent it, without having elsewhere seen anything like it; for all the ingenuity which is contained in the idea objectively only, or as it were in a picture, must exist at least in its first and chief cause, whatever that may be, not only objectively or representatively, but in truth formally or eminently.

XVIII. That the existence of God may be again inferred from the above.

Thus, because we discover in our minds the idea of God, or of an all-perfect Being, we have a right to inquire into the source whence we derive it; and we will discover that the perfections it represents are so immense as to render it quite certain that we could only derive it from an all-perfect Being; that is, from a God really existing. For it is not only manifest by the natural light that nothing cannot be the cause of anything whatever, and that the more perfect cannot arise from the less perfect, so as to be thereby produced as by its efficient and total cause, but also that it is impossible we can have the idea or representation of anything what-ever, unless there be somewhere, either in us or out of us, an original which comprises, in reality, all the perfections that are thus represented to us; but, as we do not in any way find in ourselves those absolute per-fections of which we have the idea, we must conclude that they exist in some nature different from ours, that is, in God, or at least that they were once in him; and it most manifestly follows that they are still there.

XIX. That, although we may not comprehend the nature of God, there is yet nothing which we know so clearly as his perfections.

This will appear sufficiently certain and manifest to those who have been accustomed to contemplate the idea of God, and to turn their thoughts to his infinite perfections; for, although we may not compre-hend them, because it is of the nature of the infinite not to be compre-hended by what is finite, we nevertheless conceive them more clearly and distinctly than material objects, for this reason, that, being simple, and unobscured by limits, they occupy our mind more fully.

XX. That we are not the cause of ourselves, but that this is God, and consequently that there is a God.

But, because every one has not observed this, and because, when we have an idea of any machine in which great skill is displayed, we usually know with sufficient accuracy the manner in which we obtained it, and as we cannot even recollect when the idea we have of a God was communi-cated to us by him, seeing it was always in our minds, it is still necessary that we should continue our review, and make inquiry after our author, possessing, as we do, the idea of the infinite perfections of a God: for it is in the highest degree evident by the natural light, that that which knows something more perfect than itself, is not the source of its own being, since it would thus have given to itself all the perfections which it knows; and that, consequently, it could draw its origin from no other being than from him who possesses in himself all those perfections, that is, from God.

XXI. That the duration alone of our life is sufficient to demonstrate the existence of God.

The truth of this demonstration will clearly appear, provided we consider the nature of time, or the duration of things; for this is of such a kind that its parts are not mutually dependent, and never co-existent; and, accordingly, from the fact that we now are, it does not necessarily follow that we shall be a moment afterwards, unless some cause, viz., that which first produced us, shall, as it were, continually reproduce us, that is, conserve us. For we easily understand that there is no power in us by which we can conserve ourselves, and that the being who has so much power as to conserve us out of himself, must also by so much the greater reason conserve himself, or rather stand in need of being conserved by no one whatever, and, in fine, be God.

XXII. That in knowing the existence of God, in the manner here explained, we likewise know all his attributes, as far as they can be known by the natural light alone.

There is the great advantage in proving the existence of God in this way, viz., by his idea, that we at the same time know what he is, as far as the weakness of our nature allows; for, reflecting on the idea we have of him which is born with us, we perceive that he is eternal, omniscient, omnipotent, the source of all goodness and truth, creator of all things, and that, in fine, he has in himself all that in which we can clearly discover any infinite perfection or good that is not limited by any imperfection.

XXIII. That God is not corporeal, and does not perceive by means of senses as we do, or will the evil of sin.

For there are indeed many things in the world that are to a certain extent imperfect or limited, though possessing also some perfection; and it is accordingly impossible that any such can be in God. Thus, looking to corporeal nature, since divisibility is included in local extension, and this indicates imperfection, it is certain that God is not body. And although in men it is to some degree a perfection to be capable of perceiving by means of the senses, nevertheless since in every sense there is passivity which indicates dependency, we must conclude that God is in no manner possessed of senses, and that he only understands and wills, not, however, like us, by acts in any way distinct, but always by an act that is one, identical, and the simplest possible, understands, wills, and operates all, that is, all things that in reality exist; for he does not will the evil of sin, seeing this is but the negation of being.

XXIV. That in passing from the knowledge of God to the knowledge of the creatures, it is necessary to remember that our understanding is finite, and the power of God infinite.

But as we know that God alone is the true cause of all that is or can be, we will doubtless follow the best way of philosophising, if, from the knowledge we have of God himself, we pass to the explication of the things which he has created, and essay to deduce it from the notions that are naturally in our minds, for we will thus obtain the most perfect science, that is, the knowledge of effects through their causes. But that we may be able to make this attempt with sufficient security from error, we must use the precaution to bear in mind as much as possible that God, who is the author of things, is infinite, while we are wholly finite.

XXV. That we must believe all that God has revealed, although it may surpass the reach of our faculties.

Thus, if perhaps God reveal to us or others, matters concerning himself which surpass the natural powers of our mind, such as the mysteries of the incarnation and of the trinity, we will not refuse to believe them, although we may not clearly understand them; nor will we be in any way surprised to find in the immensity of his nature, or even in what he has created, many things that exceed our comprehension.

XXVI. That it is not needful to enter into disputes regarding the infinite, but merely to hold all that in which we can find no limits as indefinite, such as the extension of the world, the divisibility of the parts of matter, the number of the stars, etc.

We will thus never embarrass ourselves by disputes about the infinite, seeing it would be absurd for us who are finite to undertake to determine anything regarding it, and thus as it were to limit it by endeavouring to comprehend it. We will accordingly give ourselves no concern to reply to those who demand whether the half of an infinite line is also infinite, and whether an infinite number is even or odd, and the like, because it is only such as imagine their minds to be infinite who seem bound to entertain questions of this sort. And, for our part, looking to all those things in which in certain senses we discover no limits, we will not, therefore, affirm that they are infinite, but will regard them simply as indefinite. Thus, because we cannot imagine extension so great that we cannot still conceive greater, we will say that the magnitude of possible things is indefinite, and because a body cannot be divided into parts so small that each of these may not be conceived as again divided into others still smaller, let us regard quantity as divisible into parts whose number is indefinite; and as we cannot imagine so many stars that it would seem impossible for God to create more, let us suppose that their number is indefinite, and so in other instances.

XXVII. What difference there is between the indefinite and the infinite.

And we will call those things indefinite rather than infinite, with the view of reserving to God alone the appellation of infinite; in the first place, because not only do we discover in him alone no limits on any side, but also because we positively conceive that he admits of none; and in the second place, because we do not in the same way positively conceive that other things are in every part unlimited, but merely negatively admit that their limits, if they have any, cannot be discovered by us.

XXVIII. That we must examine, not the final, but the efficient, causes of created things.

Likewise, finally, we will not seek reasons of natural things from the end which God or nature proposed to himself in their creation, for we ought not to presume so far as to think that we are sharers in the counsels of Deity, but, considering him as the efficient cause of all things, let us endeavour to discover by the natural light which he has planted in us, applied to those of his attributes of which he has been willing we should have some knowledge, what must be concluded regarding those effects we perceive by our senses; bearing in mind, however, what has been already said, that we must only confide in this natural light so long as nothing contrary to its dictates is revealed by God himself.

XXIX. That God is not the cause of our errors.

The first attribute of God which here falls to be considered, is that he is absolutely veracious and the source of all light, so that it is plainly repugnant for him to deceive us, or to be properly and positively the cause of the errors to which we are consciously subject; for although the address to deceive seems to be some mark of subtlety of mind among men, yet without doubt the will to deceive only proceeds from malice or from fear and weakness, and consequently cannot be attributed to God.

XXX. That consequently all which we clearly perceive is true, and that we are thus delivered from the doubts above proposed.

Whence it follows, that the light of nature, or faculty of knowledge given us by God, can never compass any object which is not true, in as far as it attains to a knowledge of it, that is, in as far as the object is clearly and distinctly apprehended. For God would have merited the appellation of a deceiver if he had given us this faculty perverted, and such as might lead us to take falsity for truth. Thus the highest doubt is removed, which arose from our ignorance on the point as to whether perhaps our nature was such that we might be deceived even in those things that appear to us the most evident. The same principle ought also to be of avail against all the other grounds of doubting that have been already enumerated. For mathematical truths ought now to be above suspicion, since these are of the clearest. And if we perceive anything by our senses, whether while awake or asleep, we will easily discover the truth, provided we separate what is clear and distinct in the knowledge from what is obscure and confused. There is no need that I should here say more on this subject; and what follows will serve to explain it still more accurately.

XXXI. That our errors are, in respect of God, merely negations, but, in respect of ourselves, privations.

But as it happens that we frequently fall into error, although God is no deceiver, if we desire to inquire into the origin and cause of our errors, with a view to guard against them, it is necessary to observe that they depend less on our understanding than on our will, and that they have no need of the actual concourse of God, in order to their production; so that, when considered in reference to God, they are merely negations, but in reference to ourselves, privations.

XXXII. That there are only two modes of thinking in us, viz., the perception of the understanding and the action of the will.

For all the modes of thinking of which we are conscious may be referred to two general classes, the one of which is the perception or operation of the understanding, and the other the volition or operation of the will. Thus, to perceive by the senses, to imagine, and to conceive things purely intelligible, are only different modes of perceiving; but to desire, to be averse from, to affirm, to deny, to doubt, are different modes of willing.

XXXIII. That we never err unless when we judge of something which we do not sufficiently apprehend.

When we apprehend anything we are in no danger of error, if we refrain from judging of it in any way; and even when we have formed a judgment regarding it, we would never fall into error, provided we gave our assent only to what we clearly and distinctly perceived; but the reason why we are usually deceived is that we judge without possessing an exact knowledge of that of which we judge.

XXXIV. That the will as well as the understanding is required for judging.

I admit that the understanding is necessary for judging, there being no room to suppose that we can judge of that which we in no way apprehend; but the will also is required in order to our assenting to what we have in any degree perceived. It is not necessary, however, at least to form any judgment whatever, that we have an entire and perfect apprehension of a thing; for we may assent to many things of which we have only a very obscure and confused knowledge.

XXXV. That the will is of greater extension than the understanding, and is thus the source of our errors.

Further, the perception of the intellect extends only to the few things that are presented to it, and is always very limited: the will, on the other hand, may, in a certain sense, be said to be infinite, because we observe nothing that can be the object of the will of any other, even of the unlimited will of God, to which ours cannot also extend, so that we easily carry it beyond the objects we clearly perceive; and when we do this, it is not wonderful that we happen to be deceived.

XXXVI. That our errors cannot be imputed to God.

But although God has not given us an omniscient understanding, he is not on this account to be considered in any wise the author of our errors, for it is of the nature of created intellect to be finite, and of finite intellect not to embrace all things.

XXXVII. That the chief perfection of man is his being able to act freely or by will, and that it is this which renders him worthy of praise or blame.

That the will should be the more extensive is in harmony with its nature; and it is a high perfection in man to be able to act by means of it, that is, freely; and thus in a peculiar way to be the master of his own actions, and merit praise or blame. For self-acting machines are not commended because they perform with exactness all the movements for which they were adapted, seeing their motions are carried on necessarily; but the maker of them is praised on account of the exactness with which they were framed, because he did not act of necessity, but freely; and, on the same principle, we must attribute to ourselves something more on this account, that when we embrace truth, we do so not of necessity, but freely.

XXXVIII. That error is a defect in our mode of acting, not in our nature; and that the faults of their subjects may be frequently attributed to other masters, but never to God.

It is true, that as often as we err, there is some defect in our mode of action or in the use of our liberty, but not in our nature, because this is always the same, whether our judgments be true or false. And although God could have given to us such perspicacity of intellect that we should never have erred, we have, notwithstanding, no right to demand this of him; for, although with us he who was able to prevent evil and did not is held guilty of it, God is not in the same way to be reckoned responsible for our errors because he had the power to prevent them, inasmuch as the dominion which some men possess over others has been instituted for the purpose of enabling them to hinder those under them from doing evil, whereas the dominion which God exercises over the universe is perfectly absolute and free. For this reason we ought to thank him for the goods he has given us, and not complain that he has not blessed us with all which we know it was in his power to impart.

XXXIX. That the liberty of our will is self-evident.

Finally, it is so manifest that we possess a free will, capable of giving or withholding its assent, that this truth must be reckoned among the first and most common notions which are born with us. This, indeed, has already very clearly appeared, for when essaying to doubt of all things we went so far as to suppose even that he who created us employed his limitless power in deceiving us in every way, we were conscious nevertheless of being free to abstain from believing what was not in every respect certain and undoubted. But that of which we are unable to doubt at such a time is as self-evident and clear as anything we can ever know.

XL. That it is likewise certain that God has foreordained all things.

But because what we have already discovered of God, gives us the assurance that his power is so immense that we would sin in thinking ourselves capable of ever doing anything which he had not ordained beforehand, we should soon be embarrassed in great difficulties if we undertook to harmonise the pre-ordination of God with the freedom of our will, and endeavoured to comprehend both truths at once.

XLI. How the freedom of our will may be reconciled with the Divine pre-ordination.

But, in place of this, we will be free from these embarrassments if we recollect that our mind is limited, while the power of God, by which he not only knew from all eternity what is or can be, but also willed and pre-ordained it, is infinite. It thus happens that we possess sufficient intelligence to know clearly and distinctly that this power is in God, but not enough to comprehend how he leaves the free actions of men indeterminate; and, on the other hand, we have such consciousness of the liberty and indifference which exists in ourselves, that there is nothing we more clearly or perfectly comprehend [so that the omnipotence of God ought not to keep us from believing it]. For it would be absurd to doubt of that of which we are fully conscious, and which we experience as existing in ourselves, because we do not comprehend another matter which, from its very nature, we know to be incomprehensible.

XLII. How, although we never will to err, it is nevertheless by our will that we do err.

But now since we know that all our errors depend upon our will, and as no one wishes to deceive himself, it may seem wonderful that there is any error in our judgments at all. It is necessary to remark, however, that there is a great difference between willing to be deceived, and willing to yield assent to opinions in which it happens that error is found. For though there is no one who expressly wishes to fall into error, we will yet hardly find any one who is not ready to assent to things in which, unknown to himself, error lurks; and it even frequently happens that it is the desire itself of following after truth that leads those not fully aware of the order in which it ought to be sought for, to pass judgment on matters of which they have no adequate knowledge, and thus to fall into error.

XLIII. That we shall never err if we give our assent only to what we clearly and distinctly perceive.

But it is certain we will never admit falsity for truth, so long as we judge only of that which we clearly and distinctly perceive; because, as God is no deceiver, the faculty of knowledge which he has given us cannot be fallacious, nor, for the same reason, the faculty of will, when we do not extend it beyond the objects we clearly know. And even although this truth could not be established by reasoning, the minds of all have been so impressed by nature as spontaneously to assent to whatever is clearly perceived, and to experience an impossibility to doubt of its truth.

XLIV. That we uniformly judge improperly when we assent to what we do not clearly perceive, although our judgment may chance to be true; and that it is frequently our memory which deceives us by leading us to believe that certain things were formerly sufficiently understood by us.

It is likewise certain that, when we approve of any reason which we do not apprehend, we are either deceived, or, if we stumble on the truth, it is only by chance, and thus we can never possess the assurance that we are not in error. I confess it seldom happens that we judge of a thing when we have observed we do not apprehend it, because it is a dictate of the natural light never to judge of what we do not know. But we most frequently err in this, that we presume upon a past knowledge of much to which we give our assent, as to something treasured up in the memory, and perfectly known to us; whereas, in truth, we have no such knowledge.

XLV. What constitutes clear and distinct perception.

There are indeed a great many persons who, through their whole lifetime, never perceive anything in a way necessary for judging of it properly; for the knowledge upon which we can establish a certain and indubitable judgment must be not only clear, but also distinct. I call that clear which is present and manifest to the mind giving attention to it, just as we are said clearly to see objects when, being present to the eye looking on, they stimulate it with sufficient force, and it is disposed to regard them; but the distinct is that which is so precise and different from all other objects as to comprehend in itself only what is clear.

XLVI. It is shown, from the example of pain, that a perception may be clear without being distinct, but that it cannot be distinct unless it is clear.

For example, when any one feels intense pain, the knowledge which he has of this pain is very clear, but it is not always distinct; for men usually confound it with the obscure judgment they form regarding its nature, and think that there is in the suffering part something similar to the sensation of pain of which they are alone conscious. And thus perception may be clear without being distinct, but it can never be distinct without likewise being clear.

XLVII. That, to correct the prejudices of our early years, we must consider what is clear in each of our simple notions.

And, indeed, in our early years, the mind was so immersed in the body, that, although it perceived many things with sufficient clearness, it yet knew nothing distinctly; and since even at that time we exercised our judgment in many matters, numerous prejudices were thus contracted, which, by the majority, are never afterwards laid aside. But that we may now be in a position to get rid of these, I will here briefly enumerate all the simple notions of which our thoughts are composed, and distinguish in each what is clear from what is obscure, or fitted to lead into error.

XLVIII. That all the objects of our knowledge are to be regarded either (1) as things or the affections of things: or (2) as eternal truths; with the enumeration of things.

Whatever objects fall under our knowledge we consider either as things or the affections of things, or as eternal truths possessing no existence beyond our thought. Of the first class the most general are substance, duration, order, number, and perhaps also some others, which notions apply to all the kinds of things. I do not, however, recognize more than two highest kinds of things; the first of intellectual things, or such as have the power of thinking, including mind or thinking substance and its properties; the second, of material things, embracing extended substance, or body and its properties. Perception, volition, and all modes as well of knowing as of willing, are related to thinking substance; on the other hand, to extended substance we refer magnitude, or extension in length, breadth, and depth, figure, motion, situation, divisibility of parts themselves, and the like. There are, however, besides these, certain things of which we have an internal experience that ought not to be referred either to the mind of itself, or to the body alone, but to the close and intimate union between them, as will hereafter be shown in its place. Of this class are the appetites of hunger and thirst, etc., and also the emotions or passions of the mind which are not exclusively mental affections, as the emotions of anger, joy, sadness, love, etc.; and, finally, all the sensations, as of pain, titillation, light and colours, sounds, smells, tastes, heat, hardness, and the other tactile qualities.

XLIX. That the eternal truths cannot be thus enumerated, but that this is not necessary.

What I have already enumerated we are to regard as things, or the qualities or modes of things. We now come to speak of eternal truths.

When we apprehend that it is impossible a thing can arise from nothing, this proposition, *ex nihilo nihil fit,* is not considered as somewhat existing, or as the mode of a thing, but as an eternal truth having its seat in our mind, and is called a common notion or axiom. Of this class are the following:—It is impossible the same thing can at once be and not be; what is done cannot be undone; he who thinks must exist while he thinks; and innumerable others, the whole of which it is indeed difficult to enumerate, but this is not necessary, since, if blinded by no prejudices, we cannot fail to know them when the occasion of thinking them occurs.

L. That these truths are clearly perceived, but not equally by all men, on account of prejudices.

And, indeed, with regard to these common notions, it is not to be doubted that they can be clearly and distinctly known, for otherwise they would not merit this appellation: as, in truth, some of them are not, with respect to all men, equally deserving of the name, because they are not equally admitted by all: not, however, from this reason, as I think, that the faculty of knowledge of one man extends farther than that of another, but rather because these common notions are opposed to the prejudices of some, who, on this account, are not able readily to embrace them, even although others, who are free from those prejudices, apprehend them with the greatest clearness.

LI. What substance is, and that the term is not applicable to God and the creatures in the same sense.

But with regard to what we consider as things or the modes of things, it is worth while to examine each of them by itself. By substance we can conceive nothing else than a thing which exists in such a way as to stand in need of nothing beyond itself in order to its existence. And, in truth, there can be conceived but one substance which is absolutely independent, and that is God. We perceive that all other things can exist only by help of the concourse of God. And, accordingly, the term substance does not apply to God and the creatures *univocally,* to adopt a term familiar in the schools; that is, no signification of this word can be distinctly understood which is common to God and them.

LII. That the term is applicable univocally to the mind and the body, and how substance itself is known.

Created substances, however, whether corporeal or thinking, may be conceived under this common concept; for these are things which, in order to their existence, stand in need of nothing but the concourse of God. But yet substance cannot be first discovered merely from its being a thing which exists independently, for existence by itself is not observed by us. We easily, however, discover substance itself from any attribute of it, by this common notion, that of nothing there are no attributes, properties, or qualities: for, from perceiving that some attribute is present, we infer that some existing thing or substance to which it may be attributed is also of necessity present.

LIII. That of every substance there is one principal attribute, as thinking of the mind, extension of the body.

But, although any attribute is sufficient to lead us to the knowledge of substance, there is, however, one principal property of every substance, which constitutes its nature or essence, and upon which all the others depend. Thus, extension in length, breadth, and depth constitutes the nature of corporeal substance; and thought the nature of thinking substance. For every other thing that can be attributed to body, presupposes extension, and is only some mode of an extended thing; as all the properties we discover in the mind are only diverse modes of thinking. Thus, for example, we cannot conceive figure unless in something extended, nor motion unless in extended space, nor imagination, sensation, or will, unless in a thinking thing. But, on the other hand, we can conceive extension without figure or motion, and thought without imagination or sensation, and so of the others; as is clear to any one who attends to these matters.

LIV. How we may have clear and distinct notions of the substance which thinks, of that which is corporeal, and of God.

And thus we may easily have two clear and distinct notions or ideas, the one of created substance, which thinks, the other of corporeal substance, provided we carefully distinguish all the attributes of thought from those of extension. We may also have a clear and distinct idea of an uncreated and independent thinking substance, that is, of God, provided we do not suppose that this idea adequately represents to us all that is in God, and do not mix up with it anything fictitious, but attend simply to the characters that are comprised in the notion we have of him, and which we clearly know to belong to the nature of an absolutely perfect Being. For no one can deny that there is in us such an idea of God, without groundlessly supposing that there is no knowledge of God at all in the human mind.

LV. How duration, order, and number may be also distinctly conceived.

We will also have most distinct conceptions of duration, order, and number, if, in place of mixing up with our notions of them that which properly belongs to the concept of substance, we merely think that the duration of a thing is a mode under which we conceive this thing, in so far as it continues to exist; and, in like manner, that order and number are not in reality different from things disposed in order and numbered, but only modes under which we diversely consider these things.

LVI. What are modes, qualities, attributes.

And, indeed, we here understand by modes the same with what we elsewhere designate attributes or qualities. But when we consider substance as affected or varied by them, we use the term modes; when from this variation it may be denominated of such a kind, we adopt the term qualities [to designate the different modes which cause it to be so named]; and, finally, when we simply regard these modes as in the substance, we call them attributes. Accordingly, since God must be conceived as superior to change, it is not proper to say that there are modes or qualities in him, but simply attributes; and even in created things that which is found in them always in the same mode, as existence and duration in the thing which exists and endures, ought to be called attribute, and not mode or quality.

LVII. That some attributes exist in the things to which they are attributed, and others only in our thought; and what duration and time are.

Of these attributes or modes there are some which exist in the things themselves, and others that have only an existence in our thought; thus, for example, time, which we distinguish from duration taken in its generality, and call the measure of motion, is only a certain mode under which we think duration itself, for we do not indeed conceive the duration of things that are moved to be different from the duration of things that are not moved: as is evident from this, that if two bodies are in motion for an hour, the one moving quickly and the other slowly, we do not reckon more time in the one than in the other, although there may be much more motion in the one of the bodies than in the other. But that we may comprehend the duration of all things under a common measure, we compare their duration with that of the greatest and most regular motions that give rise to years and days, and which we call time; hence what is so designated is nothing superadded to duration, taken in its generality, but a mode of thinking.

LVIII. That number and all universals are only modes of thought.

In the same way number, when it is not considered as in created things, but merely in the abstract or in general, is only a mode of thinking; and the same is true of all those general ideas we call universals.

LIX. How universals are formed; and what are the five common, viz., genus, species, difference, property, and accident.

Universals arise merely from our making use of one and the same idea in thinking of all individual objects between which there subsists a certain likeness; and when we comprehend all the objects represented by this idea under one name, this term likewise becomes universal. For example, when we see two stones, and do not regard their nature farther than to remark that there are two of them, we form the idea of a certain number, which we call the binary; and when we afterwards see two birds or two trees, and merely take notice of them so far as to observe that there are two of them, we again take up the same idea as before, which is, accordingly, universal; and we likewise give to this number the same universal appellation of binary. In the same way, when we consider a figure of three sides, we form a certain idea, which we call the idea of a triangle, and we afterwards make use of it as the universal to represent to our mind all other figures of three sides. But when we remark more particularly that of figures of three sides, some have a right angle and others not, we form the universal idea of a right-angled triangle, which being related to the preceding as more general, may be called species; and the right angle is the universal difference by which right-angled triangles are distinguished from all others; and farther, because the square of the side which sustains the right angle is equal to the squares of the other two sides, and because this property belongs only to this species of triangles, we may call it the universal property of the species. Finally, if we suppose that of these triangles some are moved and others not, this will be their universal accident; and, accordingly, we commonly reckon five universals, viz., genus, species, difference, property, accident.

LX. Of distinctions; and first of the real.

But number in things themselves arises from the distinction there is between them: and distinction is threefold, viz., real, modal, and of reason. The real properly subsists between two or more substances; and it is sufficient to assure us that two substances are really mutually distinct, if only we are able clearly and distinctly to conceive the one of them without the other. For the knowledge we have of God renders it certain that he can effect all that of which we have a distinct idea: wherefore, since we have now, for example, the idea of an extended and corporeal substance, though we as yet do not know with certainty whether any such thing is really existent, nevertheless, merely because we have the idea of it, we may be assured that such may exist; and, if it really exists, that every part which we can determine by thought must be really distinct from the other parts of the same substance. In the same way, since every one is conscious that he thinks, and that he in thought can exclude from himself every other substance, whether thinking or extended, it is certain that each of us thus considered is really distinct from every other thinking and corporeal substance. And although we suppose that God united a body to a soul so closely that it was impossible to form a more intimate union, and thus made a composite whole, the two substances would remain really distinct, notwithstanding this union; for with whatever tie God connected them, he was not able to rid himself of the power he possessed of separating them, or of conserving the one apart from the other, and the things which God can separate or conserve separately are really distinct.

LXI. Of the modal distinction.

There are two kinds of modal distinctions, viz., that between the mode properly so called and the substance of which it is a mode, and that between two modes of the same substance.

As for the distinction according to which the mode of one substance is different from another substance, or from the mode of another substance, as the motion of one body is different from another body or from the mind, or as motion is different from doubt, it seems to me that it should be called real rather than modal, because these modes cannot be clearly conceived apart from the really distinct substances of which they are the modes.

LXII. Of the distinction of reason.

Finally, the distinction of reason is that between a substance and some one of its attributes, without which it is impossible, however, we can have a distinct conception of the substance itself; or between two such attributes of a common substance, the one of which we essay to think without the other. This distinction is manifest from our inability to form a clear and distinct idea of such substance if we separate from it such attribute; or to have a clear perception of the one of two such attributes if we separate it from the other.

LXIII. How thought and extension may be distinctly known, as constituting, the one the nature of mind, the other that of body.

Thought and extension may be regarded as constituting the natures of intelligent and corporeal substance; and then they must not be otherwise conceived than as the thinking and extended substances themselves, that is, as mind and body, which in this way are conceived with the greatest clearness and distinctness. Moreover, we more easily conceive extended or thinking substance than substance by itself, or with the omission of its thinking or extension. For there is some difficulty in abstracting the notion of substance from the notions of thinking and extension, which, in truth, are only diverse in thought itself; and a concept is not more distinct because it comprehends fewer properties, but because we accurately distinguish what is comprehended in it from all other notions.

LXIV. How these may likewise be distinctly conceived as modes of substance.

Thought and extension may be also considered as modes of substance; in as far, namely, as the same mind may have many different thoughts, and the same body, with its size unchanged, may be extended in several diverse ways, at one time more in length and less in breadth or depth, and at another time more in breadth and less in length; and then they are modally distinguished from substance, and can be conceived not less clearly and distinctly, provided they be not regarded as substances or things separated from others, but simply as modes of things. For by regarding them as in the substances of which they are the modes, we distinguish them from these substances, and take them for what in truth they are: whereas, on the other hand, if we wish to consider them apart from the substances in which they are, we should by this itself regard them as self-subsisting things, and thus confound the ideas of mode and substance.

LXV. How we may likewise know their modes.

In the same way we will best apprehend the diverse modes of thought, as intellection, imagination, recollection, volition, etc., and also the diverse modes of extension, or those that belong to extension, as all figures, the situation of parts and their motions, provided we consider them simply as modes of the things in which they are; and motion as far as it is concerned, provided we think merely of locomotion, without seeking to know the force that produces it, and which nevertheless I will essay to explain in its own place.

LXVI. How our sensations, affections, and appetites may be clearly known, although we are frequently wrong in our judgments regarding them.

There remain our sensations, affections, and appetites, of which we may also have a clear knowledge, if we take care to comprehend in the judgments we form of them only that which is precisely contained in our perception of them, and of which we are immediately conscious. There is, however, great difficulty in observing this, at least in respect of sensations; because we have all, without exception, from our youth judged that all the things we perceived by our senses had an existence beyond our thought, and that they were entirely similar to the sensations, that is, perceptions, we had of them. Thus when, for example, we saw a certain colour, we thought we saw something occupying a place out of us, and which was entirely similar to that idea of colour we were then conscious of; and from the habit of judging in this way, we seemed to see this so clearly and distinctly that we esteemed it (i.e. the externality of the colour) certain and indubitable.

LXVII. That we are frequently deceived in our judgments regarding pain itself.

The same prejudice has place in all our other sensations, even in those of titillation and pain. For though we are not in the habit of believing that there exist out of us objects that resemble titillation and pain, we do not nevertheless consider these sensations as in the mind alone, or in our perception, but as in the hand, or foot, or some other part of our body. There is no reason, however, to constrain us to believe that the pain, for example, which we feel, as it were, in the foot is something out of the mind existing in the foot, or that the light which we see, as it were, in the sun exists in the sun as it is in us. Both these beliefs are prejudices of our early years, as will clearly appear in the sequel.

LXVIII. How in these things what we clearly conceive is to be distinguished from that in which we may be deceived.

But that we may distinguish what is clear in our sensations from what is obscure, we ought most carefully to observe that we possess a clear and distinct knowledge of pain, colour, and other things of this sort, when we consider them simply as sensations or thoughts; but that, when they are judged to be certain things subsisting beyond our mind, we are wholly unable to form any conception of them. Indeed, when any one tells us that he sees colour in a body or feels pain in one of his limbs, this is exactly the same as if he said that he there saw or felt something of the nature of which he was entirely ignorant, or that he did not know what he saw or felt. For although, when less attentively examining his thoughts, a person may easily persuade himself that he has some knowledge of it, since he supposes that there is something resembling that sensation of colour or of pain of which he is conscious; yet, if he reflects on what the sensation of colour or pain represents to him as existing in a coloured body or in a wounded member, he will find that of such he has absolutely no knowledge.

LXIX. That magnitude, figure, etc., are known far differently from colour, pain, etc.

What we have said above will be more manifest, especially if we consider that size in the body perceived, figure, motion, the situation of parts, duration, number, and those other properties which, as we have already said, we clearly perceive in all bodies, are known by us in a way altogether different from that in which we know what colour is in the same body, or pain, smell, taste, or any other of those properties which I have said above must be referred to the senses. For although when we see a body we are not less assured of its existence from its appearing figured than from its appearing coloured, we yet know with far greater clearness its property of figure than its colour.

LXX. That we may judge of sensible things in two ways, by the one of which we avoid error, by the other fall into it.

It is thus manifest that to say we perceive colours in objects is in reality equivalent to saying we perceive something in objects and are yet ignorant of what it is, except as that which determines in us a certain highly vivid and clear sensation, which we call the sensation of colours. There is, however, very great diversity in the manner of judging: for so long as we simply judge that there is an unknown something in objects, so far are we from falling into error that, on the contrary, we thus rather provide against it, for we are less apt to judge rashly of a thing which we observe we do not know. But when we think we perceive colours in objects, although we are in reality ignorant of what we then denominate colour, and are unable to conceive any resemblance between the colour we suppose to be in objects, and that of which we are conscious in sensation, yet because we do not observe this, or because there are in objects several properties, as size, figure, number, etc., which, as we clearly know, exist, or may exist in them as they are perceived by our senses or conceived by our understanding, we easily glide into the error of holding that what is called colour in objects is something entirely resembling the colour we perceive, and thereafter of supposing that we have a clear perception of what is in no way perceived by us.

LXXI. That the chief cause of our errors is to be found in the prejudices of our childhood.

And here we may notice the first and chief cause of our errors. In early life the mind was so closely bound to the body that it attended to nothing beyond the thoughts by which it perceived the objects that made impression on the body: nor as yet did it refer these thoughts to anything existing beyond itself, but simply felt pain when the body was hurt, or pleasure when anything beneficial to the body occurred, or if the body was so slightly affected that it was neither greatly benefited nor hurt, the mind experienced the sensations we call tastes, smells, sounds, heat, cold, light, colours, and the like, which in truth are representative of nothing existing out of our mind, and which vary according to the diversities of the parts and modes in which the body is affected. The mind at the same time also perceived magnitudes, figures, motions, and the like, which were not presented to it as sensations but as things of the modes of things existing, or at least capable of existing out of thought, although it did not yet observe this difference between these two kinds of perceptions. And afterwards when the machine of the body, which has been so fabricated by nature that it can of its own inherent power move itself in various ways, by turning itself at random on every side, followed after what was useful and avoided what was detrimental; the mind, which was closely connected with it, reflecting on the objects it pursued or avoided, remarked, for the first time, that they existed out of itself, and not only attributed to them magnitudes, figures, motions, and the like, which it apprehended either as things or as the modes of things, but, in addition, attributed to them tastes, odours, and the other ideas of that sort, the sensations of which were caused by itself; and as it only considered other objects in so far as they were useful to the body, in which it was immersed, it judged that there was greater or less reality in each object, according as the impressions it caused on the body were more or less powerful. Hence arose the belief that there was more substance or body in rocks and metals than in air or water, because the mind perceived in them more hardness and weight. Moreover, the air was thought to be merely nothing so long as we experienced no agitation of it by the wind, or did not feel it hot or cold. And because the stars gave hardly more light than the slender flames of candles, we supposed that each star was but of this size. Again, since the mind did not observe that the earth moved on its axis, or that its superficies was curved like that of a globe, it was on that account more ready to judge the earth immovable and its surface flat. And our mind has been imbued from our infancy with a thousand other prejudices of the same sort, which afterwards in our youth we forgot we had accepted without sufficient examination, and admitted as possessed of the highest truth and clearness, as if they had been known by means of our senses, or implanted in us by nature.

LXXII. That the second cause of our errors is that we cannot forget these prejudices.

And although now in our mature years, when the mind, being no longer wholly subject to the body, is not in the habit of referring all things to it, but also seeks to discover the truth of things considered in themselves, we observe the falsehood of a great many of the judgments we had before formed; yet we experience a difficulty in expunging them from our memory, and, so long as they remain there, they give rise to various errors. Thus, for example, since from our earliest years we imagined the stars to be of very small size, we find it highly difficult to rid ourselves of this imagination, although assured by plain astronomical reasons that they are of the greatest,—so prevailing is the power of preconceived opinion.

LXXIII. The third cause is, that we become fatigued by attending to those objects which are not present to the senses; and that we are thus accustomed to judge of these not from present perception but from preconceived opinion..

Besides, our mind cannot attend to any object without at length experiencing some pain and fatigue; and of all objects it has the greatest difficulty in attending to those which are present neither to the senses nor to the imagination: whether for the reason that this is natural to it from its union with the body, or because in our early years, being occupied merely with perceptions and imaginations, it has become more familiar with, and acquired greater facility in thinking in those modes than in any other. Hence it also happens that many are unable to conceive any substance except what is imaginable and corporeal, and even sensible. For they are ignorant of the circumstance that those objects alone are imaginable which consist in extension, motion, and figure, while there are many others besides these that are intelligible; and they persuade themselves that nothing can subsist but body, and, finally, that there is no body which is not sensible. And since in truth we perceive no object such as it is by sense alone, as will hereafter be clearly shown, it thus

happens that the majority during life perceive nothing unless in a confused way.

LXXIV. The fourth source of our errors is, that we attach our thoughts
to words which do not express them with accuracy.

Finally, since for the use of speech we attach all our conceptions to
words by which to express them, and commit to memory our thoughts
in connection with these terms, and as we afterwards find it more easy
to recall the words than the things signified by them, we can scarcely
conceive anything with such distinctness as to separate entirely what
we conceive from the words that were selected to express it. On this
account the majority attend to words rather than to things; and thus very
frequently assent to terms without attaching to them any meaning, either
because they think they once understood them, or imagine they received
them from others by whom they were correctly understood. This, however, is not the place to treat of this matter in detail, seeing the nature
of the human body has not yet been expounded, nor the existence even
of body established; enough, nevertheless, appears to have been said to
enable one to distinguish such of our conceptions as are clear and distinct
from those that are obscure and confused.

LXXV. Summary of what must be observed in order to philosophise
correctly.

Wherefore if we would philosophise in earnest, and give ourselves
to the search after all the truths we are capable of knowing, we must, in
the first place, lay aside our prejudices; in other words, we must take
care scrupulously to withhold our assent from the opinions we have
formerly admitted, until upon new examination we discover that they
are true. We must, in the next place, make an orderly review of the
notions we have in our minds, and hold as true all and only those which
we will clearly and distinctly apprehend. In this way we will observe,
first of all, that we exist in so far as it is our nature to think, and at the
same time that there is a God upon whom we depend; and after considering his attributes we will be able to investigate the truth of all other
things, since God is the cause of them. Besides the notions we have of
God and of our mind, we will likewise find that we possess the knowledge
of many propositions which are eternally true, as, for example, that
nothing cannot be the cause of anything, etc. We will farther discover
in our minds the knowledge of a corporeal or extended nature that may
be moved, divided, etc., and also of certain sensations that affect us, as
of pain, colours, tastes, etc., although we do not yet know the cause of
our being so affected; and, comparing what we have now learned, by
examining those things in their order, with our former confused knowledge of them, we will acquire the habit of forming clear and distinct
conceptions of all the objects we are capable of knowing. In these few

precepts seem to me to be comprised the most general and important principles of human knowledge.

LXXVI. That we ought to prefer the Divine authority to our perception: but that, apart from things revealed, we ought to assent to nothing that we do not clearly apprehend.

Above all, we must impress on our memory the infallible rule, that what God has revealed is incomparably more certain than anything else; and that we ought to submit our belief to the Divine authority rather than to our own judgment, even although perhaps the light of reason should, with the greatest clearness and evidence, appear to suggest to us something contrary to what is revealed. But in things regarding which there is no revelation, it is by no means consistent with the character of a philosopher to accept as true what he has not ascertained to be such, and to trust more to the senses, in other words, to the inconsiderate judgments of childhood than to the dictates of mature reason.

PART TWO: OF THE PRINCIPLES OF MATERIAL THINGS

I. THE GROUNDS on which the existence of material things may be known with certainty.

Although we are all sufficiently persuaded of the existence of material things, yet, since this was before called in question by us, and since we reckoned the persuasion of their existence as among the prejudices of our childhood, it is now necessary for us to investigate the grounds on which this truth may be known with certainty. In the first place, then, it cannot be doubted that every perception we have comes to us from some object different from our mind; for it is not in our power to cause ourselves to experience one perception rather than another, the perception being entirely dependent on the object which affects our senses. It may, indeed, be matter of inquiry whether that object be God, or something different from God; but because we perceive, or rather, stimulated by sense, clearly and distinctly apprehend, certain matter extended in length, breadth, and thickness, the various parts of which have different figures and motions, and give rise to the sensations we have of colours, smells, pain, etc., God would, without question, deserve to be regarded as a deceiver, if he directly and of himself presented to our mind the idea of this extended matter, or merely caused it to be presented to us by some object which possessed neither extension, figure, nor motion. For we clearly conceive this matter as entirely distinct from God, and from ourselves, or our mind; and appear even clearly to discern that the idea of it is formed in us on occasion of objects existing out of our minds, to which it is in every respect similar. But since God cannot deceive us, for this is repugnant to his nature, as has been already remarked, we must unhesitatingly conclude that there exists a certain object extended in length, breadth, and thickness, and possessing all those properties which we clearly apprehend to belong to what is extended. And this extended substance is what we call body or matter.

II. How we likewise know that the human body is closely connected with the mind.

We ought also to conclude that a certain body is more closely united to our mind than any other, because we clearly observe that pain and other sensations affect us without our foreseeing them; and these, the mind is conscious, do not arise from itself alone, nor pertain to it, in so far as it is a thing which thinks, but only in so far as it is united to another thing extended and movable, which is called the human body. But this is not the place to treat in detail of this matter.

III. That the perceptions of the senses do not teach us what is in reality in things, but what is beneficial or hurtful to the composite whole of mind and body.

It will be sufficient to remark that the perceptions of the senses are merely to be referred to this intimate union of the human body and mind, and that they usually make us aware of what, in external objects, may be useful or adverse to this union, but do not present to us these objects as they are in themselves, unless occasionally and by accident. For, after this observation, we will without difficulty lay aside the prejudices of the senses, and will have recourse to our understanding alone on this question, by reflecting carefully on the ideas implanted in it by nature.

IV. That the nature of body consists not in weight, hardness, colour, and the like, but in extension alone.

In this way we will discern that the nature of matter or body, considered in general, does not consist in its being hard, or ponderous, or coloured, or that which affects our senses in any other way, but simply in its being a substance extended in length, breadth, and depth. For, with respect to hardness, we know nothing of it by sense farther than that the parts of hard bodies resist the motion of our hands on coming into contact with them; but if every time our hands moved towards any part, all the bodies in that place receded as quickly as our hands approached, we should never feel hardness; and yet we have no reason to believe that bodies which might thus recede would on this account lose that which makes them bodies. The nature of body does not, therefore, consist in hardness. In the same way, it may be shown that weight, colour, and all the other qualities of this sort, which are perceived in corporeal matter, may be taken from it, itself meanwhile remaining entire: it thus follows that the nature of body depends on none of these.

V. That the truth regarding the nature of body is obscured by the opinions respecting rarefaction and a vacuum with which we are pre-occupied.

There still remain two causes to prevent its being fully admitted that the true nature of body consists in extension alone. The first is the prevalent opinion, that most bodies admit of being so rarefied and condensed that, when rarefied, they have greater extension than when condensed; and some even have subtilised to such a degree as to make a distinction between the substance of body and its quantity, and between quantity itself and extension. The second cause is this, that where we conceive only extension in length, breadth, and depth, we are not in the habit of saying that body is there, but only space and further void space, which the generality believe to be a mere negation.

VI. In what way rarefaction takes place.

But with regard to rarefaction and condensation, whoever gives his attention to his own thoughts, and admits nothing of which he is not clearly conscious, will not suppose that there is anything in those processes further than a change of figure in the body rarefied or condensed: so that, in other words, rare bodies are those between the parts of which there are numerous distances filled with other bodies; and dense bodies, on the other hand, those whose parts approaching each other, either diminish these distances or take them wholly away, in the latter of which cases the body is rendered absolutely dense. The body, however, when condensed, has not, therefore, less extension than when the parts embrace a greater space, owing to their removal from each other, and their dispersion into branches. For we ought not to attribute to it the extension of the pores or distances which its parts do not occupy when it is rarefied, but to the other bodies that fill these interstices; just as when we see a sponge full of water or any other liquid, we do not suppose that each part of the sponge has on this account greater extension than when compressed and dry, but only that its pores are wider, and therefore that the body is diffused over a larger space.

VII. That rarefaction cannot be intelligibly explained unless in the way here proposed.

And indeed I am unable to discover the force of the reasons which have induced some to say that rarefaction is the result of the augmentation of the quantity of body, rather than to explain it on the principle exemplified in the case of a sponge. For although when air or water are rarefied we do not see any of the pores that are rendered large, or the new body that is added to occupy them, it is yet less agreeable to reason to suppose something that is unintelligible for the purpose of giving a verbal and merely apparent explanation of the rarefaction of bodies, than to conclude, because of their rarefaction, that there are pores or distances between the parts which are increased in size, and filled with some new body. Nor ought we to refrain from assenting to this explanation, because we perceive this new body by none of our senses, for there is no reason which obliges us to believe that we should perceive by our senses all the bodies in existence. And we see that it is very easy to explain rarefaction in this manner, but impossible in any other; for, in fine, there would be, as appears to me, a manifest contradiction in supposing that any body was increased by a quantity or extension which it had not before, without the addition to it of a new extended substance, in other words, of another body, because it is impossible to conceive any addition of extension or quantity to a thing without supposing the addition of a substance having quantity or extension, as will more clearly appear from what follows.

VIII. That quantity and number differ only in thought from that which has quantity and is numbered.

For quantity differs from extended substance, and number from what is numbered, not in reality but merely in our thought; so that, for example, we may consider the whole nature of a corporeal substance which is comprised in a space of ten feet, although we do not attend to this measure of ten feet, for the obvious reason that the thing conceived is of the same nature in any part of that space as in the whole; and, on the other hand, we can conceive the number ten, as also a continuous quantity of ten feet, without thinking of this determinate substance, because the concept of the number ten is manifestly the same whether we consider a number of ten feet or ten of anything else; and we can conceive a continuous quantity of ten feet without thinking of this or that determinate substance, although we cannot conceive it without some extended substance of which it is the quantity. It is in reality, however, impossible that any, even the least part, of such quantity or extension, can be taken away, without the retrenchment at the same time of as much of the substance, nor, on the other hand, can we lessen the substance, without at the same time taking as much from the quantity or extension.

IX. That corporeal substance, when distinguished from its quantity, is confusedly conceived as something incorporeal.

Although perhaps some express themselves otherwise on this matter, I am nevertheless convinced that they do not think differently from what I have now said: for when they distinguish substance from extension or quantity, they either mean nothing by the word substance, or they form in their minds merely a confused idea of incorporeal substance, which they falsely attribute to corporeal, and leave to extension the true idea of this corporeal substance; which extension they call an accident, but with such impropriety as to make it easy to discover that their words are not in harmony with their thoughts.

X. What space or internal place is.

Space or internal place, and the corporeal substance which is comprised in it, are not different in reality, but merely in the mode in which they are wont to be conceived by us. For, in truth, the same extension in length, breadth, and depth, which constitutes space, constitutes body; and the difference between them lies only in this, that in body we consider extension as particular, and conceive it to change with the body; whereas in space we attribute to extension a generic unity, so that after taking from a certain space the body which occupied it, we do not suppose that we have at the same time removed the extension of the space, because it appears to us that the same extension remains there so long as it is of the same magnitude and figure, and preserves the same situation in respect to certain bodies around it, by means of which we determine this space.

XI. How space is not in reality different from corporeal substance.

And indeed it will be easy to discern that it is the same extension which constitutes the nature of body as of space, and that these two things are mutually diverse only as the nature of the genus and species differs from that of the individual, provided we reflect on the idea we have of any body, taking a stone for example, and reject all that is not essential to the nature of body. In the first place, then, hardness may be rejected, because if the stone were liquefied or reduced to powder, it would no longer possess hardness, and yet would not cease to be a body; colour also may be thrown out of account, because we have frequently seen stones so transparent as to have no colour; again, we may reject weight, because we have the case of fire, which, though very light, is still a body; and, finally, we may reject cold, heat, and all the other qualities of this sort, either because they are not considered as in the stone, or because, with the change of these qualities, the stone is not supposed to have lost the nature of body. After this examination we will find that nothing remains in the idea of body, except that it is something extended in length, breadth, and depth; and this something is comprised in our idea of space, not only of that which is full of body, but even of what is called void space.

XII. How space differs from body in our mode of conceiving it.

There is, however, some difference between them in the mode of conception; for if we remove a stone from the space or place in which it was, we conceive that its extension also is taken away, because we regard this as particular, and inseparable from the stone itself: but meanwhile we suppose that the same extension of place in which this stone was remains, although the place of the stone be occupied by wood, water, air, or by any other body, or be even supposed vacant, because we now consider extension in general, and think that the same is common to stones, wood, water, air, and other bodies, and even to a vacuum itself, if there is any such thing, provided it be of the same magnitude and figure as before, and preserve the same situation among the external bodies which determine this space.

XIII. What external place is.

The reason of which is, that the words place and space signify nothing really different from body which is said to be in place, but merely designate its magnitude, figure, and situation among other bodies. For it is necessary, in order to determine this situation, to regard certain other bodies which we consider as immovable; and, according as we look to different bodies, we may see that the same thing at the same time does and does not change place. And besides, if we suppose that the earth moves, and that it makes precisely as much way from west to east as a vessel from east to west, we will say that the person at the stern does not change his place, because this place will be determined by certain immovable points which we imagine to be in the heavens. But if at length we are persuaded that there are no points really immovable in the universe, as will hereafter be shown to be probable, we will thence conclude that nothing has a permanent place unless in so far as it is fixed by our thought.

XIV. Wherein place and space differ.

The terms place and space, however, differ in signification, because place more expressly designates situation than magnitude or figure, while, on the other hand, we think of the latter when we speak of space. For we frequently say that a thing succeeds to the place of another although it be not exactly of the same magnitude or figure; but we do not therefore admit that it occupies the same space as the other; and when the situation is changed we say that the place also is changed, although there are the same magnitude and figure as before: so that when we say that a thing is in a particular place, we mean merely that it is situated in a determinate way in respect of certain other objects; and when we add that it occupies such a space or place we understand besides that it is of such determinate magnitude and figure as exactly to fill this space.

XV. How external place is rightly taken for the superficies of the surrounding body.

And thus we never indeed distinguish space from extension in length, breadth, and depth; we sometimes, however, consider place as in the thing placed, and at other times as out of it. Internal place indeed differs in no way from space; but external place may be taken for the superficies that immediately surrounds the thing placed.

XVI. That a vacuum or space in which there is absolutely no body is repugnant to reason.

With regard to a vacuum, in the philosophical sense of the term, that is, a space in which there is no substance, it is evident that such does not exist, seeing the extension of space or internal place is not different from that of body. For since from this alone, that a body has extension in length, breadth, and depth, we have reason to conclude that it is a substance, it being absolutely contradictory that nothing should possess extension, we ought to form a similar inference regarding the space which is supposed void, viz., that since there is extension in it there is necessarily also substance.

XVII. That a vacuum in the ordinary use of the term does not exclude all body.

And, in truth, by the term vacuum in its common use, we do not mean a place or space in which there is absolutely nothing, but only a place in which there is none of those things we presume ought to be there. Thus, because a pitcher is made to hold water, it is said to be empty when it is merely filled with air; or if there are no fish in a fish-pond, we say there is nothing in it, although it be full of water; thus a vessel is said to be empty, when, in place of the merchandise which it was designed to carry, it is loaded with sand only, to enable it to resist the violence of the wind; and, finally, it is in the same sense that we say space is void when it contains nothing sensible, although it contain created and self-subsisting matter; for we are not in the habit of considering the bodies near us, unless in so far as they cause in our organs of sense impressions strong enough to enable us to perceive them. And if, in place of keeping in mind what ought to be understood by these terms a vacuum and nothing, we afterwards suppose that in the space we called a vacuum, there is not only no sensible object, but no object at all, we will fall into the same error as if, because a pitcher in which there is nothing but air, is, in common speech, said to be empty, we were therefore to judge that the air contained in it is not a substance.

XVIII. How the prejudice of an absolute vacuum is to be corrected.

We have almost all fallen into this error from the earliest age, for, observing that there is no necessary connection between a vessel and the body it contains, we thought that God at least could take from a vessel the body which occupied it, without it being necessary that any other should be put in the place of the one removed. But that we may be able now to correct this false opinion, it is necessary to remark that there is in truth no connection between the vessel and the particular body which it contains, but that there is an absolutely necessary connection between the concave figure of the vessel and the extension considered generally which must be comprised in this cavity; so that it is not more contradictory to conceive a mountain without a valley than such a cavity without the extension it contains, or this extension apart from an extended substance, for, as we have often said, of nothing there can be no extension. And accordingly, if it be asked what would happen were God to remove from a vessel all the body contained in it, without permitting another body to occupy its place, the answer must be that the sides of the vessel would thus come into proximity with each other. For two bodies must touch each other when there is nothing between them, and it is manifestly contradictory for two bodies to be apart, in other words, that there should be a distance between them, and this distance yet be nothing; for all distance is a mode of extension, and cannot therefore exist without an extended substance.

XIX. That this confirms what was said of rarefaction.

After we have thus remarked that the nature of corporeal substance consists only in its being an extended thing, and that its extension is not different from that which we attribute to space, however empty, it is easy to discover the impossibility of any one of its parts in any way whatsoever occupying more space at one time than at another, and thus of being otherwise rarefied than in the way explained above; and it is easy to perceive also that there cannot be more matter or body in a vessel when it is filled with lead or gold, or any other body however heavy and hard, than when it but contains air and is supposed to be empty: for the quantity of the parts of which a body is composed does not depend on their weight or hardness, but only on the extension, which is always equal in the same vase.

XX. That from this the non-existence of atoms may likewise be demonstrated.

We likewise discover that there cannot exist any atoms or parts of matter that are of their own nature indivisible. For however small we suppose these parts to be, yet because they are necessarily extended, we are always able in thought to divide any one of them into two or more smaller parts, and may accordingly admit their divisibility. For there is nothing we can divide in thought which we do not thereby recognize to be divisible; and, therefore, were we to judge it indivisible our judgment would not be in harmony with the knowledge we have of the thing; and although we should even suppose that God had reduced any particle of matter to a smallness so extreme that it did not admit of being further divided, it would nevertheless be improperly styled indivisible, for though God had rendered the particle so small that it was not in the power of any creature to divide it, he could not however deprive himself of the ability to do so, since it is absolutely impossible for him to lessen his own omnipotence, as was before observed. Wherefore, absolutely speaking, the smallest extended particle is always divisible, since it is such of its very nature.

XXI. It is thus also demonstrated that the extension of the world is indefinite.

We further discover that this world, or the whole of corporeal substance, is extended without limit, for wherever we fix a limit, we still not only imagine beyond it spaces indefinitely extended, but perceive these to be truly imaginable, in other words, to be in reality such as we imagine them; so that they, contain in them corporeal substance indefinitely extended, for, as has been already shown at length, the idea of extension which we conceive in any space whatever is plainly identical with the idea of corporeal substance.

XXII. It also follows that the matter of the heavens and earth is the same, and that there cannot be a plurality of worlds.

And it may also be easily inferred from all this that the earth and heavens are made of the same matter; and that even although there were an infinity of worlds, they would all be composed of this matter; from which it follows that a plurality of worlds is impossible, because we clearly conceive that the matter whose nature consists only in its being an extended substance, already wholly occupies all the imaginable spaces where these other worlds could alone be, and we cannot find in ourselves the idea of any other matter.

XXIII. That all the variety of matter, or the diversity of its forms, depends on motion.

There is therefore but one kind of matter in the whole universe, and this we know only by its being extended. All the properties we distinctly perceive to belong to it are reducible to its capacity of being divided and moved according to its parts; and accordingly it is capable of all those affections which we perceive can arise from the motion of its parts. For the partition of matter in thought makes no change in it; but all variation of it, or diversity of form, depends on motion. The philosophers even seem universally to have observed this, for they said that nature was the principle of motion and rest, and by nature they understood that by which all corporeal things become such as they are found in experience.

XXIV. What motion is, taking the term in its common use.

But motion, in the ordinary sense of the term, is nothing more than the *action by which a body passes from one place to another*. And just as we have remarked above that the same thing may be said to change and not to change place at the same time, so also we may say that the same thing is at the same time moved and not moved. Thus, for example, a person seated in a vessel which is setting sail, thinks he is in motion if he look to the shore that he has left, and consider it as fixed; but not if he regard the ship itself, among the parts of which he preserves always the same situation. Moreover, because we are accustomed to suppose that there is no motion without action, and that in rest there is the cessation of action, the person thus seated is more properly said to be at rest than in motion, seeing he is not conscious of being in action.

XXV. What motion is properly so called.

But if, instead of occupying ourselves with that which has no foundation, unless in ordinary usage, we desire to know what ought to be understood by motion according to the truth of the thing, we may say, in order to give it a determinate nature, that it is *the transporting of one part of matter or of one body from the vicinity of those bodies that are in immediate contact with it, or which we regard as at rest, to the vicinity of other bodies.* By a body as a part of matter, I understand all that which is transferred together, although it be perhaps composed of several parts, which in themselves have other motions; and I say that it is the transporting and not the force or action which transports, with the view of showing that motion is always in the movable thing, not in that which moves; for it seems to me that we are not accustomed to distinguish these two things with sufficient accuracy. Farther, I understand that it is a mode of the movable thing, and not a substance, just as figure is a property of the thing figured, and repose of that which is at rest.

PART THREE: OF THE VISIBLE WORLD

I. THAT we cannot think too highly of the works of God.

Having now ascertained certain principles of material things, which were sought, not by the prejudices of the senses, but by the light of reason, and which thus possess so great evidence that we cannot doubt of their truth, it remains for us to consider whether from these alone we can deduce the explication of all the phenomena of nature. We will commence with those phenomena that are of the greatest generality, and upon which the others depend, as, for example, with the general structure of this whole visible world. But in order to our philosophising aright regarding this, two things are first of all to be observed. The first is, that we should ever bear in mind the infinity of the power and goodness of God, that we may not fear falling into error by imagining his works to be too great, beautiful, and perfect, but that we may, on the contrary, take care lest, by supposing limits to them of which we have no certain knowledge, we appear to think less highly than we ought of the power of God.

II. That we ought to beware lest, in our presumption, we imagine that the ends which God proposed to himself in the creation of the world are understood by us.

The second is, that we should beware of presuming too highly of ourselves, as it seems we should do if we supposed certain limits to the world, without being assured of their existence either by natural reasons or by divine revelation, as if the power of our thought extended beyond what God has in reality made; but likewise still more if we persuaded ourselves that all things were created by God for us only, or if we merely supposed that we could comprehend by the power of our intellect the ends which God proposed to himself in creating the universe.

III. In what sense it may be said that all things were created for the sake of man.

For although, as far as regards morals, it may be a pious thought to believe that God made all things for us, seeing we may thus be incited to greater gratitude and love toward him; and although it is even in some sense true, because there is no created thing of which we cannot make some use, if it be only that of exercising our mind in considering it, and honouring God on account of it, it is yet by no means probable that all things were created for us in this way that God had no other end in their creation; and this supposition would be plainly ridiculous and inept in physical reasoning, for we do not doubt but that many things exist, or formerly existed and have now ceased to be, which were never seen or known by man, and were never of use to him.

PART FOUR: OF THE EARTH

I. OF WHAT is to be borrowed from disquisitions on animals and man to advance the knowledge of material objects.

I should add nothing farther to this the fourth part of the *Principles of Philosophy,* did I purpose carrying out my original design of writing a fifth and sixth part, the one treating of things possessed of life, that is, animals and plants, and the other of man. But because I have not yet acquired sufficient knowledge of all the matters of which I should desire to treat in these two last parts, and do not know whether I ever shall have sufficient leisure to finish them, I will here subjoin a few things regarding the objects of our senses, that I may not, for the sake of the latter, delay too long the publication of the former parts, or of what may be desiderated in them, which I might have reserved for explanation in those others: for I have hitherto described this earth, and generally the whole visible world, as if it were merely a machine in which there was nothing at all to consider except the figures and motions of its parts, whereas our senses present to us many other things, for example colours, smells, sounds, and the like, of which, if I did not speak at all, it would be thought I had omitted the explication of the majority of the objects that are in nature.

II. What perception is, and how we perceive.

We must know, therefore, that although the human soul is united to the whole body, it has, nevertheless, its principal seat in the brain, where alone it not only understands and imagines, but also perceives; and this by the medium of the nerves, which are extended like threads from the brain to all the other members, with which they are so connected that we can hardly touch any one of them without moving the extremities of some of the nerves spread over it; and this motion passes to the other extremities of those nerves which are collected in the brain round the seat of the soul, as I have already explained with sufficient minuteness in the fourth chapter of the *Dioptrics*. But the movements which are thus excited in the brain by the nerves, variously affect the soul or mind, which is intimately conjoined with the brain, according to the diversity of the motions themselves. And the diverse affections of the mind or thoughts that immediately arise from these motions, are called perceptions of the senses, or, as we commonly speak, sensations.

III. Of the distinction of the senses; and, first, of the internal, that is, of the affections of the mind and the natural appetites.

The varieties of these sensations depend, firstly, on the diversity of the nerves themselves, and, secondly, on the movements that are made in each nerve. We have not, however, as many different senses as there are nerves. We can distinguish but seven principal classes of nerves, of which two belong to the internal, and the other five to the external senses. The nerves which extend to the stomach, the œsophagus, the fauces, and the other internal parts that are subservient to our natural wants, constitute one of our internal senses. This is called the natural appetite. The other internal sense, which embraces all the emotions of the mind or passions, and affections, as joy, sadness, love, hate, and the like, depends upon the nerves which extend to the heart and the parts about the heart, and are exceedingly small; for, by way of example, when the blood happens to be pure and well tempered, so that it dilates in the heart more readily and strongly than usual, this so enlarges and moves the small nerves scattered around the orifices, that there is thence a corresponding movement in the brain, which affects the mind with a certain natural feeling of joy; and as often as these same nerves are moved in the same way, although this is by other causes, they excite in our mind the same feeling. Thus, the imagination of the enjoyment of a good does not contain in itself the feeling of joy, but it causes the animal spirits to pass from the brain to the muscles in which these nerves are inserted; and thus dilating the orifices of the heart, it also causes these small nerves to move in the way appointed by nature to afford the sensation of joy. Thus, when we receive news, the mind first of all judges of it, and if the news be good, it rejoices with that intellectual joy which is independent of any emotion of the body, and which the Stoics did not deny to their wise man [although they supposed him exempt from all passion]. But as soon as this joy passes from the understanding to the imagination, the spirits flow from the brain to the muscles that are about the heart, and there excite the motion of the small nerves, by means of which another motion is caused in the brain, which affects the mind with the sensation of animal joy. On the same principle, when the blood is so thick that it flows but sparingly into the ventricles of the heart, and is not there sufficiently dilated, it excites in the same nerves a motion quite different from the preceding, which, communicated to the brain, gives to the mind the sensation of sadness, although the mind itself is perhaps ignorant of the cause of its sadness. And all the other causes which move these nerves in the same way may also give to the mind the same sensation. But the other movements of the same nerves produce other effects, as the feelings of love, hate, fear, anger, etc., as far as they are merely affections or passions of the mind; in other words, as far as they are confused thoughts which the mind has not from itself alone, but from its being closely joined to the body, from which it receives impressions; for there is the widest difference between these passions and the distinct thoughts which we have of what ought to be loved, or chosen, or shunned, etc. The natural appetites, as hunger, thirst, and the others, are likewise sensations excited in the mind by means of the nerves of the stomach, fauces, and other parts, and are entirely different from the will which we have to eat and drink; but, because this will or appetition almost always accompanies them, they are therefore named appetites.

IV. Of the external senses; and first of touch.

We commonly reckon the external senses five in number, because there are as many different kinds of objects which move the nerves and their organs, and an equal number of kinds of confused thoughts excited in the soul by these motions. In the first place, the nerves terminating in the skin of the whole body can be touched through this medium by any terrene objects whatever, and moved by these wholes, in one way by their hardness, in another by their gravity, in a third by their heat, in a fourth by their humidity, etc.—and in as many diverse modes as they are either moved or hindered from their ordinary motion, to that extent are diverse sensations excited in the mind, from which a corresponding number of tactile qualities derive their appellations. Besides this, when these nerves are moved a little more powerfully than usual, but not nevertheless to the degree by which our body is in any way hurt, there thus arises a sensation of titillation, which is naturally agreeable to the mind, because it testifies to it of the powers of the body with which it is joined. But if this action be strong enough to hurt our body in any way, this gives to our mind the sensation of pain. And we thus see why corporeal pleasure and pain, although sensations of quite an opposite character, arise nevertheless from causes nearly alike.

V. Of taste.

In the second place, the other nerves scattered over the tongue and the parts in its vicinity are diversely moved by the particles of the same bodies, separated from each other and floating in the saliva in the mouth, and thus cause sensations of diverse tastes according to the diversity of figure in these particles.

VI. Of smell.

Thirdly, two nerves also or appendages of the brain, for they do not go beyond the limits of the skull, are moved by the particles of terrestrial bodies, separated and flying in the air, not indeed by all particles indifferently, but by those only that are sufficiently subtle and penetrating to enter the pores of the bone we call the spongy, when drawn into the nostrils, and thus to reach the nerves. From the different motions of these particles arise the sensations of the different smells.

VII. Of hearing.

Fourthly, there are two nerves within the ears, so attached to three small bones that are mutually sustaining, and the first of which rests on the small membrane that covers the cavity we call the tympanum of the ear, that all the diverse vibrations which the surrounding air communicates to this membrane, are transmitted to the mind by these nerves, and these vibrations give rise, according to their diversity, to the sensations of the different sounds.

VIII. Of sight.

Finally, the extremities of the optic nerves, composing the coat in the eyes called the retina, are not moved by the air nor by any terrestrial object, but only by the globules of the second element, whence we have the sense of light and colours: as I have already at sufficient length explained in the *Dioptrics* and treatise of *Meteors*.

IX. That the soul perceives only in so far as it is in the brain.

It is clearly established, however, that the soul does not perceive in so far as it is in each member of the body, but only in so far as it is in the brain, where the nerves by their movements convey to it the diverse actions of the external objects that touch the parts of the body in which they are inserted. For, in the first place, there are various maladies, which, though they affect the brain alone, yet bring disorder upon, or deprive us altogether of the use of, our senses, just as sleep, which affects the brain only, and yet takes from us daily during a great part of our time the faculty of perception, which afterwards in our waking state is restored to us. The second proof is, that though there be no disease in the brain, it is nevertheless sufficient to take away sensation from the part of the body where the nerves terminate, if only the movement of one of the nerves that extend from the brain to these members be obstructed in any part of the distance that is between the two. And the last proof is, that we sometimes feel pain as if in certain of our members, the cause of which, however, is not in these members where it is felt, but somewhere nearer the brain, through which the nerves pass that give to the mind the sensation of it.

X. That the nature of the mind is such that from the motion alone of body the various sensations can be excited in it.

In the next place, it can be proved that our mind is of such a nature that the motions of the body alone are sufficient to excite in it all sorts of thoughts, without it being necessary that these should in any way resemble the motions which give rise to them, and especially that these motions can excite in it those confused thoughts called sensations. For we see that words, whether uttered by the voice or merely written, excite in our minds all kinds of thoughts and emotions. On the same paper, with the same pen and ink, by merely moving the point of the pen over the paper in a particular way, we can trace letters that will raise in the minds of our readers the thoughts of combats, tempests, or the furies, and the passions of indignation and sorrow; in place of which, if the pen be moved in another way hardly different from the former, this slight change will cause thoughts widely different from the above, such as those of repose, peace, pleasantness, and the quite opposite passions of love and joy. Some one will perhaps object that writing and speech do not immediately excite in the mind any passions, or imaginations of things different from the letters and sounds, but afford simply the knowledge of these, on occasion of which the mind, understanding the signification of the words, afterwards excites in itself the imaginations and passions that correspond to the words. But what will be said of the sensations of pain and titillation? The motion merely of a sword cutting a part of our skin causes pain. And it is certain that this sensation of pain is not less different from the motion that causes it, or from that of the part of our body which the sword cuts, than are the sensations we have of colour, sound, odour, or taste. On this ground we may conclude that our mind is of such a nature that the motions alone of certain bodies can also easily excite in it all the other sensations, as the motion of a sword excites in it the sensation of pain.

XI. That by our senses we know nothing of external objects beyond their figure, magnitude, and motion.

Besides, we observe no such difference between the nerves as to lead us to judge that one set of them convey to the brain from the organs of the external senses anything different from another, or that anything at all reaches the brain besides the local motion of the nerves themselves. And we see that local motion alone causes in us not only the sensation of titillation and of pain, but also of light and sounds. For if we receive a blow on the eye of sufficient force to cause the vibration of the stroke to reach the retina, we see numerous sparks of fire, which, nevertheless, are not out of our eye; and when we stop our ear with our finger, we hear a humming sound, the cause of which can only proceed from the agitation of the air that is shut up within it. Finally, we frequently observe that heat and the other sensible qualities, as far as they are in objects, and also the forms of those bodies that are purely material, as, for example, the forms of fire, are produced in them by the motion of certain other bodies, and that these in their turn likewise produce other motions in other bodies. And we can easily conceive how the motion of one body may be caused by that of another, and diversified by the size, figure, and situation of its parts, but we are wholly unable to conceive how these same things can produce something else of a nature entirely different from themselves, as, for example, those substantial forms and real qualities which many philosophers suppose to be in bodies; nor likewise can we conceive how these qualities or forms possess force to cause motions in other bodies. But since we know, from the nature of our soul, that the diverse motions of body are sufficient to produce in it all the sensations which it has, and since we learn from experience that several of its sensations are in reality caused by such motions, while we do not discover that anything besides these motions ever passes from the organs of the external senses to the brain, we have reason to conclude that we in no way likewise apprehend that in external objects, which we call light, colour, smell, taste, sound, heat or cold, and the other tactile qualities, or that which we call their substantial forms, unless as the various dispositions of these objects which have the power of moving our nerves in various ways.

XII. That there is no phenomenon of nature whose explanation has been omitted in this treatise.

And thus it may be gathered, from an enumeration that is easily made, that there is no phenomenon of nature whose explanation has been omitted in this treatise; for beyond what is perceived by the senses, there is nothing that can be considered a phenomenon of nature. But leaving out of account motion, magnitude, figure, which I have explained as they exist in body, we perceive nothing out of us by our senses except light, colours, smells, tastes, sounds, and the tactile qualities; and these I have recently shown to be nothing more, at least so far as they are known to us, than certain dispositions of the objects, consisting in magnitude, figure, and motion.

XIII. That this treatise contains no principles which are not universally received; and that this philosophy is not new, but of all others the most ancient and common.

But I am desirous also that it should be observed that, though I have here endeavoured to give an explanation of the whole nature of material things, I have nevertheless made use of no principle which was not received and approved by Aristotle, and by the other philosophers of all ages; so that this philosophy, so far from being new, is of all others the most ancient and common: for I have in truth merely considered the figure, motion, and magnitude of bodies, and examined what must follow from their mutual concourse on the principles of mechanics, which are confirmed by certain and daily experience. But no one ever doubted that bodies are moved, and that they are of various sizes and figures, according to the diversity of which their motions also vary, and that from mutual collision those somewhat greater than others are divided into many smaller, and thus change figure. We have experience of the truth of this, not merely by a single sense, but by several, as touch, sight, and hearing: we also distinctly imagine and understand it. This cannot be said of any of the other things that fall under our senses, as colours, sounds, and the like; for each of these affects but one of our senses, and merely impresses upon our imagination a confused image of itself, affording our understanding no distinct knowledge of what it is.

XIV. That sensible bodies are composed of insensible particles.

But I allow many particles in each body that are perceived by none of our senses, and this will not perhaps be approved of by those who take the senses for the measure of the knowable. [We greatly wrong human reason, however, as appears to me, if we suppose that it does not go beyond the eye-sight]; for no one can doubt that there are bodies so small as not to be perceptible by any of our senses, provided he only consider what is each moment added to those bodies that are being increased little by little, and what is taken from those that are diminished in the same way. A tree increases daily, and it is impossible to conceive how it becomes greater than it was before, unless we at the same time conceive that some body is added to it. But who ever observed by the senses those small bodies that are in one day added to a tree while growing? Among the philosophers at least, those who hold that quantity is indefinitely divisible, ought to admit that in the division the parts may become so small as to be wholly imperceptible. And indeed it ought not to be a matter of surprise that we are unable to perceive very minute bodies; for the nerves that must be moved by objects to cause perception are not themselves very minute, but are like small cords, being composed of a quantity of smaller fibres, and thus the most minute bodies are not capable of moving them. Nor do I think that any one who makes use of his reason will deny that we philosophise with much greater truth when we judge of what takes place in those small bodies which are imperceptible from their minuteness only, after the analogy of what we see occurring in those we do perceive, than when we give an explanation of the same things by inventing I know not what novelties, that have no relation to the things we actually perceive.

XV. That the philosophy of Democritus is not less different from ours than from the common.

But it may be said that Democritus also supposed certain corpuscles that were of various figures, sizes, and motions, from the heaping together and mutual concourse of which all sensible bodies arose; and, nevertheless, his mode of philosophising is commonly rejected by all. To this I reply that the philosophy of Democritus was never rejected by any one because he allowed the existence of bodies smaller than those we perceive, and attributed to them diverse sizes, figures, and motions, for no one can doubt that there are in reality such, as we have already shown; but it was rejected, in the first place, because he supposed that these corpuscles were indivisible, on which ground I also reject it; in the second place, because he imagined there was a vacuum about them, which I show to be impossible; thirdly, because he attributed gravity to these bodies, of which I deny the existence in any body, in so far as a body is considered by itself, because it is a quality that depends on the relations of situation and motion which several bodies bear to each other; and, finally, because he has not explained in particular how all things arose from the concourse of corpuscles alone, or, if he gave this explanation with regard to a few of them, his whole reasoning was far from being coherent. This, at least, is the verdict we must give regarding his philosophy, if we may judge of his opinions from what has been handed down to us in writing. I leave it to others to determine whether the philosophy I profess possesses a valid coherency.

XVI. How we may arrive at the knowledge of the figures and motions of the insensible particles of bodies.

But, since I assign determinate figures, magnitudes, and motions to the insensible particles of bodies, as if I had seen them, whereas I admit that they do not fall under the senses, some one will perhaps demand how I have come by my knowledge of them. Thereupon, taking as my ground of inference the simplest and best known of the principles that have been implanted in our minds by nature, I considered the chief differences that could possibly subsist between the magnitudes, and figures, and situations of bodies insensible on account of their smallness alone, and what sensible effects could be produced by their various modes of coming into contact; and afterwards, when I found like effects in the bodies that we perceive by our senses, I judged that they could have been thus produced, especially since no other mode of explaining them could be devised. And in this matter the example of several bodies made by art was of great service to me: for I recognise no difference between these and natural bodies beyond this, that the effects of machines depend for the most part on the agency of certain instruments, which, as they must bear some proportion to the hands of those who make them, are always so large that their figures and motions can be seen; in place of which, the effects of natural bodies almost always depend upon certain organs so minute as to escape our senses. And it is certain that all the rules of mechanics belong also to physics, of which it is a part or species: for it is not less natural for a clock, made of the requisite number of wheels, to mark the hours, than for a tree, which has sprung from this or that seed, to produce the fruit peculiar to it. Accordingly, just as those who are familiar with automata, when they are informed of the use of a machine, and see some of its parts, easily infer from these the way in which the others, that are not seen by them, are made; so from considering the sensible effects and parts of natural bodies, I have essayed to determine the character of their causes and insensible parts.

XVII. That, touching the things which our senses do not perceive, it is sufficient to explain how they can be.

But here some one will perhaps reply, that although I have supposed causes which could produce all natural objects, we ought not on this account to conclude that they were produced by these causes; for, just as the same artisan can make two clocks, which, though they both equally well indicate the time, and are not different in outward appearance, have nevertheless nothing resembling in the composition of their wheels; so doubtless the Supreme Maker of things has an infinity of diverse means at his disposal, by each of which he could have made all the things of this world to appear as we see them, without it being possible for the human mind to know which of all these means he chose to employ. I most freely concede this; and I believe that I have done all that was required if the causes I have assigned are such that their effects accurately correspond to all the phenomena of nature, without determining whether it is by these or by others that they are actually produced. And it will be sufficient for the use of life to know the causes thus imagined, for medicine, mechanics, and in general all the arts to which the knowledge of physics is of service, have for their end only those effects that are sensible, and that are accordingly to be reckoned among the phenomena of nature. And lest it should be supposed that Aristotle did, or professed to do, anything more than this, it ought to be remembered that he himself expressly says, at the commencement of the seventh chapter of the first book of the *Meteorologics,* that, with regard to things which are not manifest to the senses, he thinks to adduce sufficient reasons and demonstrations of them, if he only shows that they may be such as he explains them.

XVIII. That nevertheless there is a moral certainty that all the things of this world are such as has been here shown they may be.

But nevertheless, that I may not wrong the truth by supposing it less certain than it is, I will here distinguish two kinds of certitude. The first is called moral, that is, a certainty sufficient for the conduct of life, though, if we look to the absolute power of God, what is morally certain may be false.

XIX. That we possess even more than a moral certainty of it.

Besides, there are some, even among natural, things which we judge to be absolutely certain. This certainty is founded on the metaphysical ground, that, as God is supremely good and the source of all truth, the faculty of distinguishing truth from error which he gave us, cannot be fallacious so long as we use it aright, and distinctly perceive anything by it. Of this character are the demonstrations of mathematics, the knowledge that material things exist, and the clear reasonings that are formed regarding them. The results I have given in this treatise will perhaps be admitted to a place in the class of truths that are absolutely certain, if it be considered that they are deduced in a continuous series from the first and most elementary principles of human knowledge; especially if it be sufficiently understood that we can perceive no external objects unless some local motion be caused by them in our nerves, and that such motion cannot be caused by the fixed stars, owing to their great distance from us, unless a motion be also produced in them and in the whole heavens lying between them and us: for these points being admitted, all the others, at least the more general doctrines which I have advanced regarding the world or earth, will appear to be almost the only possible explanations of the phenomena they present.

XX. That, however, I submit all my opinions to the authority of the church.

Nevertheless, lest I should presume too far, I affirm nothing, but submit all these my opinions to the authority of the church and the judgment of the more sage; and I desire no one to believe anything I may have said, unless he is constrained to admit it by the force and evidence of reason.

Catalog

If you are interested in a list of fine Paperback
books, covering a wide range of subjects
and interests, send your name and address,
requesting your free catalog, to:

McGraw-Hill Paperbacks
1221 Avenue of Americas
New York, N.Y. 10020